Microsoft® *Office 2010*
DeMYSTiFieD®

DeMYSTiFieD® Series

The Demystified Series publishes more than 125 titles in all areas of academic study. For a complete list of titles, please visit www.mhprofessional.com.

Microsoft® Office 2010

DeMYSTiFieD®

Karin Rex

New York   Chicago   San Francisco   Lisbon   London   Madrid   Mexico City
Milan   New Delhi   San Juan   Seoul   Singapore   Sydney   Toronto

The McGraw·Hill Companies

Library of Congress Cataloging-in-Publication Data

Rex, Karin.
   Microsoft Office 2010 demystified / Karin Rex.
      p. cm.
   Includes index.
   ISBN 978-0-07-176795-8 (alk. paper)
   1. Microsoft Office.   2. Business—Computer programs.   I. Title.
   HF5548.4.M525R49   2011
   005.5—dc23   2011039428

McGraw-Hill books are available at special quantity discounts to use as premiums and sales promotions, or for use in corporate training programs. To contact a representative, please e-mail us at bulksales@mcgraw-hill.com.

Microsoft® Office 2010 DeMYSTiFieD®

1 2 3 4 5 6 7 8 9 0   DOC DOC   1 0 9 8 7 6 5 4 3 2 1

ISBN   978-0-07-176795-8
MHID   0-07-176795-9

Sponsoring Editor Roger Stewart	**Technical Editor** Curt Simmons	**Composition** Cenveo Publisher Services
Editorial Supervisor Jody McKenzie	**Copy Editor** Lisa McCoy	**Illustration** Cenveo Publisher Services
Project Manager Sandhya Gola, Cenveo Publisher Services	**Proofreader** Christine Andreasen **Indexer** James Minkin	**Art Director, Cover** Jeff Weeks
Acquisitions Coordinator Joya Anthony	**Production Supervisor** George Anderson	**Cover Illustration** Lance Lekander

This book is dedicated to you, my reader.

About the Author

Karin Rex is a dedicated evangelist for all things geeky. Since 1989, Karin has owned Geeky Girl, LLC, a technology training and technical writing company based in southeastern Pennsylvania. In addition to writing books and articles, Karin develops e-learning modules as well as courses for both the virtual and traditional classrooms. Karin also teaches university courses in professional writing and technical writing.

Karin's previous books include *Internet Search Techniques* (Ziff-Davis Publishing, 1996), *The Internet Illuminated* (Skillpath Publications, 1996), *Nurturing Customer Relationships* (Nurture Institute Press, 2006), and *Computers in Clinical Practice* (American College of Physicians, 1995). In addition to these books, Karin has written a multitude of customized e-learning modules, user guides, reference manuals, tutorials, and course manuals for a wide variety of corporate clients.

Karin is a certified synchronous facilitator and instructional designer with a master's degree in professional writing. In her spare time, she knits and walks (but rarely at the same time).

About the Technical Editor

Curt Simmons is a Microsoft product expert and technical trainer. He is the author of more than 80 general computing and nonfiction titles and primarily writes about Windows operating systems and Microsoft Office products. When he is not writing and training, Curt enjoys spending time with his wife and two daughters, working on his 110-year-old Victorian home, and hanging out at the beach.

Contents

Acknowledgments

Although writing a book is a mostly solitary endeavor, it is rarely ever accomplished in a vacuum. It is with a great deal of gratitude that I would like to acknowledge the following for their invaluable assistance in making this book come alive: to Laurie for sharing the wealth; to Margot for adding me to her roster; to Roger for saying "yes" and for knowing when I needed to hear something super-duper over-the-top nice; to Joya for keeping me on task; to Curt for confirming my comprehension (not to mention boosting my ego); to Jody, Lisa, and Sandhya for editing with style and grace; and to my Mom for always believing in me. To Ken and Dave: thank you both for always being ACCESS-able. To Robin (my forever first reader): thank you for helping ensure that I got it all right and explained it all clearly and for making me laugh along the way. To my much-treasured husband and best friend John (without whom I probably would have starved during the writing of this book): thanks for letting me stay up all night and write and for never once doubting that I would git 'er dun! You are the best, and I love you.

Finally, my humblest thanks to you—my readers and students—who ask me the most amazing questions and who never fail to teach me something new every day.

Introduction

This book lets you become familiar with the Microsoft Office 2010 suite without overloading your brain with too many details. (There are plenty of other books for that!)

This book assumes three things:

- You know your way around your PC.
- You know how to use your mouse to point and click.
- You aren't afraid to explore!

Who Should Use This Book

This book is perfect for you! Why? Because you want to learn about the entire Office suite without having to buy five mammoth volumes on the topic. You want to learn the ropes, along with what's useful, what's new, and what's cool. You are my perfect reader. Enjoy!

How to Use This Book

This book is organized into six parts, spanning 18 chapters:

- **Part I:**
  Chapters 1 and 2 cover the suite of Microsoft Office 2010 applications. Here you will become familiar with what each of the individual applications provide, as well as some of the more popular universal features that can be used in all of the suite's applications.

- **Part II:**

  Chapters 3 through 5 cover the suite's word processing program: Microsoft Word. You will get started using Word; learn how to add some pizzazz to your documents; and get comfortable with page layout, viewing, and printing.

- **Part III:**

  Chapters 6 through 8 cover the suite's spreadsheet program: Microsoft Excel. You will get started with worksheets; learn the basics of working with formulas, functions, and charts; and familiarize yourself with page layout, viewing and printing.

- **Part IV:**

  Chapters 9 through 12 cover the suite's slide presentation program: Microsoft PowerPoint. You will get started with creating presentations; explore how to view and print a slide show; learn how to add pizzazz to a presentation; and discover how to orchestrate a slide show presentation.

- **Part V:**

  Chapters 13 through 14 cover the suite's personal information manager program: Microsoft Outlook. You will become familiar with e-mail, tasks, calendar, and contacts. You will also be introduced to Outlook's new Social Connector, which lets you use Outlook to connect to your personal and business social networks.

- **Part VI:**

  Chapters 15 through 18 cover the suite's database program: Microsoft Access. You will get started using databases and explore the Access interface. You will learn how to work with the four building blocks of a relational database: tables, queries, forms, and reports.

Quizzes

To cement your knowledge at the end of each chapter, enjoy taking the quick ten-question quiz. Quiz answers are in the back of the book.

Final Exam

A 100-question final exam covering all 18 chapters can be found in the back of the book. The final exam corresponds to the six sections. Exam answers are in the back of the book as well.

Part I

Exploring Office 2010

chapter 1

Exploring Office 2010 Applications

This chapter provides a quick overview of Microsoft Office 2010 applications as well as a primer on the Office ribbon—a revolutionary navigation feature common to all Office applications.

Microsoft Office 2010 is made up of a collection of applications designed to stand on their own as individual productivity tools as well as to work together seamlessly to foster easy collaboration. Employing a consistent user interface decreases the overall learning curve for the suite: learn one of the suite's applications well and you will most likely feel comfortable navigating all of the others.

CHAPTER OBJECTIVES

In this chapter, you will

- Review core Office 2010 applications
- Tour the Office 2010 ribbon

Exploring Office 2010 Applications

This book focuses on the five core Microsoft Office 2010 applications: Word, Excel, PowerPoint, Outlook, and Access. Each of these applications is described briefly in this chapter and then has its own dedicated section within the book for in-depth coverage. (Publisher and OneNote are not covered in this book.)

Word

Microsoft Word is a word processing application—the program you will use to type, format, and modify text-based documents. Word is probably the most frequently used application within the Office suite, and has been the leading word processing program in the industry for many years. Word gives you easy-to-master tools that allow you to create highly professional-looking documents.

If you need to collaborate on documents with coworkers, Word gives your team tools that will allow you to easily add comments and track changes within a document. If you're a student, Word lets you add citations, headers and footers, page numbers, and footnotes or endnotes painlessly. If you're a writer (or someone who writes a lot), you will find Word's research, thesaurus, spelling, grammar, and word count tools all helpful for your craft. Word lets you seamlessly incorporate tables, graphics, columns, hyperlinks, and artistic flairs within your documents.

Figure 1-1 displays a letter in the Microsoft Word 2010 window. The Clip Art task pane is shown on the right side of the image; the Word Home ribbon stretches across the top of the window, just under the title bar.

TIP   *Although Word can certainly be used for basic desktop publishing (creating brochures, business cards, newsletters, etc.), if you have the Microsoft Office Publisher program as part of your suite, you may want to consider using that application for desktop publishing projects instead of Word. Publisher gives you much more flexibility where page layout and design are concerned and also offers a number of tools that boost your ability to create professional-looking print media, including master design sets for brand coordination; commercial printing support; and a large number of templates for brochures, newsletters, posters, and banners.*

How Can I Use Word?

Use Microsoft Word for documents that will primarily contain words or a mix of words and graphics, such as the following:

- Letters
- Memos
- Proposals
- Business or school reports
- Résumés
- Newsletters
- Scholarly papers
- Meeting agendas

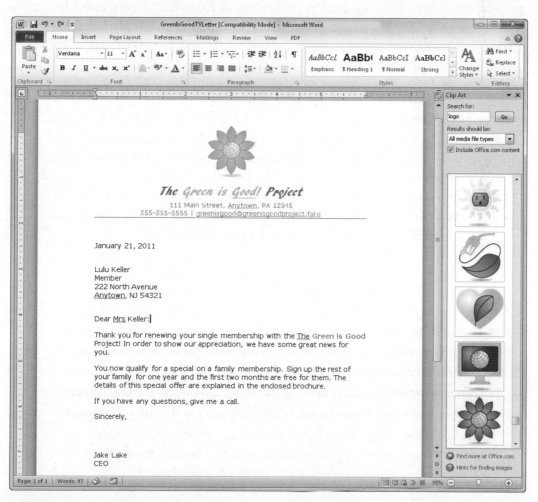

FIGURE 1-1 • Microsoft Word 2010 window

Excel

Excel is the Office suite's modern-day abacus—an electronic spreadsheet program that can be likened to a paper accounting worksheet come alive. A spreadsheet program displays a grid of rows and columns that together form numerous cells. Each cell can contain numbers, text, or formulas. A formula is an equation that can calculate or combine data based on other cells in the same or another spreadsheet. The result of the formula displayed in the cell is updated when and if the cells that equation points to changes.

While a spreadsheet is most frequently used for financial-oriented information because of its ability to organize and work with numbers and recalculate an entire spreadsheet of information instantly, you will most likely find plenty of other creative uses for this powerful tool as well. Everything from simple lists and databases to gorgeously complex charts and graphs can be created in Excel.

TIP *Microsoft Excel refers to spreadsheets as "worksheets."*

How Can I Use Excel?

Use Microsoft Excel for documents that will primarily contain numbers and other data that are best organized within a spreadsheet, such as the following:

- Budgets
- Invoices
- Lists
- Inventory
- Data analysis in pivot tables
- Charts and graphs
- Simple databases

PowerPoint

PowerPoint is a slide presentation program. A presentation program is most commonly used to create a visual backdrop to a speech, lecture, or meeting, with each slide containing a key point or supporting graphic. PowerPoint's easy-to-use templates and themes and dynamic graphic capabilities allow you to make attractive, professional presentations quite effortlessly.

A slide presentation can contain any combination of text, graphics, tables, and charts, all of which can be animated to appear at the click of the mouse or when otherwise timed, as well as speaker notes. You can even incorporate video clips into a presentation! Audience handouts can be generated easily from a presentation as well.

How Can I Use PowerPoint?

Use Microsoft PowerPoint to create graphically pleasing presentations. This includes the following:

- Presentations for a speech, class, or meeting
- Photo slideshows to show off your vacation pictures
- Graphics
- Animated charts and graphs
- Self-running presentations for a kiosk

Outlook

Outlook is a full-featured personal information management (PIM) program that provides you with e-mail, contact management (address book), scheduling (calendar), and task tracking capabilities. Outlook aims to keep you as connected and organized as you can possibly stand to be!

For the neat and tidy type, you can organize your e-mail into conversation threads, folders, and subfolders; and you can color-code and categorize appointments, tasks, e-mails, and contacts. For the lazy neat and tidy type, you can create automated rules to do some of the organizing for you.

For the well-connected type, in addition to keeping in touch with colleagues, friends, and family through e-mail, the Outlook Social Connector lets you connect to your business and personal social networks such as LinkedIn, Facebook, MySpace, SharePoint, or Windows Live Messenger.

Figure 1-2 displays Mail view in Microsoft Outlook 2010. Mail folders are shown on the left side of the window, and e-mail in the currently selected folder is listed in the center of the window. The currently highlighted e-mail message is partially displayed in the Reading pane under the list of e-mails. The To-Do bar is shown on the right side of the window; the Outlook Home ribbon stretches across the top of the window, just under the title bar.

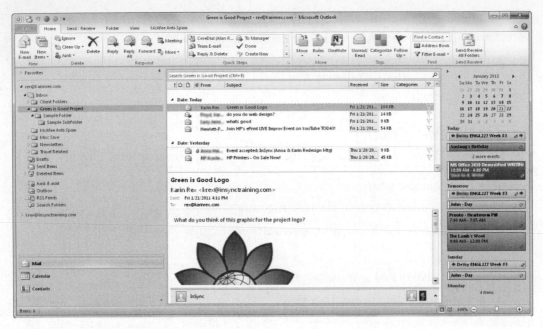

FIGURE 1-2 · Mail view in Outlook 2010 is where you will read, reply to, and organize your email.

TIP   *Although their names sound similar, Outlook is a completely different program from Outlook Express. Outlook Express is a basic e-mail program that was developed for home users as part of Internet Explorer 4.x and 5.x and that shipped with certain Windows operating systems, such as Microsoft Windows 98, Millennium Edition (Me), and Windows 2000. Outlook is a much more robust full-featured PIM that is available as part of the Microsoft Office Home and Business and Professional suites and also as a stand-alone program. In addition to ultra-advanced e-mail and contact features, Outlook provides you with calendar, task list, and scheduling capabilities.*

How Can I Use Outlook?

Use Microsoft Outlook to keep yourself in touch, organized, and in the right place at the right time. This includes the following:

- E-mail
- Contact list

- Appointment calendar
- Task list
- Social media network stream

Access

Access is the Office suite's database powerhouse, helping you manage your endless mounds of interrelated data. A database is a tool used to collect and organize data (bits of information). These bits of information can be about people (e.g., names, addresses, credit card numbers, purchasing preferences), numbers (e.g., dates, income, expenses, time), things (e.g., inventory, product SKU numbers, prices, colors), or any combination of these data. The possibilities are endless!

Many databases start as a simple list on paper or in a word processing program. Eventually the list grows larger and the data becomes difficult to contain in such a simple format. For example, you might need to be able to reorganize the list or break it into sublists; you may spot inconsistencies such as duplicate or out-of-date items; or you may start to have difficulties finding items in the list. This is where a relational database program such as Access can be very helpful. Placing your list in a database gives you the power to manipulate and organize that data in almost any way possible.

Figure 1-3 displays a table in the Microsoft Access 2010 window. The Navigation pane is shown on the left side of the image with a table displayed in the main window. The Access Home ribbon stretches across the top of the window, just under the title bar.

How Can I Use Access?

Use Microsoft Access for all of your data organization needs, such as the following:

- Maintain a customer database
- Track product inventory
- Manage your recipe collection
- Catalogue books, DVDs, CDs, or favorite collectibles
- Automate inventory
- Track an organization's membership

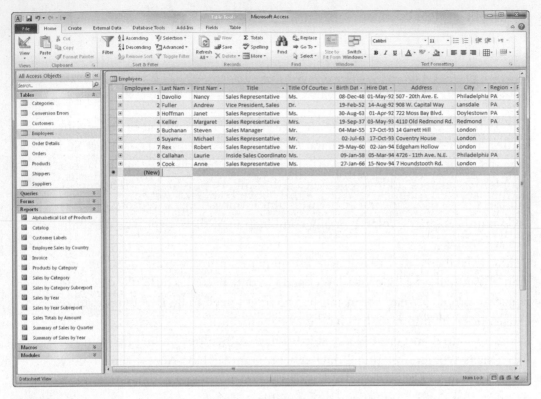

FIGURE 1-3 • The Access 2010 window gives you full control over your database.

Still Struggling

Not sure which Office applications you currently have installed? Click Start | All Programs. Scroll to and click on the Microsoft Office folder in the Programs list. The Office applications currently installed on your computer will be displayed in that folder.

Not sure which Office 2010 suite you own? Office Home and Student contains Word, Excel, PowerPoint, and OneNote. Office Home and Business contains all of those applications plus Outlook. Office Professional contains all of those applications plus Outlook, Access, and Publisher.

Office 2010 Ribbon Primer

In previous versions of Office (version 2 through version 2003), Microsoft gave us menus and toolbars (also known as command bars) as our primary tools for working within Office. Menus were organized according to related topics (in most cases), and buttons on toolbars offered a quick alternative to hunting through menus for the commands we used most frequently. These tools worked well once you were accustomed to them; however, Microsoft took the opportunity to improve upon these tools with its release of 2007, replacing menus and toolbars with "ribbons" in Word, Excel, PowerPoint, and Access.

Ribbons consist of a series of graphically pleasing tabbed command bars positioned along the top of the application window (an example is pictured in Figure 1-4). Each tab in a ribbon contains a set of related commands. The idea behind the ribbon was to organize a program's features in such a way that users can locate and use them more easily. Ribbons are contextual, meaning that certain tabs only appear when needed. For example, unless you have a graphic selected in a document, the Picture Tools Format ribbon won't be visible.

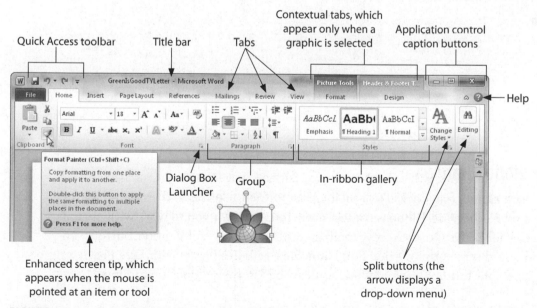

FIGURE 1-4 · Microsoft Word 2010 Home ribbon with labeled features

Size Matters

Your ribbons may look different from the ones pictured in this book. The number of commands displayed on the ribbons is dependent upon the screen real estate available. This includes the size of your monitor and your screen resolution as well as the size of the Office window itself (whether it's maximized or manually sized smaller). If you have a large monitor and use a high screen resolution, the ribbon will be able to display more commands than if you have a smaller monitor or use a lower screen resolution.

If you are using Office on two computers that have different size monitors, such as a desktop and a laptop, you will be more likely to notice this difference, as commands on the ribbons won't seem to be in the same place on both computers. Given a small space to work with, Office will automatically stack commands on the ribbon or group them under a single command to save space.

Compare the two Microsoft Word Page Layout ribbons shown in the following illustration. The top ribbon displays the commands as seen in a maximized window on a larger monitor; the bottom ribbon displays the commands as seen in a smaller window. Note how the Page Setup and Page Background sections of the ribbon have been stacked to save space. Also note how, when allowed less space, the Themes and Arrange sections of the ribbon lose their icon labels.

Ribbon Hardware

The ribbon may look like a toolbar, but its rich features and creative nuances prove otherwise. Ribbons contain numerous tools for you to work with, including tabs, the Quick Access toolbar, application control caption buttons, enhanced screen tips, Dialog Box Launchers, galleries (some with Live Preview), and split buttons, each of which is described in the sections that follow.

Tabs

The ribbon tabs stretch across the top of the ribbon, just below the title bar. In the following illustration, the PowerPoint Insert tab is currently selected. Other tab names showing in the illustration include File, Home, Design, Transitions, Animations, Slide Show, Review, and View. To view a ribbon in Office, simply click on its tab name.

As mentioned previously, ribbons are contextual, meaning that some tabs appear only when needed. For example, in Word unless the cursor is positioned in a header or footer, the Header and Footer Tools tab will not be visible.

TIP   *Double-click the current tab to hide the ribbon. Click any tab to display the ribbon. Alternatively, use the CTRL+F1 keyboard shortcut to toggle the ribbon on and off.*

Quick Access Toolbar

On the left side of the title bar is the Quick Access toolbar. This customizable toolbar contains only a few select commands by default (Save, Undo, Redo, and Customize). By default this toolbar appears just above the ribbon in the title bar; however, you can move it to under the ribbon if preferred. If you change the position of the Quick Access toolbar in one Office application, that change carries through to all of the other Office applications.

TIP   *Double-clicking a blank area of the title bar toggles the window between maximized and restored states. It's the same as clicking the Maximize and Restore buttons at the right end of the title bar.*

Customizing the Quick Access Toolbar

1. Launch the Office application in which you want to customize the Quick Access toolbar.

2. In the Quick Access toolbar, click on the Customize Quick Access Toolbar button (it's the button on the far right).

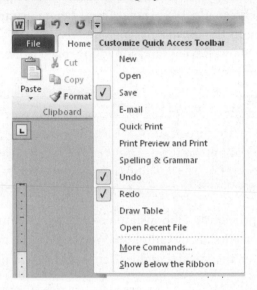

3. Choose from the list of suggested commands for that application, or choose More Commands to find and select other available commands.

Working with More Commands If a command you want to add to the Quick Access toolbar is not in the list of suggested commands in the Customize Quick Access toolbar drop-down menu, you can choose More Commands to locate additional commands. Choosing More Commands opens the Word Options Quick Access Toolbar dialog box.

TIP *If you've made changes to the Quick Access toolbar that you wish you hadn't, you can restore the toolbar to its original form. Click the Reset drop-down button in the Word Options Quick Access Toolbar dialog box and then choose Reset Only Quick Access Toolbar.*

Repositioning the Quick Access Toolbar

1. Launch the Office application in which you want to customize the Quick Access Toolbar.

2. In the Quick Access Toolbar, click the Customize Quick Access Toolbar button (it's the button on the far right).

3. Choose Show Below The Ribbon to reposition the Quick Access toolbar below the ribbon. (Note that this command will toggle between Show Below The Ribbon and Show Above The Ribbon depending on where the toolbar is currently positioned.)

Application Control Caption Buttons

As in previous versions of Office, at the very top of every window, the title bar contains the current file and application names in the center. On the right side of the title bar there are three buttons: Minimize, Maximize/Restore Down, and Close. The middle button toggles between two icons (Maximize and Restore Down) depending on the window's current state. In the following illustration, the middle button in the top half is the Maximize icon; the middle button in the bottom half is the Restore Down icon.

The Minimize button (on the left) is used to hide the window. The Maximize button is used to size the window to fill the whole screen. The Restore Down button is used to restore the screen to its previous size. The Close button closes the window as well as the program if you only have one document open at the time. These features are the same as they have been in previous versions of Office.

Still Struggling

Does it seem as though the Restore button does the same exact thing as the Maximize button? It might be because you've never manually resized that window before. Try this:

1. Click Restore Down (the icon appears as two rectangles).

2. Position the mouse pointer anywhere along the outside edge of the application window. You'll know you're in the right place when the cursor changes to a double-headed arrow.

3. With the double-headed arrow cursor, click and drag to resize the window manually.

4. Click the Maximize button to return the window to full screen.

5. Click the Restore Down button to return the window to the size it was when you manually resized the window in step 3.

Enhanced Screen Tips

In previous versions of Office, when you hovered over a toolbar button, a tiny screen tip popped up displaying the name of the command you were pointing to. Office 2010 provides enhanced screen tips. These larger pop-up windows display the name of the command as well as a brief overview of what that command is used for. Some enhanced screen tips also link to the Office Help system.

Dialog Box Launchers

Some ribbon groups have a small arrow in the lower-right corner. Clicking that arrow opens a dialog box. If you have used previous versions of Microsoft Office, you'll be familiar with dialog boxes—and very little has changed. A dialog box contains every single possible command for that group. This will include those that are already represented on the ribbon as well as esoteric commands that are infrequently used.

The following illustration shows the Microsoft Word 2010 Home ribbon with four Dialog Box Launchers circled.

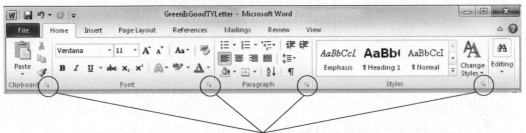

Dialog box launchers click to open a dialog box

In this illustration, clicking the Dialog Box Launcher in the bottom-right corner of the Paragraph Group would open the Paragraph dialog box, shown in the next illustration.

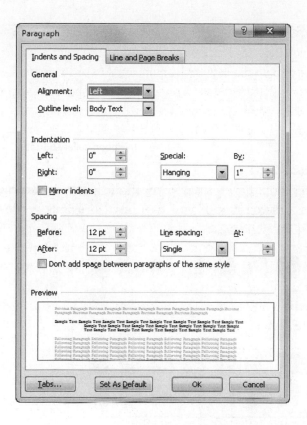

Ribbon Galleries

A ribbon gallery graphically displays a list of commands or options right in the ribbon. Additional options may be available in a pop-up window. Figure 1-5 shows the Microsoft Excel 2010 Shape Style gallery (displayed by selecting Chart Tools | Format Ribbon). Note that a single row of styles appears in the ribbon; when the drop-down arrow is clicked, additional styles appear in a pop-up window.

Some galleries provide a Live Preview of the available options. Live Preview lets you see what the change would look like simply by hovering the mouse pointer over an option (in other words, you don't have to click). As you hover over choices in a gallery, the formatting of the highlighted text or object changes instantly. To hide a gallery pop-up menu without making a selection, click the arrowhead again or click anywhere outside of the menu.

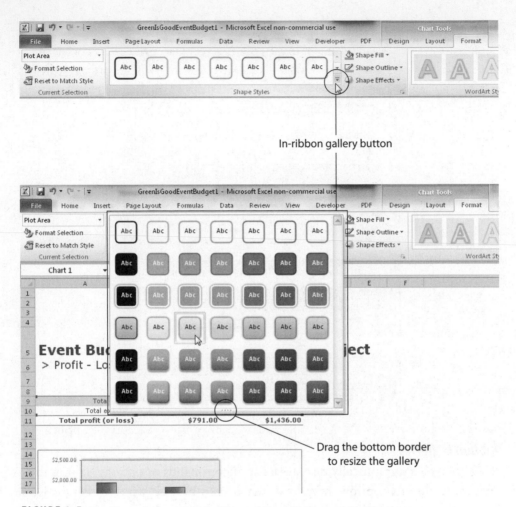

In-ribbon gallery button

Drag the bottom border
to resize the gallery

FIGURE 1-5 • The Shape Styles gallery in Microsoft Excel 2010 covers Live Preview.

TIP *Some gallery pop-up menus can be resized by dragging the bottom border. This is useful if the text or object you are formatting is hidden behind the gallery pop-up menu. You'll know if a gallery pop-up menu can be resized if, when you place the mouse pointer over the bottom border, the pointer changes to a double-headed arrow. (In addition, you will see four tiny dots at the bottom of a gallery pop-up menu if it can be resized—you can see these at the bottom of Figure 1-5.)*

Split Buttons

A split button is a button with a menu attached. Near the lower-right corner of the button you will see an arrowhead. Clicking the arrowhead displays the drop-down menu. To hide a split button menu without choosing a command, click the arrowhead again or click anywhere outside of the menu.

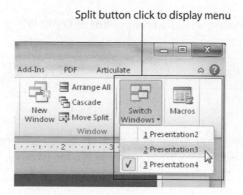

Split button click to display menu

Summary

In this chapter you learned about the applications that comprise the Office 2010 suite and took a complete tour of the suite's powerful navigation tool: the ribbon. In Chapter 2 you'll learn the basics of all of the Office 2010 applications by exploring universal features.

QUIZ

1. **True or False: Microsoft Word is a spreadsheet program best used for working with numeric data.**
   A. True
   B. False

2. **Which of the following is NOT a component of Outlook?**
   A. E-mail
   B. Spreadsheet
   C. Contact management (address book)
   D. Calendar
   E. Task tracker

3. **A spreadsheet program displays a grid of _____ made up of numerous _____ . (Fill in the blanks using the following choices.)**
   A. Cells
   B. Tabs and ribbons
   C. Rows and columns
   D. Formulas
   E. Numbers and letters

4. **A slide presentation can contain any combination of which of the following?**
   A. Charts
   B. Tables
   C. Graphics
   D. Text
   E. All of the above

5. **True or False: In PowerPoint, text, graphics, tables, and charts can be animated.**
   A. True
   B. False

6. **Microsoft Access can be used for which of the following?**
   A. Keeping an appointment calendar
   B. Writing a memo
   C. Tracking product inventory
   D. Creating a photo slide show
   E. Creating a DVD

7. **The number of commands displayed on the ribbons is dependent upon the screen real estate available. This includes which of the following? (Choose all that apply.)**
   A. Screen resolution
   B. Monitor size
   C. Window size
   D. Computer memory
   E. Dialog box size

8. **What does a ribbon gallery display?**
   A. A drop-down menu
   B. A dialog box
   C. A list of commands or options right in the ribbon itself
   D. None of the above
   E. All of the above

9. **What does clicking a split button display?**
   A. A drop-down menu
   B. A dialog box
   C. A list of commands or options right in the ribbon itself
   D. None of the above
   E. All of the above

10. **True or False: The Quick Access toolbar cannot be customized.**
   A. True
   B. False

chapter 2

Office 2010 Universal Features

The Office 2010 suite offers a high level of interface consistency across all of its applications. This means that when it comes to the important program fundamentals—such as the basics of working with documents or using cut, copy, and paste—once you learn how to manage a feature in one application, you already know how to use that feature in all of the others.

This chapter aims to dramatically shorten your learning curve and set you up for "suite" success using some of the universally shared features in Office 2010. What you will learn here can be used in any of the Microsoft Office applications, with a few exceptions as noted within the chapter.

CHAPTER OBJECTIVES

In this chapter, you will learn how to

- Use Backstage View to work with Office 2010 documents, including creating new documents, opening existing documents, and saving documents
- Use the Undo and Redo commands
- Cut, copy, and paste using the Clipboard
- Access and apply themes
- Get help

Using Backstage View to Manage Office 2010 Documents

Backstage View is a brand-new feature introduced in Office 2010. To access Backstage View in any of the Office suite applications, click the File ribbon. The commands and options organized in the Office 2010 Backstage View were found under the Office button in Office 2007, while earlier versions of the suite had File and Options menus that provided access to most of these features as well.

An easy way to remember what features you will find here is to understand that Backstage View (also known as the File ribbon or File tab) provides you with commands that will allow you to do things *to* a file (such as saving or printing it) while all of the other ribbons provide you with commands that allow you to do things *within* a file (such as formatting or editing it). To underscore that distinction, the File ribbon looks different from any of the other ribbons in one very noticeable way: the file you are working in is hidden from view when the Backstage View is active. Figure 2-1 shows an example of Backstage View in Word.

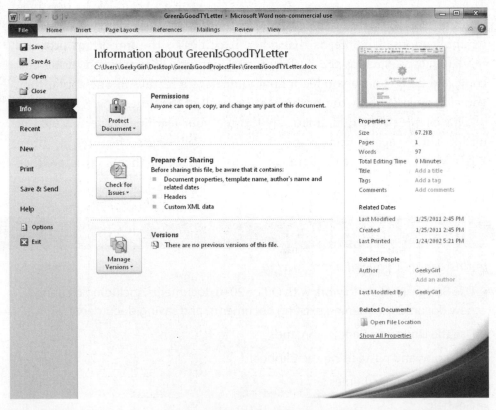

FIGURE 2-1 · The Info pane displays document properties, lets you set document permissions, and prepares a file for sharing.

TIP   *Since the File ribbon looks so different from the other ribbons, you may be tempted to click the Close button in the top-right corner of the window when you want to leave that Backstage View. Don't! Instead, you can press the ESC key or simply click on any of the other tab names (e.g., Home, Insert, etc.). Clicking the Close button in the top-right corner of the screen or on the Exit link in the left pane will close the document (as well as the application if only a single document was open). You will be prompted to save the document if you've made any changes.*

The left pane of Backstage View displays a list of commands. The larger portion of the Backstage View window displays related information or additional options for the command that is currently selected in the left pane. As illustrated in Figure 2-2, commands in the left pane are exactly the same in Word, Excel, and PowerPoint and only slightly different in Access and Outlook. So again—once you become familiar with one File ribbon, you are familiar with them all.

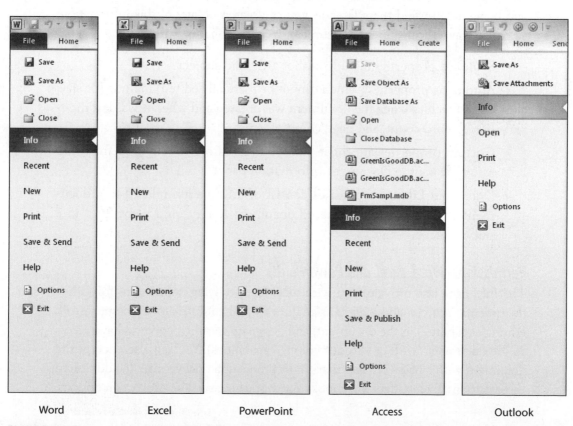

Word   Excel   PowerPoint   Access   Outlook

FIGURE 2-2 • Features on the File ribbon in Microsoft Office 2010 Backstage View are similar throughout the suite.

Backstage View Info Pane

What is displayed in the Backstage View Info pane depends on the current state of the open file. In Word, Excel, and PowerPoint, the Info pane includes the following areas: Document Properties, Permissions, Prepare For Sharing, and Versions. An example is pictured in Figure 2-1.

The Access and Outlook Info panes are unique to those programs. The Access Info pane offers options for compacting and repairing a database and password-protecting a database. The options in the Outlook Info pane depend on what you are looking at when you click the File ribbon (i.e., inbox, e-mail message, contact, task, or appointment). Since the Access and Outlook Info panes are quite different, they are not included in this chapter.

Document Properties (Word, Excel, and PowerPoint)

The Info pane lists document properties, also known as metadata. These properties identify and describe a document, and can be a great help in organizing documents and being able to find them later, as you can search on any of this information. There are several categories of document properties that may display:

- **Standard properties** include author, title, and subject.

- **Automatic properties** (which cannot be manually edited) include file size, dates (such as when the document was created and when it was last modified), word count, and page count.

- **Custom properties** are those that you (or an organization) defines and assigns using the Document Information panel.

- **Document Library properties** consist of information related to a document that is stored in a shared document library on a website or in a public folder.

Permissions (Word, Excel, and PowerPoint)

The Info pane also provides you with tools for specifying permissions for Office documents. You can add a digital signature to authenticate a document, restrict editing capabilities in the document, and designate specific people to have access to the document (with or without editing capabilities). You can also encrypt the document with a password and mark a document as a final version. In addition to these options, Excel offers workbook- and worksheet-specific protection options.

Prepare for Sharing (Word, Excel, and PowerPoint)

The Prepare For Sharing drop-down menu on the Info pane offers options to prepare a document for sharing with others. You can check a document for personal information or hidden properties (such as tracked changes, comments, or text marked as hidden) that you might not want others to see. You can test the document for accessibility issues (such as images missing descriptive captions or slides missing titles) to ensure that readers with disabilities will be able to read the document.

In addition, if you will be sharing documents with others who may have an older version of the program, you can check the document for features that would not be compatible with earlier versions.

Versions (Word, Excel, and PowerPoint)

Office 2010's AutoSave feature is set to automatically save a version of your document every 10 minutes. The Versions drop-down menu on the Info pane works in conjunction with this setting to allow you to recover a document, whether you accidentally closed it without saving or would simply like to return to a slightly earlier version of a document.

Recovering an Existing Document in Word, Excel, and PowerPoint   If you've made modifications to an existing file (one that had previously been saved with a name) and the file was closed without being saved, you can recover a document using the following steps.

1. Click the File ribbon.
2. Choose Info.
3. Click Manage Versions.

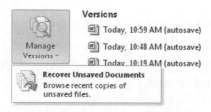

4. Choose Recover Unsaved. (In Word, this will say *Recover Unsaved Documents*; in Excel, *Recover Unsaved Workbooks*; and in PowerPoint, *Recover Unsaved Presentations*.) A list of unsaved files displays in a new window.

5. Select a file and click Open.

6. Click the Save As button in the yellow bar at the top of the document.

7. Type a name for the file in the File Name field.

8. Navigate to the folder where you want the file saved.

9. Click Save.

Recovering a New Document in Word, Excel, and PowerPoint If you created a brand new file and the file was closed without being saved, you can recover a document using the following steps.

1. Click the File ribbon.

2. Choose Recent.

3. Click the Recover Unsaved Documents button in the lower-right corner of the window (instead of the word *Documents*, you will see *Workbooks* in Excel and *Presentations* in PowerPoint). The saved drafts folder will open in a new window.

4. Select a file and click Open.

5. Click the Save As button in the yellow bar at the top of the document.

6. Type a name for the file in the File Name field.

7. Navigate to the folder where you want the file saved.

8. Click Save.

Modifying AutoSave Options in Word, Excel, and PowerPoint AutoSave options can be modified to suit your preferences.

1. Click the File ribbon.

2. Choose Options.

3. Choose Save. The AutoSave options are under the Save Documents heading, as pictured here.

Customize how documents are saved.

Save documents

Save files in this format: Word Document (*.docx)

☑ Save AutoRecover information every 2 minutes

☑ Keep the last autosaved version if I close without saving

AutoRecover file location: C:\Users\GeekyGirl\AppData\Roaming\Microsoft\Word\ Browse...

Default file location: C:\Users\GeekyGirl\Documents\ Browse...

4. Modify the settings as desired found under the Save Documents heading. For example, you can change the number of minutes between AutoSaves, turn AutoSave off completely, choose not to keep the last autosaved version of a document if you close without saving, or change your file save locations.

Still Struggling

Wondering where automatically saved files are stored on your hard drive?

- In Windows 7 and Vista, the file path is: C:\Users\<user name>\AppData\ Roaming\Microsoft\<Application_Name>

- In Windows XP, the file path is c:\Documents and Settings\<user name>\ Application Data\Microsoft\<App Name>

Creating a New Office 2010 Document

Launching Word, Excel, or PowerPoint presents you with a new, blank file in which you can immediately begin working. You can also use the New command on the File ribbon (pictured in PowerPoint in Figure 2-3) to create a new file in all Office applications with the exception of Outlook. (Note that since Outlook is quite different with regard to creating new files—such as e-mails, contacts, tasks, and appointments—this topic will be covered in that application's section of this book.)

The New pane gives you the option of starting with a completely blank *document* (Word), *workbook* (Excel), *presentation* (PowerPoint), or *database* (Access), starting with an available template (and/or theme in PowerPoint) or starting with a template from the Microsoft Office website. A template is a preformatted document layout that serves as the basis for a brand-new file. In addition to being preformatted, most templates include suggested text that you can modify to suit your own purposes. Table 2-1 offers a few examples of the types of templates available in Office.

Using a template can save you loads of time and ensure a professional look and feel to your documents. If this cookie-cutter design approach doesn't quite appeal to you, then you can still save time by customizing an existing template to suit your own purpose and sense of design and then saving it with a new name.

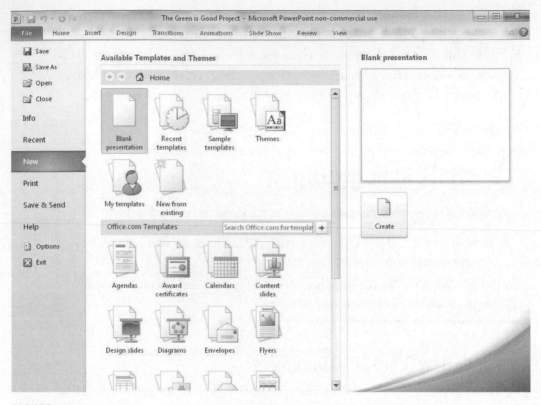

FIGURE 2-3 · The New pane lets you create a new, blank document or start from a template.

TABLE 2-1	File Ribbon Recent Pane (Excel 2010)		
Word	• Resumes • Fax cover pages • Cover letters • To-do lists • Memos	• Reports • Agendas • Flyers • Newsletters • Meeting minutes	• Letters • Envelopes • Forms • Proposals • Labels
Excel	• Billing statements • Invoices • Time cards • Charts	• Expense reports • Loan amortization • Sales reports • Receipts	• Blood pressure tracker • Personal monthly budgets
PowerPoint	• Presentations • Diagrams • Calendars	• Awards certificates • Greeting cards • Photo albums	• Quiz show • Training deck • Pitch book
Access	• Assets database • Projects web database • Expense reports and tracker	• Contacts database • Sales pipeline • Student list • Inventory tracker	• Charitable contributions database • Personal or business account ledger

Simply create a new document based on a template and then modify any design element you wish—text styles, themes (color combinations), backgrounds, and so on.

In addition to the sample templates available under the Available Templates heading, hundreds of templates are available from the Office.com website.

TIP *Use the CTRL-N keyboard shortcut to quickly open a new blank file in Word, Excel, and PowerPoint and to open the New pane on the File ribbon in Access.*

Creating a New File in Word, Excel, PowerPoint, or Access

1. Click the File ribbon.
2. Choose New.
3. Do one of the following:
   - To start with a blank file, click Blank under the Available Templates heading.
   - To start with a template, navigate to and select the desired template under the Available Templates or Office.com Templates headings.
4. Click the Create button.

TIP *Already have an existing file that would be a perfect starting point for your new file? To base a new file on one of your own existing files, choose New From Existing under the Available Templates heading. Navigate to and select the file you want to use as the basis for your new document, and click Create New.*

Opening an Existing Office 2010 File

Need to work with a file you created previously? The Open dialog box allows you to navigate to and open any of your existing files.

TIP *To help confine the search for a file, the Open dialog box lists only files created in the program you are currently in. This is controlled by the drop-down menu on the right side of the File Name field. If you are in Access, for example, the drop-down menu will default to Microsoft Access; if you are in Word, the drop-down menu will default to All Word Documents. This is helpful to know if you are look-ing for a specific file type, such as a template. A template file won't be listed in the Open dialog box if the drop-down menu is set to All Word Documents. So if you are in Word and looking for a template, choose All Word Templates from this drop-down menu to display only templates in the Open dialog box.*

Opening an Existing File in Word, Excel, PowerPoint, or Access

1. Click the File ribbon.
2. Choose Open. Figure 2-4 shows an example of the Open dialog box in PowerPoint 2010.
3. Navigate to the folder where the file is stored, and select it.
4. Click Open.

TIP *Use the CTRL-O keyboard shortcut to quickly access the Open dialog box in Word, Excel, PowerPoint, and Access.*

Opening a Recently Viewed File in Word, Excel, PowerPoint, or Access

If you've recently worked with a file, the Recent pane on the File ribbon makes it easy for you to locate and open that file.

1. Click the File ribbon.
2. Choose Recent. (In Word, this will say *Recent Document*; in Excel, *Recent Workbooks*; in PowerPoint, *Recent Presentations*; and in Access, *Recent Databases*.) Figure 2-5 shows an example of the Recent pane on the File ribbon in Excel 2010.
3. Choose a file to open from the Recent list. The file opens immediately.

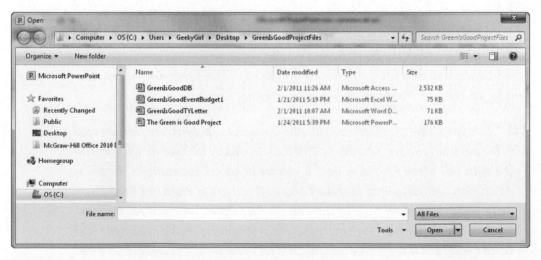

FIGURE 2-4 • The Open dialog box (shown here in PowerPoint 2010) lets you navigate to and open a file.

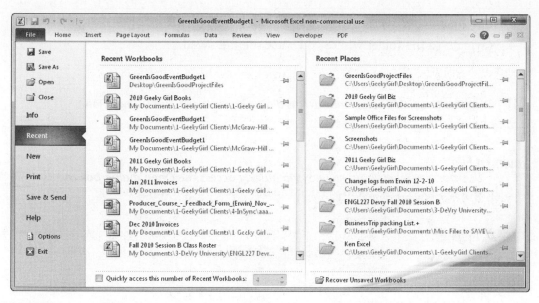

FIGURE 2-5 · The Recent pane (shown here in Excel 2010) lists files and folders you have worked with recently.

> **TIP** *If the file you wish to open doesn't appear in the Recent list, you might be able to find it by navigating within the folders displayed on the right side of the Recent pane, under Recent Places.*

Saving an Office 2010 Document

There are two commands for saving a file: Save and Save As. If you are saving a document for the first time, you will want to save it with a unique name and place it in a folder where you can find it again. The Save As command allows you to do this. (Note that if you are saving a file for the very first time, either command will open the Save As dialog box.) If you open an existing document and then want to save a copy of it with a different name, you should use the Save As command.

After you use the Save As command to save a file with a unique name and specific location you will then use the Save command to periodically save the file while you are working in it.

Saving a File with a New Name

1. Click the File ribbon.
2. Click Save As.

3. Type a name for the file in the File Name field.

4. Navigate to the folder where you want the file saved.

5. Click Save.

TIP *Press F12 to quickly access the Save As dialog box in Word, Excel, PowerPoint, and Access.*

Saving a File

1. In the Quick Access toolbar, click the Save button (pictured here).

Save button

TIP *Use the CTRL+S keyboard shortcut to quickly save a file in Word, Excel, Power-Point, and Access. Alternatively, you can save a file from the File ribbon by clicking the Save command.*

Undo and Redo

The Undo and Redo buttons on the Quick Access toolbar (pictured here) allow you to cancel or re-create, respectively, the last action taken. For example, if you delete text or a graphic and then realize you want it back, the Undo command will get it back for you. If you then decide that you want that text or graphic gone after all, the Redo command will redo the deletion for you. The Undo and Redo commands work with hundreds of actions within Office.

Undo   Redo

The drop-down menu attached to the Undo button lets you look through a list of actions you've recently taken. Choosing an item in that list undoes all of the actions that occurred since that action. Undo and Redo are not unlimited;

each Office application has its own limit as to the number of actions you can undo or redo.

TIP *Use the CTRL-Z keyboard shortcut to quickly undo the previous action.*

Undoing an Action

1. Click the Undo button.
2. Repeat as necessary, or select an action in the Undo drop-down list.

Redoing an Action

1. Click the Redo button.
2. Repeat as necessary.

Working with the Clipboard in Office 2010

The Clipboard is a temporary holding area in your computer's working memory that allows you to copy or move text or objects within a document, between two different files or even between two different applications (in most cases).

When you use the Copy or Cut commands in Office, the text or object you are copying or moving gets placed into the Clipboard memory. When you use the Paste command, the most recent item placed into the Clipboard will be copied or moved to the current cursor location. The item remains in the Clipboard, so if you want to paste it multiple times, you can. The Cut, Copy, and Paste commands (and their various options) are located on the Home ribbon in all of the Office 2010 applications (pictured in Figure 2-6).

The Office Clipboard

The Office Clipboard can store up to 24 items, which can be accessed by clicking the Clipboard Dialog Box Launcher (the arrow on the bottom-right area of the Clipboard group on the Home ribbon).

Pasting Using the Clipboard Dialog Box

1. Position the mouse pointer where you want the item pasted.
2. Click the Clipboard Dialog Box Launcher button.

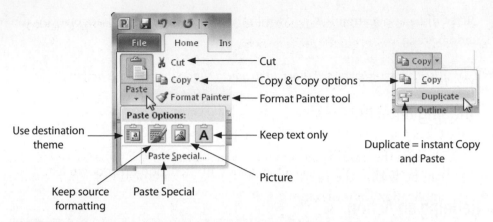

FIGURE 2-6 · Cut (Move), Copy, and Paste options are located on the Home ribbon.

3. Scroll through the Clipboard to locate the item you wish to paste, and right-click it.

4. Choose Paste.

Options for working in the Office Clipboard, such as choosing when the Clipboard dialog box should open, can be modified by clicking the Options drop-down menu at the bottom of the dialog box.

TIP *When you launch the Office Clipboard dialog box, it is positioned on the left side of the window in its own pane. You can float this pane anywhere on your screen by dragging it by its title bar. Resize the floating pane by dragging any of its edges. To redock and expand the pane, simply drag it toward the top-left corner of the screen until it docks.*

Copying Text or Objects

1. Select the text or object you wish to copy.

2. Click Copy the Home ribbon.

3. Position the mouse pointer where you want the item pasted. This can be within the same document, in another document, or in another application (in most cases).

4. Click the Paste button on the Home ribbon. To paste the item multiple times, simply click Paste as many times as needed.

TIP   *Use the CTRL-C keyboard shortcut to quickly copy an item. Use the CTRL-V keyboard shortcut to quickly paste an item.*

Moving Text or Objects

1. Select the text or object you wish to move.
2. Click Cut on the Home ribbon.
3. Position the mouse pointer where you want the item to be moved to. This can be within the same document, in another document, or in another application (in most cases).
4. Click the Paste button on the Home ribbon. If you want to paste the item multiple times, simply click Paste multiple times.

TIP   *Use the CTRL+- keyboard shortcut to quickly cut an item. Use the CTRL-V keyboard shortcut to quickly paste an item.*

Exploring Office 2010 Themes

A theme is an attractive designer-coordinated collection of fonts, effects, color combinations, table formats, and graphic concepts. Using a theme can help give your files a professional and consistent look and feel. Using a theme ensures that all of a document's elements complement one another stylistically. If you are *not* the creative type, using a theme can solve your design deficiencies. If you *are* the creative type, you can start with a theme, customize it to suit, and then save it with a unique name for future use.

Themes are shared across all of the Office 2010 applications, so if you want to coordinate your letters with your spreadsheets and charts as well as your database reports, presentations, and e-mail messages, you can! The same theme names, such as *Aspect*, *Elemental*, or *Opulent*, are used consistently in each of the Office applications.

Although themes are shared across all Office 2010 applications, how they are used in Outlook (e-mail) and Access (reports and tables) is a little different from how they are used in Word, Excel, and PowerPoint; thus, applying themes in Outlook and Access is not covered in this chapter.

Applying a Theme in Word, Excel, and PowerPoint

1. Open the Word, Excel, or PowerPoint file in which you want to apply a theme.

2. Do one of the following:
   - In Word or Excel, choose the Page Layout ribbon.
   - In PowerPoint, choose the Design ribbon.

3. Click the Themes drop-down menu (pictured in Figure 2-7), and do one of the following:
   - To use one of the Office predefined themes, select it under the Built-In heading.

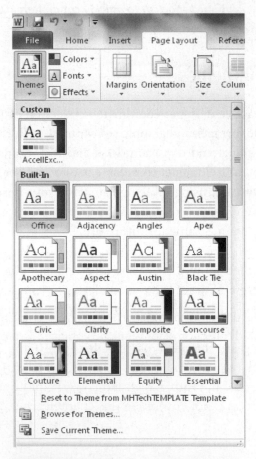

FIGURE 2-7 • The Themes drop-down list (shown here in Word) is split into distinct sections: Custom, Built-In, and From Office.com.

- To use a custom theme that you created previously, select it under the Custom heading.
- To use a theme from the Office.com website, scroll down and select it under the From Office.com heading.

Scroll through the document and note the changes.

Customizing a Theme and Saving It

The easiest way to create your own theme is to start with a built-in theme, customize it to your liking, and then save the modified theme with a unique name. Your custom themes will appear under the Custom heading in the Themes drop-down menu.

1. Apply a theme to a file.
2. Use the Colors, Fonts, and Effects drop-down menus in the Theme group to modify the colors, fonts, and effects in the current theme as desired.
3. When your theme is complete, choose Save Current Theme from the Themes drop-down menu.
4. Type a name for your theme in the File Name field.
5. The Save As Type drop-down list should default to Office Theme. This saves the theme in the same location as all of the other themes thereby ensuring that it will appear under the Custom heading in the Themes drop-down menu.

 Still Struggling

Confused about the difference between a theme and a template? A theme is a designer-coordinated collection of fonts, color combinations, table formats, and graphic concepts. A template is a preformatted document that serves as the basis for a brand-new file. A template can use a theme as its basis, but it will also contain other elements such as placeholders and suggested text.

Help!

Help is integrated into each of the Office 2010 applications. This means you will be able to get help with a program even if you are not connected to the Internet. Additional help is available online. You can browse Help contents or search for specific keywords.

Browsing Help Contents

1. Click the Help button (round blue question mark) that appears in the top-right corner of the application, or press the F1 key on the keyboard.

2. To display the table of contents, click the Table Of Contents button (pictured in Figure 2-8). Note that this button is a toggle; click it again if you wish to hide the table of contents.

3. Click a topic category in the table of contents.

4. Click one or more subtopics if necessary to reach the desired information.

5. Close the Help window by clicking the Close button (the red X) in the top-right corner of the window.

TIP   *The Search field near the top-left area of the Help window has a drop-down menu attached to it. The drop-down menu (pictured here) contains your most recent searches. Choose from this list to quickly return to a Help topic you recently looked at.*

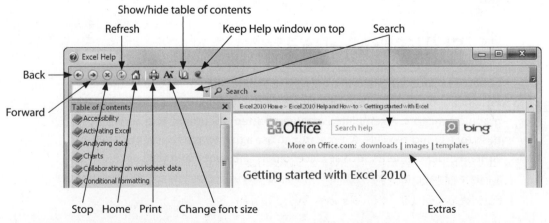

FIGURE 2-8 · The Office 2010 Help window and toolbar allow you to get online or in-application help.

Searching Help Contents

1. Click the Help button (round blue question mark) that appears in the top-right corner of the application, or press the F1 key on the keyboard.

2. Type what you are looking for in either of the search fields at the top of the Help window and press ENTER. Search results can contain articles, links, templates, training, videos, and more.

3. Click a search result link to view it.

4. Close the Help window by clicking the Close button (the red X) in the top-right corner of the window.

TIP   *By default, a search will look in all Help resources, both local and online, and deliver all types of results. To narrow your search to a specific resource (such as content from Office.com) or a type of result (such as templates), search using the Search field in the top-left corner of the Help window and narrow your search using the Search drop-down list to the right of that Search field.*

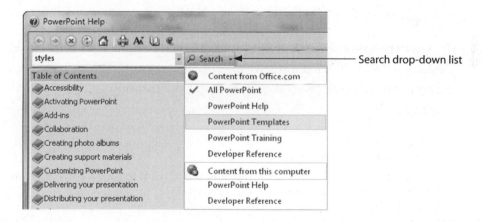

Summary

This chapter introduced you to working with documents in Backstage View as well as some of the universally shared features across the Office suite, including Undo and Redo, the Clipboard, themes, and Help. In Chapter 3 you'll begin focusing specifically on Microsoft Word 2010.

QUIZ

1. True or False: Backstage View only appears in Word, Excel, and PowerPoint. There is no Backstage View in Access or Outlook.

    A. True
    B. False

2. On which ribbon will you find options for managing versions?

    A. File
    B. Home
    C. Design
    D. Review
    E. View

3. By default, Office 2010's _____ feature is set to automatically save a version of your document every _____ minutes. (Fill in both blanks using the following choices.)

    A. Save As
    B. 10
    C. Permissions
    D. 3
    E. AutoSave

4. What is the keyboard shortcut for creating a new document in Word, Excel, PowerPoint, and Access?

    A. CTRL-S
    B. F1
    C. CTRL-V
    D. CTRL-N
    E. None of the above

5. True or False: If you open an existing document and want to save a copy of it with a new name, you must use the Save As command.

    A. True
    B. False

6. Which of the following best describes a theme?

    A. A preformatted document that serves as the basis for a brand-new file
    B. A designer-coordinated collection of fonts, color combinations, table formats, and graphic concepts
    C. Neither of the above

7. **What is the keyboard shortcut for pasting cut or copied text or graphics in a document?**
   A. CTRL-S
   B. CTRL-V
   C. F12
   D. CTRL-N
   E. None of the above

8. **Which of the following buttons does not appear in the Help window toolbar?**
   A. Print
   B. Table Of Contents
   C. Change Font Size
   D. Save
   E. Back

9. **What is the keyboard shortcut for saving a file?**
   A. CTRL-S
   B. CTRL-V
   C. CTRL-F7
   D. CTRL-N
   E. None of the above

10. **True or False: The Undo and Redo buttons on the Quick Access toolbar allow you to cancel or recapture the last action taken.**
    A. True
    B. False

Part II

Microsoft Word

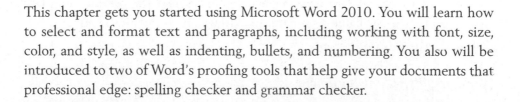

chapter **3**

Getting Started with Word

This chapter gets you started using Microsoft Word 2010. You will learn how to select and format text and paragraphs, including working with font, size, color, and style, as well as indenting, bullets, and numbering. You also will be introduced to two of Word's proofing tools that help give your documents that professional edge: spelling checker and grammar checker.

CHAPTER OBJECTIVES

In this chapter, you will learn how to

- Build a new document
- Work with text (click and type, selecting, deleting, and formatting)
- Work with paragraphs (formatting marks, alignment, and indenting)
- Proof a document

Building a New Document

As you learned in Chapter 2, launching Word presents you with a new, blank document in which you can immediately begin working. You can also use the New command on the File ribbon to create a new file in Word. Doing so displays the New pane, which gives you the option of starting with a completely blank document, starting with an available template, or starting with a template from the Microsoft Office website.

Creating a New File in Word

1. Click the File ribbon.
2. Choose New.
3. Do one of the following:
   - To start with a blank document, click Blank (located under the Available Templates heading).
   - To start with a template, navigate to and select the desired template under the Available Templates or Office.com Templates heading.
4. Click the Create button.

Working with a Blank Document

A blank document gives you the opportunity to completely build your file from scratch. A new, blank document is always based on a default template named Normal.dotx, which can be tailored to suit your personal preferences. For example, you can change the Normal template's font, size, and style as well as line spacing and paragraph spacing, among other items.

Changing the Default Font for the Normal Template

1. Create a new, blank document.
2. On the Home tab, click the Font Dialog Box Launcher.
3. Click the Font tab (if necessary).
4. Choose a font from the Font list.
5. Choose a font style from the Font Style list.
6. Choose a font size from the Size list (or type a size in the Size field).

7. Click the Set As Default button.

8. Click OK.

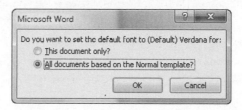

9. Do one of the following:

   - To change the default font for the open document only, click This Document only?

   - To change the default font for the open document as well as all future documents created from the Normal template, click All Documents Based On The Normal template?

10. Click OK.

TIP *If the font size you wish to use does not appear in the Size list (for example, size 13), type it in the Size field.*

Changing Paragraph and Spacing Settings for the Normal Template

1. Create a new, blank document.

2. On the Home tab, click the Paragraph Dialog Box Launcher. The Paragraph dialog box opens (pictured in Figure 3-4).

3. Click the Indents And Spacing tab (if necessary).

4. Under the Indentation heading, modify the current settings as needed. For example, if you want the paragraphs to have a 0.25" indent for the first line of every paragraph, change the number in the Left field to 0.25.

5. Under the Spacing heading, modify the current settings as needed. For example, if you want the paragraphs to have 6 points of spacing after each of them, change the number in the After field to 6 pt. If you want lines to have more (or less) spacing between them, make a selection under the Line Spacing drop-down list.

6. Click the Set As Default button.

7. Click OK.

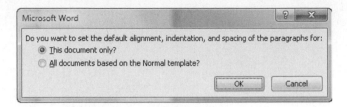

8. Do one of the following:

- To change the default font for the open document only, click This Document Only?

- To change the default font for the open document as well as all future documents created from the Normal template, click All Documents Based On The Normal template?

9. Click OK.

TIP   *The Paragraph dialog box also allows you to set up default tabs for your documents (click the Tabs button on the Indents And Spacing tab) as well as line and page break options (click the Line And Page Breaks tab).*

Working with a Template

You may recall from Chapter 2 that a template is a preformatted document layout that serves as the basis for a brand-new file. In addition to being preformatted, most templates include suggested text that you can modify to suit your purposes. Figure 3-1 shows an example of a resume template called "Origin." Note that the text within square brackets is directing you to add a specific type of information, such as a job title or degree.

To modify text in a template, simply follow the instructions written within the square brackets. For example, if the template says [Type your address] then you can click anywhere within the brackets to select the entire placeholder and then begin typing your address. When you begin typing, the old text will be replaced by the new text. Where dates are requested in a template, you can type a date or click the Pick The Date drop-down menu to select from a calendar (pictured here).

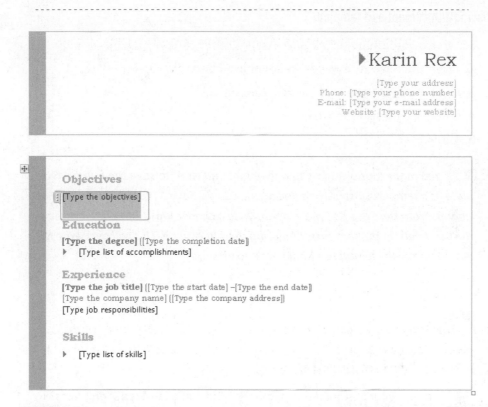

FIGURE 3-1 • Word 2010 template example showing the Origin resume template

You can tailor a template to suit your own needs and then save it as a new template. You can also save any document you've created from scratch as a template. Saving a document as a template allows you to create additional new documents based on the template. One benefit of saving a document as a template is that you are protecting the document from being easily overwritten. The first time you save a document that is based on a template, the Save As dialog box will open (even if you chose the Save command). This reminds you to give the file a unique name and save it in a specific location where you can find it again.

TIP   *A Word document has a .docx file extension. A Word template has a .dotx file extension. Word templates that also include macros (an automated series of instructions) have a .docm extension.*

Saving a Document as a Template

1. On the File ribbon, click Save As.
2. From the Save As Type drop-down list, choose Word Template.
3. Type a unique name in the File Name field.
4. Choose a location for the file.
5. Click Save.

TIP *If you make modifications to a template and want to save the revised template as a template instead of a document, use the Save As command on the File ribbon. From the Save As Type drop-down list, choose Word Template and save the document in the same location using the same name. This will overwrite the old version of the template with the revised version.*

Still Struggling

Want to save your custom templates in the same folder as Word's templates? To find the path to that folder:

1. In Word, click the File ribbon and then click Options.
2. In the Word Options dialog box, click Advanced and scroll all the way to the bottom.
3. At the bottom of the Advanced pane, click the File Locations button.
4. Click User Templates and then click Modify.
5. The file path for user templates can be seen at the top of the window—jot it down so you know where to navigate the next time you save a custom template. An example is pictured here.

Working with Text

To add text to a Word document, simply start typing. Text is added wherever the cursor is blinking. In a new, blank document that is based on the default Normal template, this will be one inch from the left margin and one inch from the top margin. Text will automatically wrap to the next line when you've run out of space in the current line. There is no need to press the ENTER key at the end of every line—only press ENTER at the end of a paragraph. As you type, you can use the BACKSPACE key to delete in a backward direction and the DELETE key to delete in a forward direction.

Click And Type

Word's Click And Type feature allows you to begin a line of text anywhere on the page instead of adhering to the existing left margin. Just double-click anywhere on the page and begin typing. The text you are typing will be automatically aligned (left, center, or right) depending on where on the page you have double-clicked. For example, double-clicking near the center of a page causes text to center-align; double-clicking nearer to the left margin will left-align text; double-clicking nearer the right margin will right-align text.

Just before you double-click to place the cursor, you can preview the alignment by looking at the mouse pointer. The illustration on the right shows the alignment cursors.

Align left   Align center   Align right

Note that Click And Type will not work in bulleted or numbered lists, or in paragraphs formatted using multiple columns or indents. Click And Type also will not function near graphics that use top or bottom text wrapping.

TIP *Word's Click And Type feature only works when you are in Print Layout view. Choose Print Layout on the View ribbon.*

Selecting Text

To format, cut, or copy text, you must select (or highlight) it first. The following illustration shows an example of text that is not selected (on the left) and text that is selected (on the right).

This text is not selected. This text is selected.

TABLE 3-1 Popular Text Selection Methods

To select...	Do this:
Any amount of text	Click and drag with your mouse pointer.
A single word	Double-click in the middle of the word.
A single sentence	CTRL-click in a sentence.
A single paragraph	Triple-click in the middle of the paragraph.
A single line of text	Position the mouse pointer to the left of the text (the cursor will look like an arrow) and click.
Multiple lines of text	Position the mouse pointer to the left of the text (the cursor will look like an arrow) and then click and drag.
The entire document	CTRL-A

There are numerous ways to select text in a document. Table 3-1 lists some of the most popular methods.

TIP *To learn additional ways to select text—including methods that involve using only the keyboard—search on "select text" in the Word Help file.*

Deleting Text

In addition to using the BACKSPACE and DELETE keys to delete individual characters while you are typing, you can select larger chunks of text for deletion.

1. Select (highlight) the text you wish to delete.

2. Press the BACKSPACE or DELETE key.

Formatting Text

There are numerous ways to format text, including font, size, style, color, and case. You can choose formatting options *before* typing, or you can type first and then format *afterward*. When using the first method, you must turn on the formatting option(s) you want to use, type the text you want formatted that way, and then turn off the formatting option. (This can be cumbersome unless you make good use of keyboard shortcuts.) When using the second method, you must first select the text you want formatted.

Changing the Font

1. A font can be loosely defined as a complete character set (a–z, plus numbers and symbols) of a particular typeface, such as Arial or Times Roman. Fonts can be businesslike, whimsical, ornate, humdrum, or exciting. Fonts can add personality to a document and enhance readability when used properly. Select the text you wish to format.

2. Click the Home ribbon.

3. Choose a font from the Font drop-down list (pictured here).

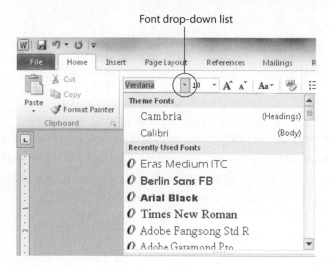

Font drop-down list

TIP *Avoid using more than one or two fonts in a document. Using multiple fonts in a document can give it the disjointed look of a ransom note and make the text difficult to read.*

Changing Text Size

1. Select the text you wish to format.

2. Click the Home ribbon.

3. Do one of the following:

- Choose a size from the Size drop-down list.
- Type a size in the Size field.
- Click the Grow Font or Shrink Font button.

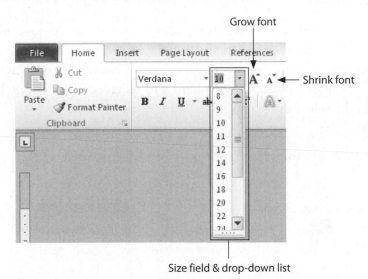

TIP   *If you enjoy using keyboard shortcuts, you can resize selected text using the keyboard instead of the mouse. To increase the size of selected text, use CTRL-SHIFT->. To decrease the size of selected text, use CTRL-SHIFT-<. (Watch the Size field on the Home ribbon as you do this to see the text size update.)*

Changing Text Style and Color

Styles augment the font by letting you apply bold, italic, underline, strikethrough, subscript, and superscript to selected text. Note that the Underline button drop-down list offers a variety of underline styles, such as a dotted or double underline. Likewise, the Color button also provides a drop-down list of color choices. Some style buttons, such as Bold and Italic, are "toggle switches"— clicking the button a second time will turn off the style.

1. Select the text you wish to format.
2. Click the Home ribbon.

3. Use the various style buttons (pictured in Figure 3-2) to add one or more styles to the selected text. For example, to make the selected text bold, click the Bold button.

TIP *Keyboard shortcuts can also be used to modify the style of selected text. For example, to make text bold, use* CTRL-B; *to make it italic, use* CTRL-I; *and to make it underlined, use* CTRL-U.

Highlighting Text

The Text Highlight Color button allows you to mimic the effect of highlighting text in a hard copy document. The current highlight color is displayed on the button; however, clicking the arrow attached to the button provides you with other color options.

1. Select the text you wish to format.

2. Click the Home ribbon.

3. Click the Text Highlight Color button to apply the current highlight color, or click the arrow attached to the button to choose a different color.

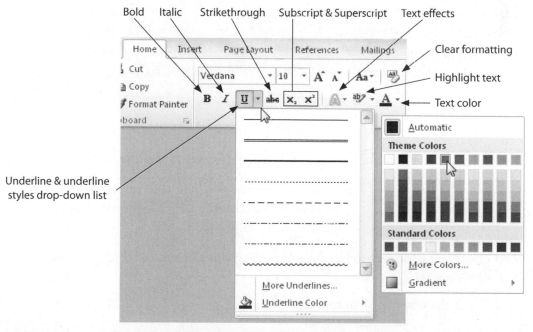

FIGURE 3-2 · Text formatting options appear on the Word 2010 Home ribbon.

TIP *To remove highlighting, click the Text Highlight Color button drop-down list arrow and select No Color.*

Changing Text Case

If you accidentally typed an entire sentence in all caps or an entire paragraph in all lowercase, you do not have to retype the text to fix the issue. Instead, use the Change Case button.

1. Select the text you wish to change the case for.
2. Click the Home ribbon.
3. Click the Change Case button, and choose the appropriate case for the text:
   - Sentence Case capitalizes the first letter in every sentence.
   - Lowercase changes all of the selected text to lowercase letters.
   - Uppercase changes all of the selected text to capital letters.
   - Capitalize Each Word capitalizes every word in the selection.
   - Toggle Case changes uppercase letters to lowercase letters and vice versa.

TIP *The keyboard shortcut SHIFT-F3 cycles through lowercase, uppercase, and sentence case. Select the text, and use the SHIFT-F3 keyboard shortcut one or more times to change the case.*

Adding Text Effects

Text effects are a fun way to jazz up text, letting you add glow effects, shadows, or reflections.

1. Select the text you wish to format.

2. Click the Home ribbon.

3. Click the Text Effects button, and choose the appropriate effect for the text. You can choose one of the instant effects displayed in the drop-down menu, or click one of the four options at the bottom of the menu to choose from additional effects, including outlines, shadows, reflections, and glows.

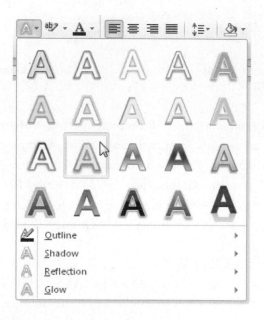

Clearing All Formatting

1. Select the text you wish to clear the formatting from.

2. Click the Clear Formatting button.

Formatting Paragraphs

Most paragraph formatting commands can be found in the Paragraph group on the Home ribbon (pictured in Figure 3-3). Paragraph formatting options apply to entire paragraphs, as opposed to one or more words within a paragraph. To apply paragraph formatting to a single paragraph, simply click in it (there is no need to select the text in the paragraph). To apply paragraph formatting to multiple paragraphs, select all or part of each of the paragraphs you wish to format. You can also choose your formatting options before you begin typing.

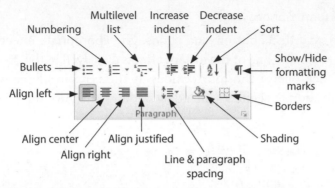

FIGURE 3-3 · Paragraph formatting options appear in the Paragraph group on the Word Home ribbon.

TIP *Paragraph formats are "stored" in the paragraph mark at the end of the paragraph. You will not see this paragraph mark unless you have clicked the Show Formatting Marks button. Because the paragraph formatting gets stored in the paragraph mark, you can select and copy a paragraph mark from one paragraph and then paste it over a paragraph mark in another paragraph. This serves to copy each of the paragraph formatting options from one paragraph to another.*

Showing/Hiding Formatting Marks

By default, formatting marks are hidden. The Show/Hide Formatting Marks button (located in the Paragraph group on the Home ribbon) toggles formatting marks on and off. Formatting marks include all of those pictured here.

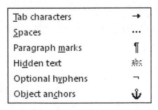

Changing Alignment

Text can be aligned on a page in one of four ways:

- Left (aligned to the left margin of the page, producing a ragged right edge)
- Centered (centered between the left and right margins of the page)
- Right (aligned to the right margin of the page, producing a ragged left edge)
- Justified (aligned to both the left and right margins with no ragged edge)

To choose any of these options:

1. Select the paragraph(s) you want to format.

2. Click an alignment button in the Paragraph group on the Home ribbon.

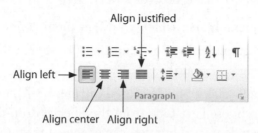

TIP   *Depending on line length, justified text alignment can cause unattractive rivers of white space running through a page because the spacing between words is adjusted to spread out between the margins. For this reason, it is infrequently used.*

Indenting Text

Indenting a line of text by pressing the SPACEBAR a few times is not considered a good practice. Instead, use the Increase Indent and Decrease Indent commands to indent a paragraph. Or, if it's only the first line in a paragraph that you want indented, press the TAB key. This will ensure that all of your indents are uniform.

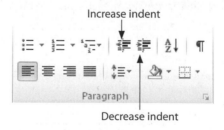

Indenting All Lines in One or More Paragraphs

1. Select the paragraph(s) you want to indent.

2. Do one of the following:

   • Click the Increase Indent button to push the paragraph away from the left margin.

   • Click the Decrease Indent button to push the paragraph closer to the left margin.

Indenting Just the First Line in One or More Paragraphs To indent only the first line of one or more paragraphs, you have a choice between simply pressing the TAB key in front of each paragraph as you are typing and using the First Line Indent setting in the Paragraph dialog box (described here).

1. Select the paragraph(s) in which you want the first line indented.

2. Click the Paragraph Dialog Box Launcher (located in the lower-right corner of the Paragraph group).

3. In the Paragraph dialog box (pictured in Figure 3-4), under the Indentation heading, choose First Line from the Special drop-down list. The default first line indent is .5" but you can change it to suit your document of course.

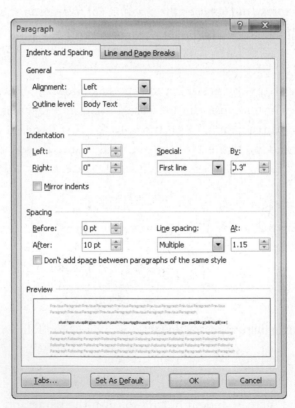

FIGURE 3-4 • The Paragraph dialog box lets you control indents and spacing as well as line and page breaks.

4. Modify the indent width in the By field if necessary. You can type a number directly in the field or use the up and down arrows to change the number.

5. Click OK.

Setting Line and Paragraph Spacing

Line spacing is the spacing between each line in a paragraph. Paragraph spacing is the extra spacing *before* and/or *after* paragraphs. The following illustration shows an example of both line spacing and paragraph spacing. The paragraphs on the left use single line spacing and have six extra points after each paragraph. The paragraphs on the right use double line spacing and have no extra space between paragraphs.

1. Select the paragraph(s) you want to format.

2. Click the Line And Paragraph Spacing button in the Paragraph group of the Home ribbon. A drop-down menu of options appears.

3. To modify the line spacing, choose from the line spacing settings at the top of the menu or select Line Spacing Options to open the Paragraph dialog box (pictured in Figure 3-4) to customize the line spacing.

4. To modify the paragraph spacing, choose one of the following:

   • Add Space Before Paragraph

   • Remove Space After Paragraph.

Adding Bullets

The Bullet button is a split button. Clicking the left side of the button assigns the default bullet point to the selected paragraph. Clicking the right side of the button produces a drop-down list of alternative bullet points (pictured here).

Using bullet points applies a hanging indent to the paragraph and wraps the text neatly within the confines of the indent.

The lines in this paragraph are spaced as Single. The paragraphs have no extra space above or below. The lines in this paragraph are spaced as Single.

- Clicking on the Bullets button indents the paragraph and applies a hanging indent.
- Clicking on the Bullets button indents the paragraph and applies a hanging indent.

The lines in this paragraph are spaced as Single. The paragraphs have no extra space above or below. The lines in this paragraph are spaced as Single.

1. Select the paragraph(s) where you want to add bullets.
2. Do one of the following:
   - Click the left side of the Bullet button to format the paragraph using the currently selected bullet type.
   - Click the right side of the Bullet button to choose a button from the bullet library.

Numbering Text

The Numbering button is a split button. Clicking the left side of the button assigns the default number style to the selected paragraph. Clicking the right side of the button produces a drop-down list of alternative numbering schemes (pictured here).

Using Numbering applies a hanging indent to the paragraph and wraps the text neatly within the confines of the indent.

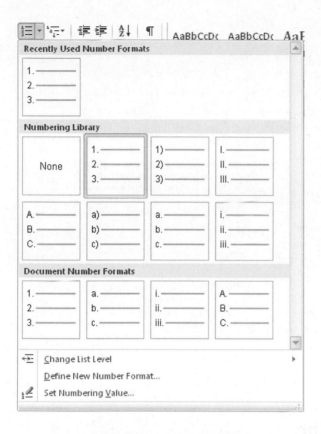

The lines in this paragraph are spaced as Single. The paragraphs have no extra space above or below. The lines in this paragraph are spaced as Single.

1. Clicking on the Numbering button indents the paragraph and applies a hanging indent.
2. Clicking on the Numbering button indents the paragraph and applies a hanging indent.

The lines in this paragraph are spaced as Single. The paragraphs have no extra space above or below. The lines in this paragraph are spaced as Single.

1. Select the paragraph(s) where you want to add numbers.

2. Do one of the following:

- Click the left side of the Numbering button to format the paragraph using the currently selected numbering style.

- Click the right side of the Numbering button to choose a button from the numbering library.

Proofing a Document

As you work in a file, spelling and grammar are checked automatically. When a spelling error is found, the word in question has a squiggly red underline (as shown in the top paragraph of the following illustration). When a grammar error is found, the phrase in question has a squiggly green underline (as shown in the bottom paragraph of the illustration).

Thank you for renewing your single membership with The Green is Good Project! In order to show our apreciation, we have some great news for you.

You now qualifies for a special on a family membership. If you sign up the rest of your family for one year, the first two months are free for them. The details of this special offer is explained in the enclosed brochure.

Correcting Spelling Errors

1. Right-click the misspelled word.

2. Choose the correct spelling from the drop-down menu.

Still Struggling

Word's spelling checker flags words in a document that are not in its dictionary. Sometimes the flagged words are not actually misspelled. For example, obscure technical terms or proper names with unusual spellings will usually be flagged. You can add these words to Word's dictionary so that they will no longer be flagged. Simply right-click a word and choose Add To Dictionary from the drop-down menu.

Correcting Grammar Errors

1. Right-click the questionable grammar.

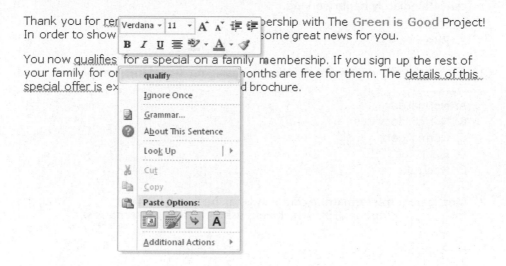

2. Choose the appropriate correction from the drop-down menu.

Changing Proofing Settings

1. Click the File ribbon.
2. Choose Options.
3. Click Proofing.
4. Check or uncheck settings as desired under the When Correcting Spelling And Grammar heading. For example, if you do not want spelling and grammar to be checked as you type, clear the Check Spelling As You Type and Mark Grammar Errors As You Type check boxes.

Summary

In this chapter you got off to a quick start using Microsoft Word 2010. You learned how to select and format text and paragraphs and were introduced to Word's spelling and grammar checkers. In Chapter 4 you will learn how to add pizazz to your document by including graphics, tables, page numbers, headers, and footers.

QUIZ

1. True or False: Launching Word presents you with a new, blank file in which you can immediately begin working.
   A. True
   B. False

2. A new, blank document is always based on a default template named _____.
   A. Normal.doc
   B. Normal.docx
   C. Normal.dotx
   D. Blank.doc
   E. New.doc

3. Most paragraph formatting commands can be found in the _____ Group on the _____ ribbon. (Fill in the blanks using the following choices.)
   A. Insert
   B. Paragraph
   C. Page Setup
   D. Page Layout
   E. Home

4. How do you change font size?
   A. Use the CTRL-SHIFT-> or CTRL-SHIFT-< keyboard shortcut
   B. Choose a size from the Size drop-down list
   C. Type a size in the Size field.
   D. Click the Grow Font or Shrink Font button
   E. All of the above

5. True or False: You cannot modify Word's Normal template in any way.
   A. True
   B. False

6. How do you quickly select a single word?
   A. Triple-click the word
   B. CTRL-CLICK the word
   C. Double-click the word
   D. Use the CTRL-A keyboard shortcut
   E. All of the above

7. **When a spelling error is found, the word in question has a _____ .**
   A. Squiggly green underline
   B. Double underline
   C. Dotted underline
   D. Squiggly red underline
   E. None of the above

8. **When a grammar error is found, the phrase in question has a _____ .**
   A. Squiggly green underline
   B. Double underline
   C. Dotted underline
   D. Squiggly red underline
   E. None of the above

9. **What does clicking the Clear Formatting button do?**
   A. Removes all text formatting
   B. Removes all text and paragraph formatting
   C. Removes all paragraph formatting
   D. None of the above
   E. All of the above

10. **True or False: Thanks to Word's automatic word wrap feature, there is no need to press the ENTER key at the end of every line—just press ENTER at the end of a paragraph.**
    A. True
    B. False

chapter 4

Adding Pizzazz to a Word Document

This chapter introduces you to some Word features that can help your documents appear professional and appealing. Add interest (style! zing! pizzazz!) to your documents by including eye-catching graphics and well-styled tables. Bolster readability and organization in longer documents by including attractive headers, footers, and page numbers.

CHAPTER OBJECTIVES

In this chapter, you will learn how to

- Insert and modify clip art and pictures
- Insert and modify tables
- Add headers and footers
- Work with page numbering

Inserting and Working with Graphics

You can add a variety of graphics in Office 2010 documents, including clip art (Office-supplied artwork provided for decorative purposes), pictures (photographs or other artwork you own), shapes (rectangles, circles, banners, and more that are drawn using tools provided in Office), SmartArt (visual representation of information created in Office), and charts (graphic representations of data).

Inserting and working with graphics works basically the same across all of the Office applications. Clip art and pictures will be covered in this chapter. Shapes and SmartArt will be covered in the PowerPoint section of the book, and charts will be covered in the Excel section of the book.

Inserting Clip Art

1. Position the cursor where you want to insert the clip art.
2. On the Insert ribbon, click Clip Art. The Clip Art dialog box appears.
3. In the Search field at the top of the Clip Art dialog box, type a keyword that represents the type of graphic you want to find, and press ENTER. In the following illustration, the search keyword is "recycle."

4. Scroll through the choices, and click the artwork you want to insert.

TIP   *Don't feel limited by the artwork available in the Clip Art dialog box. The Office.com website is constantly updating its collection of clip art. Click the Find More At Office.com link at the bottom of the Clip Art dialog box.*

Inserting a Picture

1. Position the cursor where you want to insert the picture.
2. On the Insert ribbon, click Picture. The Insert Picture dialog box appears.
3. Navigate to and select the picture you want to use.
4. Click Insert.

Deleting Graphics

1. Click the graphic you wish to delete.
2. Press the BACKSPACE or DELETE key on the keyboard.

TIP   *Accidentally delete something you didn't mean to? Don't forget the Undo command: CTRL-Z or click the Undo button on the Quick Action toolbar.*

Modifying Graphics

Once you've inserted a piece of clip art or a picture into an Office document, you may want to modify it in some way. Office 2010 allows you to resize, rotate, crop, style, recolor, and position graphics.

TIP   *Double-clicking a graphic selects the graphic and displays the Picture Tools Format ribbon. If you single-click a graphic, the Picture Tools Format ribbon will be available but you will have to click on it to view it. Save time and double-click a graphic when you want to select it!*

Sizing a Graphic by Clicking and Dragging

Click the artwork you wish to resize. A border containing eight sizing handles will surround the selected graphic

1. Drag any of the border handles to resize. (Note that the green handle above the border outline is for rotating an image, not resizing it. You will learn more about rotating later in this chapter.)

TIP *Drag a resizing handle outward to make the image larger; drag it inward to make the image smaller. The image aspect ratio will remain intact as you drag.*

Sizing a Graphic by Specifying Its Dimensions

1. Select the graphic you want to resize.
2. On the Pictures Tools Format ribbon, locate the Size group.
3. In the Size group, provide the desired dimensions in the Height or Width fields. Note that, by default, the aspect ratio of the picture will be retained, so you only need to provide one dimension and the other dimension will be adjusted appropriately.

TIP *If you don't want the aspect ratio of a graphic to be retained, click the Size Dialog Box Launcher, uncheck Lock Aspect Ratio on the Size tab, and click OK. This will allow you to change the height and width of a graphic independent from one another. (This tip applies to sizing a graphic by clicking and dragging as well.)*

Rotating a Graphic

1. Click the artwork you want to rotate. At the top of the selected graphic, there will a green handle above the border outline.
2. Drag the green handle to rotate the image.

TIP *Want to get more specific in your graphic rotation? (For example, want to rotate a graphic at a 90-degree angle?) Double-click the graphic and, on the Picture Tools Format ribbon, select an option from the Rotate button drop-down menu. For even more options, choose More Rotating Options to open the Layout dialog box, where you can type a specific rotation degree in the Rotation field.*

Cropping a Graphic

A graphic can be cropped for reshaping purposes (from a rectangle to a square, for example) or to remove a portion of it that you don't want to show (an overflowing trash can in an otherwise great picture of your family in front of the Coliseum, for example). In Figure 4-1, the original graphic is the square image at the left. If you needed a rectangular picture instead, the image can be

FIGURE 4-1 • You can crop a graphic in a variety of ways.

cropped to suit, as shown in the middle image. If all you wanted from the pictures was a headshot of the woman, you could crop out everything else, as shown in the third image.

The Crop tool is on the Picture Tools Format ribbon. Office 2010 offers several cropping options:

- Cropping manually by clicking and dragging
- Cropping to a specific shape automatically
- Cropping to accommodate a specific aspect ratio
- Cropping to fill or fit an area

1. Select the graphic you want to crop.
2. On the Pictures Tools Format ribbon, locate the Crop button in the Size group.

3. Do one of the following:

- Click the top part of the Crop button to indicate that you will manually crop the graphic. Then click and drag the bar handles attached to the picture's border.

- Click the bottom part of the Crop button to choose an option from the Crop button menu:

    - If cropping to a shape, select the shape from the submenu.

    - If cropping to a specific aspect ratio, select the aspect ratio from the submenu.

    - If cropping to fill or fit an area, select that option and then manually crop the graphic by clicking and dragging the bar handles attached to the picture's border.

TIP *With regard to the fill or fit cropping options: To remove part of a picture but still fill the shape with as much of the picture as possible, use the Fill option (the original aspect ratio will be maintained but some of the picture edges may not display). To force all of a picture to fit into a shape, choose the Fit option (the original aspect ratio will be maintained).*

Styling a Graphic

The Office 2010 Picture Tools Format ribbon offers numerous tools for restyling graphics. The Picture Styles gallery lets you choose from a variety of frames and rotation effects. The Effects menu lets you add shadows; reflections; glows; soft, hard, or beveled edges; and 3-D rotations to an image. The Artistic Effects menu lets you choose from creative effects, such as line drawing, film grain, glowing edges, and photocopy. The following illustration shows just a few of the available options (the original picture is the one on the left).

1. Select the graphic you want to style.

2. Do one or more of the following to achieve the effect(s) you are looking for:

   - On the Pictures Tools Format ribbon, locate the Picture Styles group and select a style

   - On the Pictures Tools Format ribbon, click the Picture Effects drop-down menu (on the right side of the Picture Styles group), and select an effect.

   - On the Pictures Tools Format ribbon, locate the Artistic Effects button (in the Adjust group), and select a style.

TIP *All of the effects covered here offer Live Preview. You can "try on" a style or effect by simply hovering over the style or effect name. (In other words, you don't have to click.)*

Recoloring a Graphic

Office 2010 lets you recolor a graphic by changing its color saturation (the intensity of the color), color tone (increasing or decreasing the color temperature to affect a change in the color cast), or coloring scheme (such as sepia or black and white).

1. Select the graphic you want to recolor.

2. On the Pictures Tools Format ribbon, locate the Adjust group, and click the Color button.

3. Do one of the following:

   - Select a color option under the Color Saturation, Color Tone, or Recolor headings or click More Variations for additional choices.

   - Choose Picture Color Options to open the Format Picture dialog box, where there are additional options.

Resetting a Graphic

To undo stylistic changes made to a graphic or to return it to its original size, use the Reset Picture button on the Picture Tools Format ribbon.

1. Select the graphic you want to reset.

2. On the Pictures Tools Format ribbon, locate the Size group, and click the Reset Picture button.

3. Do one of the following:

- Choose Reset Picture to undo any stylistic modifications you may have made to the graphic.
- Choose Reset Picture & Size to undo any stylistic modifications you may have made to the graphic and to restore the graphic to its original size.

Still Struggling

If you are using and modifying a large number of pictures in a document, the file size may become excessively large. You can reduce the file size by compressing pictures used in the document. Select a picture and, on the Picture Tools Format ribbon, click the Compress Pictures button. To compress all of the pictures in the document, uncheck the Apply Only To This Picture check box. To delete portions of pictures you may have cropped, leave the Delete Cropped Areas Of Pictures check box checked. Next, select a resolution and then click OK. Note that compressing pictures will reduce the quality of the images. In most cases, however, the quality difference will not be noticeable.

Positioning a Graphic

By default, graphics are inserted in line with text at the cursor. An *inline* graphic keeps its location relative to the text that surrounds it. Another option for positioning a graphic is to float it. A *floating* graphic keeps its location relative to the page and lets text wrap around it.

1. Select the graphic you want to position.
2. On the Pictures Tools Format ribbon, locate the Arrange group and click the Position button.
3. Do one of the following:

- Choose an option under the With Text Wrapping heading to float the graphic.
- Choose an option under the In Line With Text heading to keep the graphic's location relative to the text that surrounds it.

- Choose More Layout Options to open the Layout dialog box for additional choices. (Click the Help button at the upper-right corner of the dialog box for assistance with these options.)

Inserting and Working with Tables

Tables organize text and graphics into columns and rows. Word offers an amazing array of tools for creating and working with tables. Figure 4-2 showcases three different styles of tables. In addition to helping enhance a document's professional appeal, tables can add readability to a document by making dense information easier to grasp. Trying to explain any of the three tables in Figure 4-2 in paragraph form would be a daunting task, for example.

Inserting a Table

Word provides numerous ways to create a table. In this chapter, two of the most straightforward methods are discussed: Quick Tables and the Table drop-down menu grid. To create a plain table from scratch, use the Table drop-down menu grid; to create a styled table based on another table (similar to using a template), use the Quick Tables approach. Both of these methods are accessible from the Insert ribbon in Word.

ITEM	NEEDED
Books	1
Magazines	3
Notebooks	1
Paper pads	1
Pens	3
Pencils	2
Highlighter	2 colors
Scissors	1 pair

ITEM	NEEDED
	1
	3
	2
	1 pair

Enrollment in local colleges, 2012

College	New students	Graduating students
Undergraduate		
Cedar University	110	103
Elm College	223	214
Maple Academy	197	120
Pine College	134	121
Oak Institute	202	210
Graduate		
Cedar University	24	20
Elm College	43	53
Maple Academy	3	11
Pine College	9	4
Oak Institute	53	52
Total	998	908

Source: Fictitious data, for illustration purposes only

FIGURE 4-2 • A variety of attractive tables can be created in Word 2010.

Using Quick Tables

Use Word's Quick Table tool as a starting point to quickly create a fully styled table. Simply choose a table style you like, replace the placeholder text with your own data, and you are done!

1. Position the cursor where you want the table to be placed.

2. From the Insert ribbon, choose Table and then Quick Table.

3. Scroll through the table examples, and choose a table style that suits the type of table you had in mind. For example, if you want to create a table with subheads, choose one of the sample tables that already has subheads.

4. Modify the table (replacing the sample text with your own, adding or deleting rows or columns, etc.) to suit your own text and purpose. (See "Modifying a Table" later in this chapter for additional tips and techniques.)

Using the Table Menu Drop-down Grid

Use Word's Table menu drop-down grid to quickly create a basic table. The following illustration shows the Table menu drop-down grid with a 3 × 3 (9 cell) table chosen.

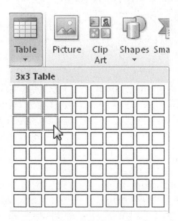

1. Position the cursor where you want the table to be placed.

2. From the Insert ribbon, choose Table.

3. Drag across the grid at the top of the menu to choose the number of rows and columns you want the table to have, and then release. (Note that you are limited to an eight-row, ten-column table using the grid. To create a larger table, use the Insert Table command instead.)

4. Add text and formatting to the table to suit your needs. (See "Modifying a Table" later in this chapter for additional tips and techniques.)

TIP   *If you would prefer to use a dialog box approach to creating a table rather than clicking and dragging the Table button drop-down grid, choose Insert Table from the Table button menu. Complete the Number Of Columns and Number Of Rows fields, and then click OK.*

Modifying a Table

After a table has been created, it can still be modified. You can add or delete rows and columns, resize row height or column width, and resize the entire table. Most of these modifications require that you select a portion of the table first. Table 4-1 describes how to select content in preparation for modifying it.

TABLE 4-1 Selecting Content in a Word Table

To Select Content in This...	Do This...	Or This...
Cell	Click in the cell, and then choose Table Tools | Layout Ribbon | Table Group | Select | Cell	Position the mouse pointer on the right edge of the cell (the cursor will be a black arrow pointing toward the cell content), and click.
Row	Click in the row, and then choose Table Tools | Layout Ribbon | Table Group | Select | Row	Position the mouse pointer on the left edge of the row (the cursor will be a white arrow pointing toward the cell content), and click. (Click and drag to select multiple rows.)
Column	Click in the column, and then choose Table Tools | Layout Ribbon | Table Group | Select | Column	Position the mouse pointer at the top edge of the column (the cursor will be a black arrow pointing down), and click. (Click and drag to select multiple columns.)
The entire table	Click in the table, and then choose Table Tools | Layout Ribbon | Table Group | Select | Table	Click in the table, and then click the four-headed arrow just outside of the top-left portion of the table.

Resizing a Table

1. Click in the table.

2. Click and drag the resizing handle (pictured in Figure 4-3) near the bottom-right corner of the table. As you drag, the dotted lines represent the new size and shape of the table. Drag outward to make the table larger; drag inward to make the table smaller.

TIP   *Hold down the SHIFT key while dragging to retain the table's current aspect ratio.*

Changing Column Width

1. Position the mouse pointer on the right edge of the column you want to resize. You are in the correct place when the cursor resembles a double-headed arrow pointing left and right (pictured in Figure 4-3).

2. Drag to the left to make the column smaller; drag to the right to make the column wider.

Changing Row Height

1. Position the mouse pointer on the bottom edge of the row you want to resize. You are in the correct place when the cursor resembles a double-headed arrow pointing up and down (pictured in Figure 4-3).

2. Drag up to decrease the row height; drag down to increase the row height.

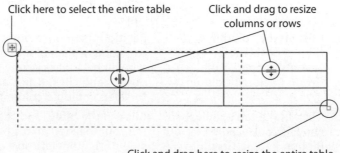

Click here to select the entire table

Click and drag to resize columns or rows

Click and drag here to resize the entire table

FIGURE 4-3 ·

TIP   *Double-clicking instead of dragging will resize the row height or column width to suit the text it contains.*

Deleting Rows and Columns

1. Select the row or column you want to delete.
2. Do one of the following:
   1. Right-click the selected row or column, and choose Delete Rows or Delete Columns.
   2. On the Table Tools Layout ribbon, click the Delete button (Rows & Columns group), and then choose Delete Rows or Delete Columns.

Adding Rows and Columns

1. Select a row or column adjacent to where you want to add a new row or column.
2. Do one of the following:
   - Right-click the selected row or column, and choose from among the following:
     - Insert | Insert Columns To The Left
     - Insert | Insert Columns To The Right
     - Insert | Insert Rows Above
     - Insert | Insert Rows Below
   - On the Table Tools Layout ribbon, in the Rows & Column Group, click the appropriate Insert button (pictured here).

TIP   *Select multiple rows or columns to add multiple rows or columns. For example, if you select two rows and choose Insert Rows Above, two rows will be added above the selected two rows.*

? Still Struggling

Want to turn a table into text? Convert it! Select the table and on the Table Tools Layout ribbon, click the Convert To Text button. In the Convert Table To Text dialog box, choose how you want the text separated: paragraph marks, tabs, commas, or another character. Click OK. If you don't like the results, use the Undo command and try another separator to see if that works better for you.

Working with Headers and Footers

Headers are positioned at the top of a document within the document's margin. Footers are positioned at the bottom of a document within the document's margin. Headers and footers typically contain document titles, page numbers, chapter or section titles, copyright statements, graphic logos or decoration, dates, and other such identifying or organizing information.

Figure 4-4 features active header and footer areas as shown in Print Layout view. ("Active" means the cursor is in the header or footer as opposed to being elsewhere in the body of the document.) When the cursor is in the body of the document, headers and footers appear grayed out. Double-clicking in an existing header or footer moves the cursor there and activates the Header and Footer Tools Design ribbon.

TIP   *You must be in Print Layout view to modify headers or footers.*

Exploring the Header & Footer Tools Ribbon

When the cursor is in a header or footer, you can use options available on the Header & Footer Tools ribbon (pictured here) to change header or footer style, add dates or graphics, and navigate between headers and footers.

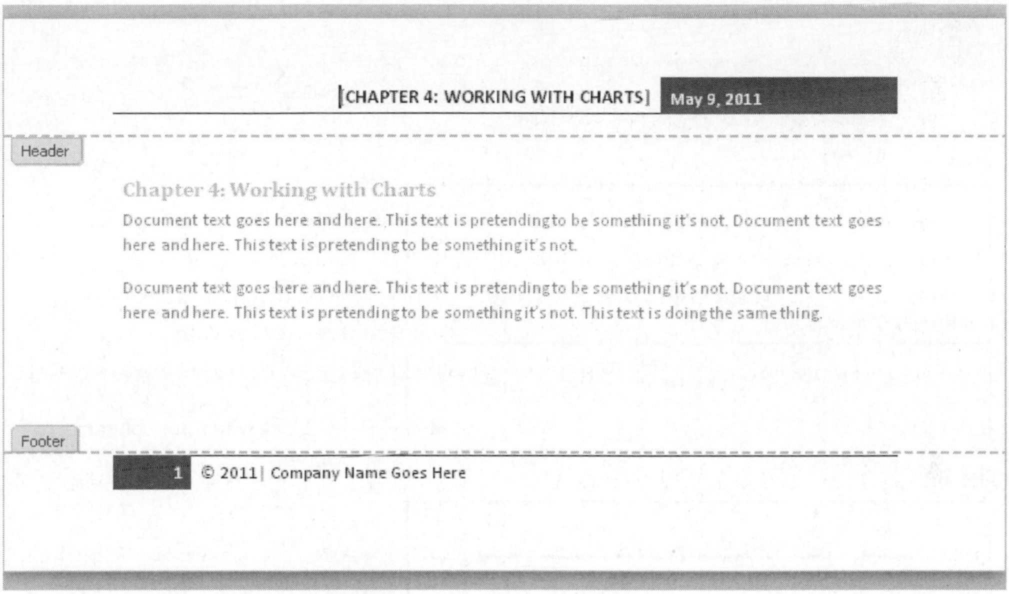

FIGURE 4-4 • When active, header and footer areas appear at the very top and very bottom of each page.

The Options group provides tools for making the first page of a document different from the others (if you were writing a report, for example, you might not want the header or footer to be on the cover page), making odd pages and even pages different from one another (look at the header for this book as an example), and hiding the text in the body of a document (so you can focus on the headers and footers).

The Position group lets you modify where headers and footers are positioned relative to the top and bottom of the page. You can type a number in the field provided or use the UP and DOWN ARROW keys to choose a number. The Insert Alignment command lets you add an alignment tab (left, center, right) within a header or footer.

The Close Header And Footer button places the cursor in the body of the document and hides the Header & Footer Tools Design ribbon.

TIP   *Instead of using the Close Header And Footer button, you can just double-click anywhere in the body of the document.*

Inserting a Header or Footer

Clicking the Header or Footer button on either the Insert or Header & Footer Tools Design ribbon produces a menu of options. Figure 4-5 displays the Header

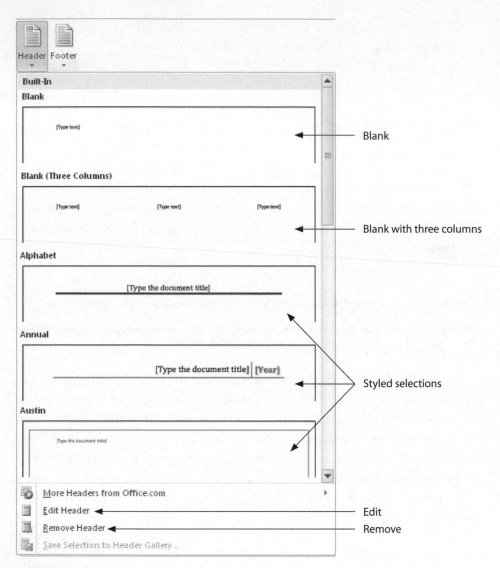

FIGURE 4-5 · The Microsoft Word 2010 Header button drop-down list provides a variety of header styles.

menu; the Footer menu is similar. The top style is blank; the second style is blank with three alignment tabs: left, center, and right (a very popular choice for headers and footers). The rest of the styles (both in the list as well as available on Office.com) provide suggested text (some of which is automatically drawn from the document itself, such as the title or location) as well as stylistic additions such as colorful rules (lines) and decorative page numbers.

1. Click the Header or Footer button.

2. Choose one of the built-in styles listed. Your cursor is placed in the header or footer area of the document and the Header & Footer Tools Design ribbon is displayed.

3. Replace the text in the square brackets with text personalized for your document.

4. Click the Close Header And Footer button in the Header & Footer Tools Design ribbon.

TIP *Want to try on different styles for a header or footer? The Header and Footer buttons both appear on the Header & Footer Tools Design ribbon. Try on as many styles as you like by selecting styles from the Header or Footer drop-down menus.*

Modifying a Header or Footer

You must be in Print Layout view to modify the headers or footers in a document (from the View ribbon click the Print Layout button). Double-clicking in an existing header or footer activates the Header & Footer Tools Design ribbon and places the cursor wherever you clicked.

Choosing a Different Style for a Header or Footer

1. Change to Print Layout view (if necessary), and double-click in the header or footer you want to modify.

2. Click the Header or Footer button, and select another style. (Note that selecting another style may mean that you will have to modify the text as well.)

3. Click the Close Header And Footer button in the Header & Footer Tools Design ribbon.

Inserting a Date or Time into a Header or Footer

1. Change to Print Layout view (if necessary), and double-click in the header or footer you want to modify.

2. Position the cursor where you want to add the date or time.

3. Click the Insert Date & Time button in the Header & Footer Tools Design ribbon. The Date & Time dialog box appears.

4. Make a selection from the available formats.

5. Select the Update Automatically check box if you want the date or time to be updated each time you open the document.

6. Click OK.

Inserting a Picture into a Header or Footer

1. Change to Print Layout view (if necessary), and double-click in the header or footer you want to modify.

2. Position the cursor where you want to add the graphic.

3. Click the Picture button in the Header & Footer Tools Design ribbon.

4. Navigate to and select the picture you want to use.

5. Click OK.

6. Modify the picture as necessary.

Inserting Clip Art into a Header or Footer

1. Change to Print Layout view (if necessary), and double-click in the header or footer you want to modify.

2. Position the cursor where you want to add the artwork.

3. Click the Clip Art button in the Header & Footer Tools Design ribbon.

4. Find the picture you want to use, and click it to insert it.

5. Modify the artwork as necessary.

Deleting a Header or Footer

1. Change to Print Layout view (if necessary), and double-click in the header or footer you want to modify.

2. Click the Header or Footer button in the Header & Footer Tools Design ribbon, and choose Remove Header or Remove Footer.

Working with Page Numbers

If all you want in a header or footer is a page number, using the Page Number button on the Header & Footer Tools Design ribbon can be more straightforward than using the Header or Footer buttons. Clicking the Page Number

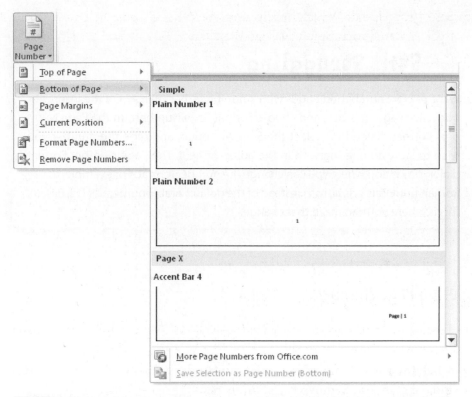

FIGURE 4-6 • Numerous page numbers options appear on the Header & Footer Tools Design ribbon.

button displays a short menu of choices (pictured in Figure 4-6), such as Top of Page and Bottom of Page. The submenu for either of these options offers plain page number options as well as decorative options.

Inserting Page Numbers

1. Change to Print Layout view (if necessary).
2. From On the Insert ribbon click Page Numbers.
3. Choose Top of Page or Bottom of Page.
4. From the submenu, select the style of page number you wish to use.

Still Struggling

Want to start numbering pages with a number other than 1? On the Insert ribbon, click Page Numbers and choose Format Page Numbers. In the Page Numbers Format dialog box, select the Start At option, and type the number you wish to start numbering with in the adjacent field. The Page Number Format dialog box is also where you can change the number format. For example, to use Roman numerals (i, ii, iii, iv, v) instead of the default Arabic numerals (1, 2, 3, 4, 5), this is where you can make that change.

Deleting Page Numbers

1. Change to Print Layout view (if necessary), and double-click in the header or footer you want to modify.
2. Click the Page Numbers button in the Header & Footer Tools Design ribbon, and choose Remove Page Numbers.

Summary

In this chapter you learned to use some Word features that can help your documents appear professional and appealing. You learned how to add visual interest to your documents by including attention-grabbing graphics and professional-looking tables. You also learned how to bolster readability and organization in longer documents by including attractive headers, footers, and page numbers. Chapter 5 focuses on page layout, viewing, and printing.

QUIZ

1. **True or False: Inserting and working with graphics works basically the same across all of the Office applications.**
   A. True
   B. False

2. **What kind of graphics can be added to a Word document?**
   A. Clip art
   B. Photographs
   C. Shapes
   D. SmartArt
   E. All of the above

3. **When using the click-and-drag method to resize a graphic, drag outward to make the image _____ ; drag inward to make the image _____ . (Fill in the blanks using the following choices.)**
   A. bluer
   B. smaller
   C. more transparent
   D. larger
   E. less transparent

4. **Which of the following can be done to a table?**
   A. Resizing the table
   B. Making a column wider
   C. Increasing a row's height
   D. Adding or deleting columns or rows
   E. All of the above

5. **True or False: When resizing a graphic by dragging, if you don't want the aspect ratio of a graphic to be retained, click the Size Dialog Box Launcher, deselect Lock Aspect Ratio on the Size tab, and click OK.**
   A. True
   B. False

6. **If all you need in a header or footer is a page number, using the _____ button on the _____ ribbon can be much more straightforward than using the Header or Footer buttons.**
   A. Header & Footer Tools
   B. Page Number
   C. Insert
   D. View
   E. Home

7. **Which of the following will allow you to select an entire row in a table? (Choose all that apply.)**
   A. Triple-click anywhere in the row
   B. Click in the row, and then choose Table Tools | Layout Ribbon | Table Group | Select > Row.
   C. Position the mouse pointer on the left edge of the row (the cursor will be a white arrow pointing toward the cell content), and click.
   D. Click the four-headed arrow to the left of the row.
   E. None of the above

8. **True or False: In addition to being on the Insert ribbon, the Header and Footer buttons both appear on the Headers & Footers Toolbar ribbon.**
   A. True
   B. False

9. **A(n) _____ keeps its location relative to the text that surrounds it. A(n) _____ keeps its location relative to the page and lets text wrap around it. (Fill in the blanks using the following choices.)**
   A. floating graphic
   B. transparent graphic
   C. round graphic
   D. larger graphic
   E. inline graphic

10. **True or False: To undo any stylistic changes you made to a graphic or to return it to its original size, use the Reset Picture button on the Picture Tools Format ribbon.**
    A. True
    B. False

chapter **5**

Page Layout, Viewing, and Printing in Word

This chapter provides an overview of Microsoft Word 2010's page layout, document viewing, and printing options. Setting document margins, page orientation, and page size and being able to control where page breaks are placed are all useful tools for making documents look as professional as possible. Being able to view and work in a document in multiple ways, such as Print Layout, Full Screen Reading, or Outline view is practical as well. Print and print preview options in Word are also explored.

CHAPTER OBJECTIVES

In this chapter, you will learn how to

- Change page margins, orientation, and size
- Insert and delete page breaks
- Use the various views available on the View ribbon
- Preview a document before printing
- Print a document

Working with Pages

The Page Layout ribbon (pictured here) is where the most frequently used page-related commands, such as margins, orientation, and size, are found. Additional page-related commands can be located in the Page Setup dialog box, shown in Figure 5-1, which is available by clicking the Page Setup Dialog Box Launcher button (located in the lower-right corner of the Page Setup group).

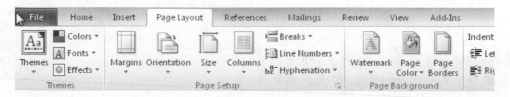

Changing Margins

Page margins refer to the space between the edge of the page and the body of the document. Document text and graphics are positioned in the body of the document. Headers, footers, and page numbers, which you learned about in the previous chapter, are positioned within the margins of the document.

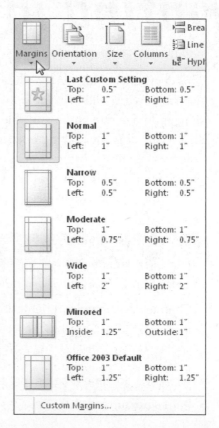

Word's default margins—referred to as Normal—are set to 1" for all four margins: top, bottom, left, and right. If you are trying to fit more text on a page, you can decrease the size of the page margins to give the body of the document more space. You might, for example, change the margins to .5" all around. If you are using headers, footers, or page numbers in a document, you will need to be careful about encroaching upon the space these page elements need. In this case, you may choose to only modify the left and right margins to .5" and leave the top and bottom at 1" so that the header or footer fits comfortably.

1. On the Page Layout ribbon, click Margins.

2. From the Margins menu, do one of the following:

- Choose one of the suggested margin settings (Normal, Narrow, Moderate, etc.).

- Choose Custom Margins to open the Page Setup dialog box with the Margins tab displayed (pictured in Figure 5-1), and then provide the desired custom margin settings in the Top, Bottom, Left, and Right fields.

TIP *The top choice in the Margins menu is Last Custom Settings. Choose this option to set the margins to match whatever custom margins you used previously.*

Sections are not covered in this book, but you can learn more about them in Help.

Still Struggling

If you are working with a double-sided document, such as a manual or book, you may want to use mirrored margins (available from the Margins menu as well as from the Page Setup dialog box). Instead of left and right margins, you will set *inside* and *outside* margins. The margins of the left page will mirror those on the right page. Depending on how the document will be bound, you may also wish to add a gutter margin to accommodate the binding and to make certain that none of the text is buried by the binding. A gutter margin can be set in the Page Setup dialog box.

Setting Page Orientation

Page orientation refers to whether the page is taller than it is wide (portrait) or wider than it is tall (landscape). Word's default page orientation is set to portrait.

1. On the Page Layout ribbon, click Orientation.

2. Choose Portrait or Landscape.

TIP *Using the Page Setup dialog box along with Word's Section feature, you can choose to combine portrait and landscape pages in the same document. This is useful if you are writing a report in portrait mode and have a large table or graphic that would be better suited to a landscape-orientated page. Learn more about sections in the Word Help file.*

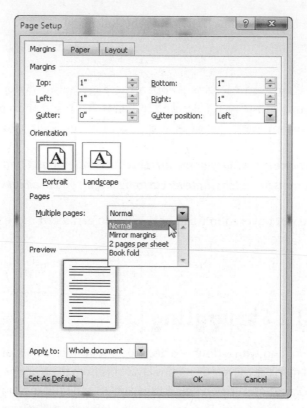

FIGURE 5-1 · The Word Page Setup dialog box offers three tabs: Margins, Paper, and Layout.

Specifying a Page Size

Word's default page size is set to 8.5" × 11"; however, a variety of other page sizes can be accommodated.

1. On the Page Layout ribbon, click Size.

2. From the Size menu, do one of the following:

   • Choose one of the suggested page sizes (A4, Legal, Executive, etc.).

   • Choose More Paper Sizes to open the Page Setup dialog box with the Paper tab displayed, and then provide the desired custom margin settings in the Width and Height fields.

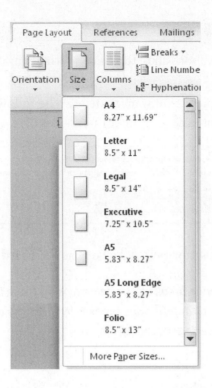

TIP *Check your printer user manual to see what paper sizes the printer can accommodate and how to position the paper in the paper tray.*

Working with Page Breaks

As text and graphics are added to a document, page breaks are automatically inserted in accordance with page margins. Sometimes a page breaks in an awkward location. For example, if an automatic page break happens right after a subheading, the text that goes with that subheading becomes visually disconnected from it. In this case, you might choose to insert a manual page break in front of the subheading. This will force the subheading to join its text on the next page.

Inserting a Page Break

1. Position the cursor where you want the page break to be added.
2. On the Page Layout ribbon, click Breaks.
3. From the Breaks menu, choose Page Break.

Deleting a Page Break

1. On the Home ribbon, click the Show Formatting Marks button to view formatting marks.

2. Select the page break you want to delete. The following illustration shows a selected page break.

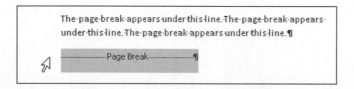

3. Press the BACKSPACE or DELETE key on the keyboard.

TIP   *Only a manual page break can be deleted using these instructions. The only way to get rid of an automatic page break is by inserting a manual page break where it will affect the desired change.*

? Still Struggling

Wondering why your page background did not print? To save printer ink, Word's defaults are set to prevent page background colors and images from printing. However, this can be changed. On the File ribbon, click Options and then Display. Then, select the Print Background Colors And Images check box. Click OK and print the document.

Page color will not extend to the edge of the paper, since your printer has limits on how close to the page edge it can print, so your page will have a white border around the edges.

Changing Page Color

Tired of plain white pages? Document pages in Word can have a background color, including gradient, pattern, or texture. You can also specify a picture as a page color.

TIP *Be aware of how a page color can affect a document's readability. If the main objective of a document is to be read, then you should avoid busy backgrounds such as gradients, patterns, texture, or pictures. Just because a feature is possible, doesn't mean you should necessarily use it! Consider readability first.*

Adding a Page Color

1. On the Page Layout ribbon, click Page Color.
2. From the Page Color menu, do one of the following:
   - Choose a suggested theme or standard color from the menu.
   - Choose More Colors to open the Colors dialog box and choose a color.
   - Choose Fill Effects to open the Fill Effects dialog box, where you can specify a gradient, pattern, texture, or picture for the page.

Removing a Page Color

1. On the Page Layout ribbon, click Page Color.
2. From the Page Color menu, choose No Color.

Adding a Page Border

Placing a border around a page can give it a crisp, professional look.

Adding a Page Border

1. On the Page Layout ribbon, click Page Borders. The Borders And Shading dialog box appears.
2. In the Borders And Shading dialog box, do one of the following:
   - Select Box, Shadow, or 3-D under the Setting heading, and then use the Style, Color, Width, or Art drop-down menus to customize the border.
   - Select Custom under the Setting heading. Use the Style, Color, Width, or Art drop-down menus to customize the border; and then, in the Preview area, use the border buttons or click the diagram to apply custom borders to the page.
3. Click OK.

Removing a Page Border

1. On the Page Layout ribbon, click Page Borders. The Borders And Shading dialog box appears.
2. On the Page Border tab, under the Setting heading, click None.
3. Click OK.

Viewing and Printing

The View ribbon (pictured in the following illustration) is where commands related to viewing a document, such as layouts and zoom settings, are found

- The Document Views group gives you one-click access to each of Word's view types: Print Layout, Full Screen Reading, Web Layout, Outline, and Draft.
- The Show group lets you show or hide the ruler, table gridlines, and navigation pane.
- The Zoom group allows you to modify the screen size of a document.

The Print pane on the File ribbon is where you will go to preview how a document will print as well as to print a document. Several page layout options are also available on this pane. See the section "Printing and Previewing" for more information on the Print pane.

Exploring Document Viewing Options

As mentioned previously, Word offers five document views: Print Layout, Full Screen Reading, Web Layout, Outline, and Draft. To change to a view, click the View ribbon, and then click the desired layout in the Document Views group. Each view is described in the sections that follow.

Print Layout

Print Layout is the default layout for all documents in Word. This "What You See Is What You Get" (WYSIWYG) view represents how the document will look when printed. The paper edges and the margins surrounding the body of the document are visible in this view.

TIP   *Want more screen real estate in Print Layout view? You can choose to hide the white space that separates pages in the document. Position the mouse pointer in the gray area between any two pages. The cursor changes to a double-headed arrow when you are in the right place (pictured here). Double-click to hide the white space. Double-click in the same place to show the white space again.*

Full Screen Reading

Full Screen Reading view displays the document for maximum ease of reading. The text is larger and the ribbons, status bar, and taskbar are all hidden. It is important to note that this view does *not* represent how a document will print—in fact, it is usually quite different!

Tools for reading, navigating, and review are available in the toolbar at the top of the screen (see Figure 5-2). In this view, you can highlight text in the document, add comments, search for text, translate text, and use Word's research tools.

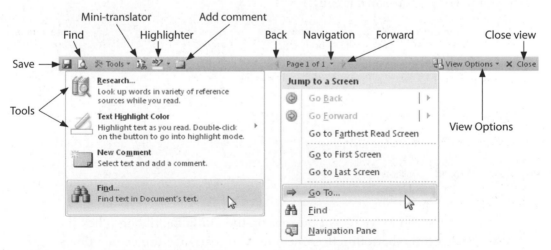

FIGURE 5-2 · The Full Screen View Toolbar offers a variety of Tools and Navigation Menus.

The View Options drop-menu (near the top-right corner of the window) lets you increase or decrease text size, read one or two pages at a time, and modify margins. None of these options affects the actual document; they only affect the current view of the document. To type in this mode, choose Allow Typing from the View Options menu. In addition, you can use Word's reviewing features, such as Track Changes, by selecting those options in the View Options menu.

Web Layout

Web Layout view displays how a document would look if viewed as a web-page. In this view, text will wrap to accommodate the size of the window it is in, as opposed to wrapping according to any page margins you may have set.

You use Web Layout view to create, view, and edit pages as they'll appear online when opened in a browser. Word's Save As command (located on the File ribbon) lets you save a document in a Web-compatible format.

Outline

Outline view is used to create, view, and modify outlines. When you are in Outline view, the Outlining ribbon (pictured here) makes it easy to create a quick outline. Buttons on the Outline Tools group let you promote (green arrows pointing to the left) or demote (green arrows pointing to the right) outline topics as well as to filter the outline so that it displays only certain levels of text (the Show Level drop-down menu).

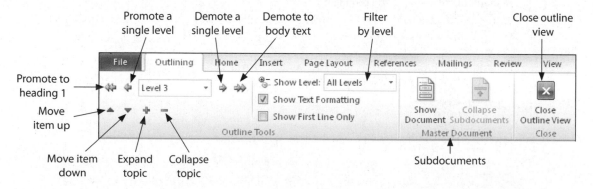

The Move Up and Move Down buttons on the Outlining ribbon (click the gray triangles on the bottom-left corner) let you rearrange topics in a document, or you can simply click and drag topics within the document.

The Expand and Collapse buttons on the Outlining ribbon let you expand (click the plus sign) or collapse (click the minus sign) individual topics within the outline. You can use the buttons on the Outlining ribbon or those positioned next to the topics in the outline to collapse or expand topics.

Draft

Draft view displays the document as a continuous page without margins, headers, footers, page numbers, or graphics, allowing you to totally focus on the text. In this view, a dotted line shows where pages break. Advantages to this view include faster refreshing (if you have a slow computer, this can be helpful) and a less cluttered page. It's important to note that Word will switch itself from Draft view to Print Layout view whenever you try to do something that cannot be accomplished in Draft view, such as inserting a picture.

Zoom

The Zoom group, located on the View ribbon, lets you control how a document displays on screen:

- Click the One Page button to fit one entire page of a document on the screen.
- Click the Two Pages button to fit two entire pages of a document on the screen.
- Click the Page Width button to fill the screen with the full width of a document.
- Click the 100% button to view the document at 100 percent of its size.
- Click the Zoom button to open the Zoom dialog box, where you can customize your zoom percentage or choose from additional preset zoom percentages.

Printing and Previewing

Office 2010 brings printing and previewing together into one neat window! The Print pane on the File ribbon (pictured in Figure 5-3) provides a preview of the printed document as well as page layout commands such as paper orientation, page size, and margins. Here, you can choose a specific printer if you have more than one, specify which pages in a document are to be printed, and,

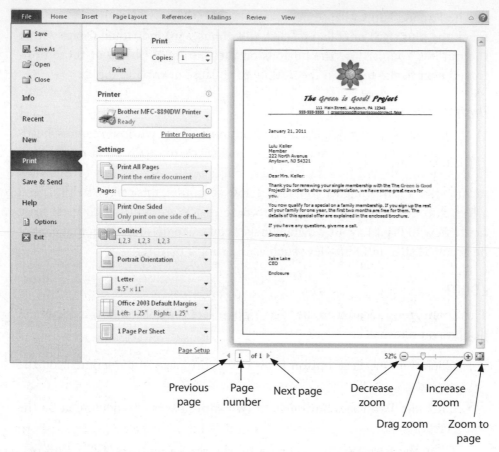

Previous page
Page number
Next page
Decrease zoom
Increase zoom
Drag zoom
Zoom to page

FIGURE 5-3 • In Word 2010, print and preview options are all on the File ribbon's Print pane.

if your printer has duplex printing and/or collating features, set those options as well.

Previewing a Document

1. Click the File ribbon.
2. Click Print. The document preview is displayed on the right side of the Print pane:
   - To navigate between pages in the preview, use the Previous Page and Next Page buttons at the bottom-left corner of the preview pane, or type a number in the Page Number field.

- To zoom the preview screen, use the Decrease Zoom and Increase Zoom buttons at the bottom-right corner of the Preview pane, or drag the zoom indicator on the line between the buttons. To return to single-page view click the Zoom To Page button.

Printing a Document

1. Click the File ribbon.
2. Click Print.
3. In the Print pane, make any necessary changes, including the following:
   - Choose a printer from the Printer drop-down menu.
   - Specify which pages to print from the Print All Pages drop-down menu, or type a page range in the Pages field (e.g., **1-3** or **1,3,5**).
   - If your printer has duplex printing and/or collating features, specify those options using the Print One Sided and Collated drop-down menus (these options will only be available if your printer is capable of them.)
   - Change the page orientation in the Orientation drop-down menu.
   - Change the page size in the Size drop-down menu.
   - Change the page margins in the Margins drop-down menu.
   - Choose how many pages you want to print on a single sheet in the Page Per Sheet menu.
4. Click Print.

TIP *To quickly access the Print pane on the File ribbon, press CTRL-P on the keyboard.*

Summary

This chapter provided you with an overview of Microsoft Word 2010's page layout, document viewing, and printing options. You learned how to set page margins, orientation, and size and how to control where pages break are placed. You explored Word's various document views and learned how to preview a document before printing, as well as how to print a document. In Chapter 6, you will get started with the Office 2010 spreadsheet program: Excel.

QUIZ

1. True or False: The View ribbon is where the most frequently used page-related commands, such as margins, orientation, and size, are accessed.
   A. True
   B. False

2. Which of the following is *not* on the Page Layout ribbon?
   A. Margins
   B. Orientation
   C. Size
   D. Full Screen Reading view
   E. Watermark

3. _____ page orientation refers to when the page is taller than it is wide; _____ page orientation refers to when a page is wider than it is tall. (Fill in the blanks using the following choices.)
   A. Narrow
   B. Even
   C. Landscape
   D. Letter
   E. Portrait

4. Which of the following is a document view in Word?
   A. Print Layout
   B. Full Screen Reading
   C. Web Layout
   D. Outline
   E. Draft
   F. All of the above

5. True or False: Watermarks are included when printing.
   A. True
   B. False

6. Which of the following does/do not display in Full Screen Reading view? (Choose all that apply.)
   A. Pictures
   B. Page break
   C. Ribbons
   D. Status bar
   E. Task bar

7. **True or False: Word's defaults are set to print page background colors and images.**
   A. True
   B. False

8. **Which of the following zoom views displays one entire page?**
   A. 100%
   B. Page width
   C. One page
   D. Two pages
   E. None of the above

9. **Which of the following is not /are not option(s) in the Print pane of the File ribbon? (Choose all that apply.)**
   A. Orientation
   B. Margin
   C. Breaks
   D. Watermark
   E. Printer

10. **True or False: Print Preview only allows you to view the very first page in a document.**
    A. True
    B. False

Part III

Microsoft Excel

chapter 6

Getting Started with Excel Worksheets

This chapter gets you started using Microsoft Excel 2010. You will discover some key spreadsheet-related terminology, create a new Excel workbook, and learn how to add and delete data in a worksheet. Then you'll get comfortable with all of the formatting basics needed to create a professional-looking worksheet.

CHAPTER OBJECTIVES

In this chapter, you will learn how to

- Describe the parts of a worksheet
- Build a new worksheet
- Add and delete data in Excel
- Work with rows and columns
- Format cell content
- Format cells

Excel Terminology

As you read in Chapter 1, Excel is the Office suite's modern-day abacus—an electronic spreadsheet program that can be likened to a paper accounting worksheet come alive. A spreadsheet program displays a grid of rows and columns that together make up numerous cells. Each cell can contain numbers, text, or formulas. Excel is primarily used for documents that will contain numbers and other data that are best organized within a spreadsheet, such as budgets, invoices, inventory tracking, lists, data analysis, charts, and graphs.

Excel uses some terminology that you may be unfamiliar with unless you've worked in a spreadsheet program before. If you have, then skip this section of the chapter; if you haven't, then review the terms and definitions in Table 6-1. Figure 6-1 offers a graphical representation of many of terms defined.

TABLE 6-1 Excel Terminology

Term	Definition
Cell/Cell Address/Cell Reference/Active Cell	A *cell* is a single addressable rectangular block within a worksheet. A cell's *address* or *reference* (the two terms are used interchangeably) is based on the intersection of a column and a row. For example, the intersection of column B with row 12 is called B12. The column letter is always stated before the row number in a cell reference. The *active* or *selected cell* is the cell the cursor is currently in. The address of the active cell is displayed just above the row number headings.
Cell Range	A *cell range* consists of a group of adjacent cells. Cell ranges are expressed by separating the address of the first cell in the range and the address of the last cell in the range with a colon. For example, cells J9 through J21 would be written as J9:J21; cells J9 through L14 would be expressed as J9:L14.
Column	A *column* is a vertical series of cells in a worksheet. There are 256 columns within the default Excel worksheet. After columns A through Z, the lettering begins with AA, AB, AB, and so on—all the way through to IV.
Column Heading	A *column heading* is the letter at the top of a column.
Formula	A *formula* consists of an equation that performs an operation in a worksheet. For example, the formula =B3+B4+B5 would add the three numbers in those cells.
Formula Bar	The *formula bar* is located just above the column headings in a worksheet and always displays the contents of the current cell. If a group of cells is selected, the formula bar will display the contents of the cell in the top-left corner of the group. You can edit the contents of a cell in the formula bar or directly in the cell itself.

TABLE 6-1 Excel Terminology *(Continued)*	
Term	**Definition**
Function	A *function* is a predefined, built-in formula. One example is the SUM function—=SUM(B3:B5)—which would add the numbers in cells B3, B4, and B5.
Labels	A *label* is text that identifies a series of values in a row or column. In Figure 6-1, there are labels for each of the years (2008, 2009, and 2010) and for each of the states (PA, NY, NJ, and DE).
Row	A *row* is a horizontal series of cells in a worksheet. By default, there are 65,536 rows in an Excel worksheet.
Row Heading	A *row heading* is the number at the beginning of a row.
Values	*Values* consist of data in a cell (numbers, letters).
Workbook	Excel refers to a spreadsheet file as a *workbook*.
Worksheet/ Spreadsheet	An Excel workbook can contain multiple *worksheets*. Each worksheet consists of 65,536 rows and 256 columns for a total of 1,678,336 cells. By default, new workbooks contain three worksheets, but you can add more as needed. The maximum number of worksheets is limited by your computer's available memory.

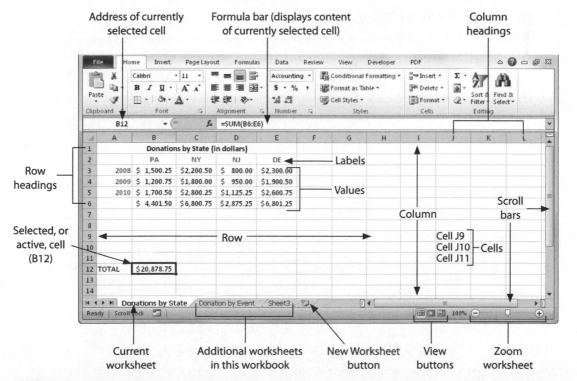

FIGURE 6-1 • Understanding worksheet terminology will help you use Excel more effectively. Table 6-1 details many of the terms pictured here.

Building a New Worksheet

As you learned in Chapter 2, launching Excel presents you with a new, blank workbook in which you can immediately begin working. You can also use the New command to create a new workbook in Excel. The New pane offers you the option of starting with a completely blank workbook, starting with an available template, or starting with a template from the Microsoft Office website.

Creating a New Worksheet

1. Click the File ribbon.
2. Choose New.
3. Do one of the following:
   - To start with a blank worksheet, click Blank.
   - To start with a template, navigate to and select the desired template under the Available Templates or Office.com Templates headings.
4. Click the Create button.

Working with a Blank Document

A blank workbook gives you the opportunity to build a worksheet completely from scratch. A new, blank workbook is always based on a default template named book.xlt, and a new, blank worksheet is always based on a default template named sheet.xlt. A few modifications, such as font, size, default view, and default number of worksheets in a workbook, can be modified to suit your preferences.

Changing the Default Font for Workbooks

1. Create a new, blank document.
2. On the File ribbon, click Options.
3. On the General tab, select a font from the Use This Font drop-down list.

4. Choose a font size from the Font Size list.

5. Click OK.

TIP *The new default font will not affect the currently opened workbook or any previously created workbooks. The change will take place only after you have exited and then restarted the Excel program.*

Changing the Default Number of Worksheets in New Workbooks

1. Create a new, blank document.

2. On the File ribbon, click Options.

3. On the General tab, type a number in the Include This Many Sheets field (or use the up and down arrows to change the current number).

4. Click OK.

Working with a Template

You may recall from Chapter 2 that a template is a preformatted document layout that serves as the basis for a brand-new file. In addition to being preformatted, many Excel templates include placeholder values and/or blank fields with labels that you can modify to suit your own purposes, as well as built-in formulas and functions that will automatically calculate once the pertinent information has been added. Figure 6-2 shows an example of a blank loan

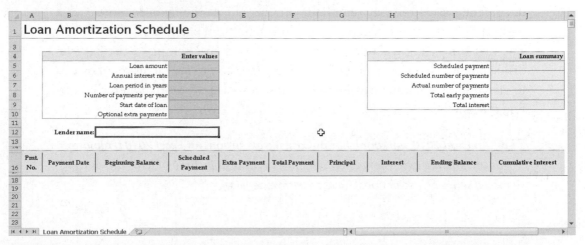

FIGURE 6-2 · A blank Loan Amortization template is pictured here. Figure 6-3 displays the completed template for comparison.

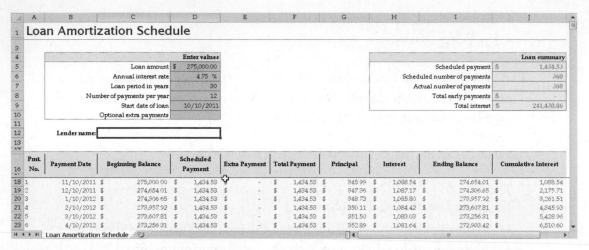

FIGURE 6-3 · A completed Loan Amortization template is pictured here. Figure 6-2 displays the blank template for comparison

amortization template. Once you enter data into the shaded cells (the amount of the loan, interest rate, loan period, number of payments in a year, and starting date), the entire table is populated with the loan data, as pictured in Figure 6-3. Change the numbers in the shaded cells and the entire worksheet is automatically recalculated.

You can tailor a template to suit your own needs and then save it as a new template. You can also save any document you've created from scratch as a template. Saving a document as a template allows you to create additional, new documents based on that template. One benefit of saving a document as a template is that you are protecting the document from being easily overwritten. The first time you save a document that is based on a template, the Save As dialog box will open (even if you chose the Save command). This reminds you to give the file a unique name and save it in a specific location where you can find it again.

TIP *An Excel 2010 workbook has an .xlsx file extension. An Excel 2010 template has an .xltx file extension. Excel templates that also include macros (an automated series of instructions) have an .xltm extension.*

Saving a Document as a Template

1. On the File ribbon, click Save As.
2. From the Save As Type drop-down list, choose Excel Template. The default location will be selected for you automatically.
3. Type a unique name in the File Name field.
4. Click Save.

TIP *If you make modifications to a template and want to save the revised template as a template instead of a workbook, use the Save As command on the File ribbon. From the Save As Type drop-down list, choose Excel Template and save the file in the same location using the same name. This will overwrite the old version of the template with the revised version.*

Adding and Deleting Data in Excel

You can add text, numbers, dates, or times into a cell. You can also opt to have Excel automatically fill adjacent cells with a known series using the AutoFill feature.

Adding Data

To add values (text, numbers) to an Excel worksheet, click in a cell and begin typing. Some things to keep in mind include the following:

- Unlike typing in a Microsoft Word document, text typed into an Excel cell will not automatically wrap within the cell. Instead, as long as nothing is in its way (such as text in the adjacent cell), the content will stretch across as many cells as needed. An example of this is pictured in cell A1 in the following illustration. If data exists in the cell adjacent to the one you are typing in, the text will fill the current cell width but then appear to truncate; however, the Formula bar will display the text in its entirety when the cell is selected (see cell A3 and the Formula bar in the following illustration for an example). If a cell is not wide enough to display the number it contains, a series of pound signs (#####) displays in the cell instead of the number. Cell A5 in the illustration shows an example of a number that is too wide for its cell. If desired, you can adjust the column width and/or text-wrap feature after you are finished typing.

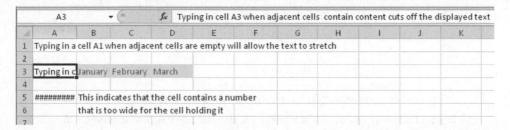

- As you type in a cell, you can use the BACKSPACE key to delete in a backward direction.
- When you are finished typing in a cell, press the ENTER key to move the cursor to the cell directly below, or press the TAB key to move the cursor to the cell directly to the right.

TIP   *Use the keyboard combination ALT-ENTER to insert a line break within a cell.*

Working with AutoComplete

If the first few characters of what you are typing match an entry in the same column, Excel's AutoComplete feature will offer to complete the entry for you. Note that this applies only to entries consisting of just text or text and number combinations; AutoComplete will not make suggestions for entries containing only numbers, dates, or times). To accept Excel's suggestion, press ENTER. To ignore Excel's suggestion, simply keep typing. To delete the suggestion, press BACKSPACE.

TIP   *You can turn off the AutoComplete feature if you wish. On the File ribbon, choose Options and then Advanced. Under the Editing Options heading, clear the Show AutoComplete Suggestions check box.*

Working with AutoFill

The Excel Fill handle (the small black handle at the bottom-right corner of a selected cell) offers a way to quickly fill a group of adjacent cells with data. The Fill handle can be used to copy the contents of a cell into one or more adjacent cells, or to fill adjacent cells or rows with a known series. A series can consist of numbers, dates, or, in some cases, text. The following illustration shows a series of month names (January through June) being created using the Fill handle.

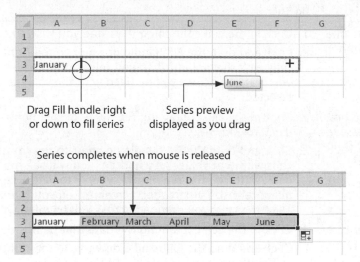

Table 6-2 offers a few examples of how the Excel Fill handle can be used. For additional ideas, investigate this topic in Excel Help.

Still Struggling

If you open a worksheet that was created by someone else and cannot modify it, it may be because the worksheet has been protected from having data changed accidentally. If you have permission from the worksheet owner to make changes in it, then you can unprotect it by clicking Unprotect Sheet on the Review ribbon. In some cases, you may need a password to unprotect a sheet.

Deleting Data

In addition to using the BACKSPACE key to delete individual characters while typing in a cell, you can select one or more cells and delete the content in those cells.

1. Click in the cell whose contents you wish to delete (click and drag to select multiple cells).

2. Press the DELETE key.

TABLE 6-2 Excel 2010 Fill Handle Options

To Accomplish This...	Do This...
Copy the contents of a cell into one or more adjacent cells	1. Click in the cell containing the value you wish to copy. 2. Click and drag the Fill handle down or to the right to fill adjacent cells with that value. When you release the mouse, all of the cells you dragged across will be filled with the value in the first cell selected.
Copy a series of month or day names into one or more adjacent cells	1. Click in the cell containing the name of the month (i.e., January) or day (i.e., Monday). 2. Click and drag the Fill handle down or to the right to fill adjacent cells with that value. As you drag, you will see month or day names attached to the mouse pointer to help keep track of how many cells you've dragged across. When you release the mouse, all of the cells you dragged across will be filled with the series.
Copy a simple series of dates (e.g., 5/9/11, 5/10/11, 5/1/11) into one or more adjacent cells	1. Click in the cell containing the date that begins the series. 2. Click and drag the Fill handle down or to the right to fill adjacent cells with the series of dates. As you drag, you will see a date attached to the mouse pointer to help keep track of how many cells you've dragged across. When you release the mouse, all of the cells you dragged across will be filled with the series of dates.
Copy a series of numbers or noncongruent dates into one or more adjacent cells	To use the Fill handle with numbers, you need to "teach" Excel how you want the series to progress. To do this, you type the first two or more numbers (or noncongruent dates) in the series and then select both cells. For example, if you wanted to have 30 adjacent cells filled with the numbers 1 through 30, you would type a **1** in the first cell and a **2** in the next cell, and then select both before dragging the Fill handle. By typing the first two numbers first, you've "taught" Excel how you want the numbers in the series to progress. You can use the Fill handle with almost any type of series of numbers, including dates. To create a series of dates that incremented by 7 days, for example, you would type the first date (e.g., **January 1**) in the first cell and the next date in the next cell (e.g., **January 8**). Select both dates and then drag the handle to fill adjacent cells with dates that increase on a weekly basis.

TIP   *The BACKSPACE key will only delete the contents of the currently selected cell and will not delete the contents of multiple selected cells.*

Working with Rows and Columns

The height and width of rows and columns in Excel can be modified to suit your spreadsheet design:

- Row height is measured in points (1 point is equal to 1/72 inch or 0.035 cm). The default row height is 12.75 points (approximately 1/6" or 0.4 cm).

- Column width is measured by the number of characters (in default font size) that the column can accommodate. Column width goes from 0, which would effectively hide the column, to 255. The default column width is 8.43 characters.

Changing Row Height or Column Width

The most direct way to change the height of a row or the width of a column is to position the mouse pointer on the line separating two row or column headings (the pointer will resemble a double-headed arrow, as pictured in the following illustration) and then dragging it to modify the height or width. For rows, drag down to increase the height or up to decrease the height. For columns, drag right to increase the width or left to decrease the width. The illustration shows the mouse pointer being used to increase the height of row 3 as well as the width of column C.

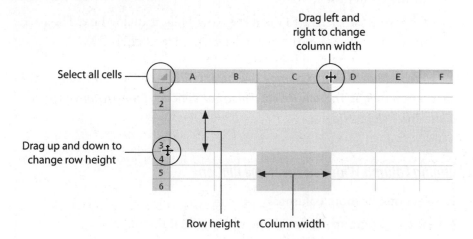

When using this method there are a few additional tips to keep in mind:

- If you select multiple rows, the height of all the selected rows will be changed at the same time. If you select multiple columns, the width of all the selected columns will be changed at the same time.
- Double-clicking on the line causes the row height or column width to adjust so that it automatically fits the content it contains (referred to in Excel as "AutoFit").
- To AutoFit all rows and columns in the worksheet, click in the Select All cell (pictured in the illustration, just above the row 1 heading and just to the left of the column A heading), and then double-click any line separating two rows and then any line separating two columns.

You can also change row height or column width using the Home ribbon as outlined in the following section.

Changing Row Height on the Home Ribbon

1. Select one or more rows.
2. In the Cells group on the Home ribbon, click Format.
3. Do one of the following:
   - Choose Automatic Row Height to size the row height to automatically fit the content it contains.
   - Choose Row Height to open the Row Height dialog box. Then type a height (in points) in the Row Height field, and click OK.

TIP *Here's another way to change row height: Right-click a row heading and choose Row Height. The Row Height dialog box appears. Type a height (in points) in the Row height field.*

Changing Column Width on the Home Ribbon

1. Select one or more columns.
2. In the Cells group on the Home ribbon, click Format.
3. Do one of the following:
   - Choose Automatic Column Width to size the column to automatically fit the content it contains.

- Choose Column Width to open the Column Width dialog box. Then type a height (in number of characters) in the Column Width field, and click OK.

TIP   *Here's another way to change column width: Right-click a column heading and choose Column Width. The Column Width dialog box appears. Type a width (in number of characters) in the Column Height field.*

Inserting Rows

The most direct way to insert a row is to right-click the row heading where you want the new row inserted and choose Insert from the menu. The new row will be inserted above the selected row. (To insert multiple rows, select multiple rows.) You can also insert one or more rows using the Home ribbon as outlined here.

Inserting Rows on the Home Ribbon

1. Select the row where you want the new row inserted. (If you want multiple rows inserted, begin by selecting multiple rows.)
2. In the Cells group on the Home ribbon, click Insert Sheet Rows.

Deleting Rows

The most direct way to delete a row is to right-click the row heading where you want the new row inserted and choose Delete from the menu. (To delete multiple rows, begin by selecting multiple rows.) You can also delete one or more rows using the Home ribbon as outlined here.

Inserting Rows on the Home Ribbon

1. Select the row(s) you want to delete.
2. In the Cells group on the Home ribbon, click Delete Sheet Rows.

Inserting Columns

The most direct way to insert a column is to right-click the column heading where you want the new column inserted and choose Insert from the menu. The new column will be inserted to the left of the original column. (To insert multiple columns, select multiple columns.) You can also insert one or more columns using the Home ribbon as outlined here.

Inserting Columns on the Home Ribbon

1. Select the column where you want the new column inserted. (If you want multiple columns inserted, begin by selecting multiple columns.)
2. In the Cells group on the Home ribbon, click Insert Sheet Columns.

Deleting Columns

The most direct way to delete a column is to right-click the column heading where you want the new column inserted and choose Delete from the menu. (To delete multiple columns, begin by selecting multiple columns.) You can also delete one or more columns using the Home ribbon as outlined here.

Inserting Rows on the Home Ribbon

1. Select the column(s) you want to delete.
2. In the Cells group on the Home ribbon, click Delete Sheet Columns.

Excel Formatting Basics

There are numerous ways to format cell values, including font, size, style, and color. You can also format the cells themselves with a background color and border. In addition, Excel gives you numerous options for formatting number styles (percentage, currency, etc.). You can choose formatting options before adding values to a cell, or you can type first and format afterward. Regardless of the method you use, you must first select the cells you want formatted.

Selecting Cells, Rows, and Columns

There are numerous ways to select cells in a worksheet. Table 6-3 lists some of the most popular methods.

Changing Font, Size, Style, and Color

As you may recall from Chapter 3, a font can be loosely defined as a complete character set (a–z, plus numbers and symbols) of a particular typeface, such as Arial or Times Roman. The creative use of fonts, along with size, style, and color choices, can add personality to a document and enhance readability when used

TABLE 6-3 Selecting Cells in Excel 2010	
To select...	**Do this...**
A single cell	Click in the cell (or use the keyboard arrow keys to move to the cell).
A single row	Click in the row heading (numbered).
A single column	Click in the column heading (lettered).
Multiple adjacent rows	Click in the first row's heading, drag toward the last row's heading, and then release.
Multiple nonadjacent rows	Click in the first row's heading, hold down the CTRL key, and click in each additional row heading.
Multiple adjacent columns	Click in the first column's heading, drag toward the last column's heading, and then release.
Multiple nonadjacent columns	Click in the first column's heading, hold down the CTRL key, and click in each additional column heading.
Multiple adjacent cells	Do either of the following: • Click in the first cell, drag toward the last cell, and then release. • Click in the first cell, hold down the SHIFT key, and then click in the last cell.
Nonadjacent cells	Select the first cell (or range of cells), hold down the CTRL key, and then click in each additional cell (or click and drag in each additional range of cells) you wish to select.
All cells	Click in the Select All cell (just above the row 1 heading and to the left of the column A heading).

properly. Font, size, style, and color options can all be found on the Font group of the Home ribbon (pictured in Figure 6-4).

1. Select the cells you wish to format.

2. From the Home ribbon, choose a font from the Font drop-down list.

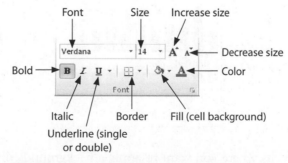

FIGURE 6-4 • The Excel 2010 Font Group on the Home Ribbon provides numerous formatting options.

3. From the Home ribbon, choose a size from the Size drop-down list, type a size in the Size field, or use the Increase Size and Decrease Size buttons to change the font size.

4. From the Home ribbon, choose bold or italic by clicking the Bold or Italic button.

5. From the Home ribbon, choose an underline style from the Underline button menu (single or double).

6. From the Home ribbon, choose a color from the Color button menu.

TIP *If you enjoy using keyboard shortcuts, you can resize the values in selected cells using the keyboard instead of the mouse. To increase the size of selected text, press CTRL-SHIFT->. To decrease the size of selected text, press CTRL-SHIFT-<. (Watch the Size field on the Home ribbon as you do this to see the size increase or decrease.) Keyboard shortcuts can also be used to modify the style of selected text: Press CTRL-B to make text bold, press CTRL-I to make text italic, and press CTRL-U to underline text.*

Filling a Cell with Color

The Fill Colors button on the Font group can be used to apply a background color in worksheet cells. Colors that coordinate with the current theme are pictured at the top of the menu, while standard colors appear farther down. Additional colors are available by clicking on More Colors. The No Fill command lets you remove a fill color. The Fill Colors menu is pictured here.

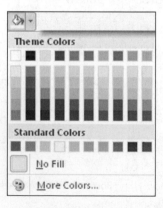

1. Select the cells where you want to apply a background color.

2. From the Home ribbon, click the Fill Colors button.

3. Choose a theme or standard color from the Fill Colors menu, or click More Colors to choose from additional colors.

Adding Borders to Cell Gridlines

By default, worksheet gridlines do not print. As you will learn in Chapter 8, you can change this default in the Page Setup dialog box; however, most worksheet designers prefer to be more selective about how borders appear. The Borders button in the Font group lets you design cell borders for your worksheet.

In the Borders menu, popular border styles are shown under the Borders heading. These borders are applied by first selecting cells and then choosing the type of border you want to use for those cells. Alternatively, you can draw borders on a worksheet by using the commands under the Draw Borders heading. This second method does not require that you select cells first.

Applying Borders to Selected Cells

1. Select the cells where you want a border to appear.
2. From the Home ribbon, click the Borders button.
3. Under the Borders heading, choose the type of border you wish to apply to the selected cells.

TIP *To remove a border, select the cells and choose No Border from the Borders menu.*

Drawing Borders

1. From the Home ribbon, click the Borders button.
2. Under the Draw Borders heading, choose a line color and line style if desired.
3. Under the Draw Borders heading, choose Draw Border to draw an outside border surrounding a group of cells, or choose Draw Border Grid to draw a grid of borders.
4. Click and drag in the worksheet to draw borders.

TIP *To remove a border, choose Erase Border from the Borders menu and then drag the mouse over the borders you wish to erase.*

Formatting Numbers

By default, numbers typed into a cell are formatted with the Excel General format, which means no special formatting is applied. Special formatting may be needed to add meaning to numbers in Excel. For example, to show that a number refers to currency, you might want a dollar sign, comma separators, and a decimal point. The Number group on the Home ribbon (pictured in Figure 6-5) offers one-click access to a few of the more popular number formats available, including Currency, Percentage, and Commas. The General drop-down menu offers additional options.

1. Select the cells you wish to format.

2. From the Home ribbon, click a number format button (currency, percentage, commas) on the Number group.

3. If needed, use the Increase Decimals button to show more precise values by showing more decimal places or use the Decrease Decimals button to show less precise values by showing fewer decimal places.

TIP   *For additional number format options, click the Number Dialog Box Launcher (located at the bottom-right corner of the Number group) to open the Format Cells dialog box with the Number tab displayed. Choose a number category from the list on the left, and then select the format from the samples on the right and click OK.*

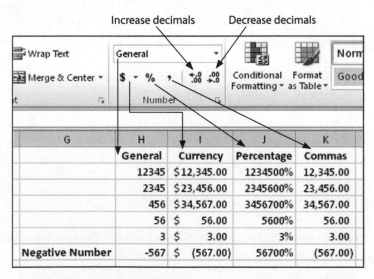

G	H General	I Currency	J Percentage	K Commas
	12345	$12,345.00	1234500%	12,345.00
	2345	$23,456.00	2345600%	23,456.00
	456	$34,567.00	3456700%	34,567.00
	56	$ 56.00	5600%	56.00
	3	$ 3.00	3%	3.00
Negative Number	-567	$ (567.00)	56700%	(567.00)

FIGURE 6-5 · The Number Group on the Home Ribbon provides formatting options for numeric cell content

Alignment Options

Values in cells can be aligned horizontally (between the left and right edges of the cell) as well as vertically (between the top and bottom edges of the cell). The Alignment group on the Home ribbon offers one-click access to the alignment options used most often. Additional options can be found by clicking the Alignment Dialog Box Launcher (located in the lower-right corner of the group).

The Alignment group also offers access to several other alignment options:

- **Orientation** lets you angle cell content counterclockwise or clockwise or position it vertically (top down) as well as rotate content up or down.

- **Wrap Text** lets you have cell content appear on multiple lines.

- **Merge & Center** lets you center or align data that spans several columns or rows.

Figure 6-6 showcases a few examples of cell alignment options.

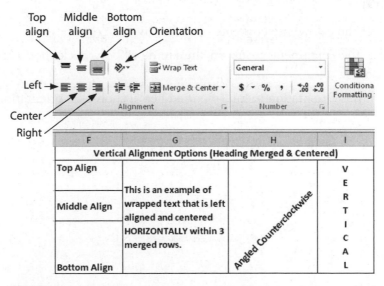

FIGURE 6-6 · The Alignment group on the Home ribbon provides a variety of alignment options for cell content.

Aligning Cell Values Horizontally

1. Select the cell(s) you want to align horizontally (between the left and right edges of the cell).

2. From the Alignment group on the Home ribbon, choose Left, Center, or Right.

Aligning Cell Values Vertically

1. Select the cell(s) you want to align vertically (between the top and bottom edges of the cell).

2. From the Alignment group on the Home ribbon, choose Top Align, Middle Align, or Bottom Align.

Changing Orientation

The Orientation button menu lets you angle cell content counterclockwise or clockwise or position it vertically (top down) as well as rotate content up or down. Figure 6-6 shows an example of cell content that has been angled counterclockwise (column H) as well as cell content that has a vertical orientation (column I).

1. Select the cell whose contents you want to angle or rotate.

2. From the Alignment group on the Home ribbon, click the Orientation button.

3. From the Orientation menu (pictured here), choose an orientation.

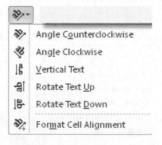

Using the Wrap Command

The Wrap Text button lets you have cell content appear on multiple lines. Figure 6-6 shows an example of cell content that has been wrapped (column G).

1. Select the cell(s) you want to wrap.
2. From the Alignment group on the Home ribbon, click the Orientation button.

TIP   *Press ALT-ENTER to insert a line break within a cell.*

Using the Merge & Center Command

The Merge & Center button lets you center or align data that spans several columns or rows. In Figure 6-6, the heading spanning columns F through I is an example of using Merge & Center.

1. Select the cells you want to merge and center.
2. From the Alignment group on the Home ribbon, click the Merge & Center button.

TIP   *The Merge & Center button also offers a menu containing additional merging options (pictured here). Click the down arrow on the right side of the button to access these commands: Merge Across (without centering), Merge Cells (works both horizontally and vertically), and Unmerge Cells (to unmerge previously merged cells).*

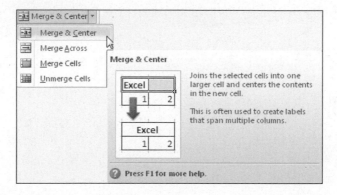

Still Struggling

Remember to refer back to Chapter 2 for common program functionality, such as Backstage View (document properties and permissions, opening existing files, and saving files); using undo and redo; working with the Office Clipboard (cut, copy, and paste); working with themes; and getting help.

Summary

This chapter got you started using Microsoft Excel 2010. You discovered some key spreadsheet-related terminology, learned how to create a new Excel workbook, and learned how to add and delete data in a worksheet. You also became comfortable with all of the formatting basics needed to make a professional-looking worksheet. In Chapter 7 you will delve into formulas, functions, and charts—three features that help make Excel such a powerful business tool.

QUIZ

1. **True or False: An Excel workbook can contain multiple worksheets.**
   A. True
   B. False

2. **Which feature allows to you to fill adjoining cells with a series?**
   A. AutoComplete
   B. Orientation
   C. Merge & Center
   D. AutoFill
   E. None of the above

3. **The _____ is located just above the column headings in a worksheet and always displays the _____ of the current cell. (Fill in the blanks using the following choices.)**
   A. ribbon
   B. Formula bar
   C. title bar
   D. name
   E. contents

4. **Which feature lets you have cell content appear on multiple lines?**
   A. Merge & Center
   B. Wrap
   C. Orientation
   D. AutoFill
   E. Top Align

5. **True or False: The height and width of rows and columns in Excel cannot be modified to suit your spreadsheet design.**
   A. True
   B. False

6. **How can you change the width of a column?**
   A. Drag the line separating two column headings
   B. Double-click the line separating two column headings
   C. Right-click a column heading and choose Column Width
   D. Click Format in the Cells group on the Home ribbon
   E. All of the above

7. **What does the Increase Decimals button do?**

   A. Shows more precise values by showing more decimal places
   B. Shows less precise values by showing more decimal places
   C. Shows less precise values by showing fewer decimal places
   D. Shows more precise values by showing fewer decimal places
   E. None of the above

8. **True or False: By default, worksheet gridlines print.**

   A. True
   B. False

9. **A(n) _____ consists of a(n) _____ that performs an operation on a worksheet. (Fill in the blanks using the following choices below.)**

   A. formula
   B. screen tip
   C. list of commands
   D. equation
   E. cell

10. **True or False: Excel refers to a spreadsheet file as a workbook.**

    A. True
    B. False

chapter 7

Exploring Excel Formulas, Functions, and Charts

This chapter familiarizes you with three features that help make Excel such a powerful business tool: formulas, functions, and charts. Learning to create your own formulas gives you a deeper understanding of what makes Excel tick. Being able to take advantage of Excel's impressive array of built-in functions will turn any novice user into a power user. Finally, Excel's charting feature will help make your data shine.

CHAPTER OBJECTIVES

In this chapter, you will be able to

- Define the components of a formula
- Use Excel Quick functions, the function library, and the Insert Function dialog box
- Copy a formula or function
- Chart data on a worksheet
- Format a chart
- Add a sparkline

Working with Formulas and Functions

As you may recall from Chapter 6, a *formula* consists of an equation that performs an operation on a worksheet. The following are a few simple examples of formulas along with a brief explanation of what the formula does:

=A3+B3+C3+D4 adds the numbers in each of the fours cells specified

=B3-22 subtracts 22 from the number in cell B3

=C3*D4 multiplies the number in cell C3 by the number in cell D4

=E5/A2 divides the number in cell E5 by the number in cell A2

=D5*7% multiplies the value in cell D5 by 7 percent

The ability to dynamically calculate values that are dependent on other values in the worksheet is what makes Excel so useful. Change one of the values that a formula uses, and the result is recalculated instantly!

Understanding Formula Components

You may have noticed that all of the examples noted earlier begin with an equal sign (=). The equal sign tells Excel that what is coming next is a calculation. A formula will not calculate without the equal sign at the beginning. In the following illustration, the only difference between the formula in cell B6 (which calculated properly) and the formula in cell C6 (which did not calculate) is that the formula in cell B6 has an equal sign at the beginning. (Look in the Formula bar above the column headings to see the formula.)

B6		▼	f_x	=B3+B4+B5	
◢	A	B	C	D	E
1		Donations by State (in dollars)			
2		PA	NY	NJ	DE
3	2008	$1,500.25	$2,200.50	$ 800.00	$2,300.00
4	2009	$1,200.75	$1,800.00	$ 950.00	$1,900.50
5	2010	$1,700.50	$2,800.25	$1,125.25	$2,600.75
6		$4,401.50	C3+C4+C5		
7					
8					

A formula can contain cell references, mathematical operators, values, text, or functions. Formulas may be typed directly into the cell or in the *Formula bar* (located just above the column headings in a worksheet).

The Formula bar, shown in Figure 7-1, displays the cell reference for the currently selected cell, the Insert Function button, and the contents of

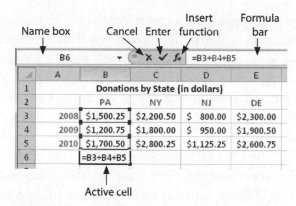

FIGURE 7-1 • The Excel Formula Bar lets you work with functions.

the currently selected cell. When the cursor is active in the Formula bar, two additional buttons appear as well: Cancel (which does the same thing as the ESC key on the keyboard) and Enter (which does the same thing as the ENTER key on the keyboard).

Cell References

As you read in Chapter 6, a cell reference (sometimes referred to as a *cell address*) is based on the intersection of a column and a row. For example, the intersection of column B and row 12 is called B12. The column letter is always stated before the row number in a cell reference. You can use a combination of cell references and values in a formula—for example, =C3*20% multiplies the value in cell C3 by 20 percent.

Cell Ranges If a formula will be calculating a great number of cells, it would be time-consuming to write each of the cell references out individually. For example, to add the values in cells D5 through D10, you might type =D5+D6+D7+D8+D9+D10. Imagine if you were writing a formula to add the values in cells D5 through D500. That would be a lot of typing! So Excel gives us a way to indicate a range of cells by using a colon between the first and last cell references. D5 through D500, for example, can be expressed as D5:D500. Much simpler! Of course, a cell range can only be used to indicate a range of adjoining cells. To select all of the cells containing numbers in Figure 7-1, the range would be written as B3:E5.

Relative Cell References versus Absolute Cell References Cell references can be *relative* or *absolute*. In a relative reference, the address of a cell is based on the relative position of the cell containing the formula and the cell that is referred to in the formula. If the formula is copied, the reference will automatically adjust.

In an absolute cell reference, a formula will point to a specific cell that remains the same regardless of whether the formula is copied. To differentiate between a relative and absolute cell reference, dollar signs are added to the absolute cell reference. Instead of A3 (a relative cell reference), an absolute cell reference would look like this: A3. In some cases you may want a cell reference that is relative for the row but absolute for the column, in which case the dollar sign would appear before the column only: $A3. Likewise, in other cases you may want a cell reference that is relative for the column but absolute for the row, in which case the dollar sign would appear before the row only: A$3.

TIP   *To change a relative cell reference to an absolute cell reference, you can type the dollar signs yourself, or you can highlight the cell reference and press F4 to change the reference to an absolute one. The F4 key cycles through all four types of references: absolute, absolute row/relative column, relative row/absolute column, and relative.*

Mathematical Operators

Operators are the symbols used to tell Excel what type of calculation the formula is to perform. For basic mathematical operations, such as addition, subtraction, or multiplication, use the arithmetic operators shown in Table 7-1.

In addition to mathematical operators, Excel permits the use of comparison operators (used to compare two values), as well as a text concatenation operator (used to connect two values to produce one continuous text value). You can learn more about these operators in the Excel Help file.

TABLE 7-1   Mathematical Operators Used in Excel

Operator	Example of Usage in a Formula	What It Does
+	=C3+C4	Addition
–	=C3–C4	Subtraction
*	=C3*C4	Multiplication
/	=C3/C4	Division
%	=C3*20%	Percent
^	=C3^C4	Exponentiation

Still Struggling

Math-challenged? Two things to keep in mind: 1) You don't *have* to write your own formulas if you don't want to—Excel provides numerous functions that you can use instead of trying to build formulas by hand. 2) The Internet provides a great deal of information on the topic of writing Excel formulas. In addition to the articles and tutorials available on the Office.com website, many more resources can be found by typing **Excel formulas** into your favorite search engine. If you are a visual learner who might prefer a video to an article, you might search for **Excel formulas video** instead.

Order of Operations Excel follows the standard order of mathematical operations, performing calculations from left to right according to the order of operator precedence. Standard operator precedence states that anything inside of parentheses will always be calculated first. Next come exponents and roots, followed by multiplication and division, and finally, addition and subtraction.

You can control the order of calculations by using parentheses to group calculations you want performed first. Figure 7-2 steps you through two formulas that look the same except for the use of parentheses to control the order of operations. Take note of how different the final results are. (Note that while numbers are used in this example for easy reading, cell references could be used in place of any or all of the numbers in either formula.)

=50+2*8/4-2		=(50+2)*(8/4)-2	
Step 1: 2*8	RESULT=16	Step 1: (50+2)	RESULT=52
Step 2: 16/4	RESULT=4	Step 2: (8/4)	RESULT=2
Step 3: 50+4	RESULT=54	Step 3: 52*2	RESULT=104
Step 4: 54-2	**FINAL RESULT: 52**	Step 4: 104-2	**FINAL RESULT: 102**

FIGURE 7-2 · Parentheses are used to control the order in which formula operations are performed.

Writing a Simple Formula

In the three simple steps below, a simple formula will be created that sums the values in cells B3 through B5 in the following worksheet.

	A	B	C	D	E
1		Donations by State (in dollars)			
2		PA	NY	NJ	DE
3	2008	$ 1,500.25	$2,200.50	$ 800.00	$2,300.00
4	2009	$ 1,200.75	$1,800.00	$ 950.00	$1,900.50
5	2010	$ 1,700.50	$2,800.25	$1,125.25	$2,600.75
6	TOTAL				
7	AVERAGE				
8					

1. Select cell B6.
2. Type an equal sign (=) to begin the formula.
3. Type **B3+B4+B5** and press ENTER.

Working with Functions

You may recall from Chapter 6 that a *function* is a predefined, built-in formula. Excel provides dozens of functions so you don't have to write formulas if you don't want to. (This will likely come as a welcome surprise to those who are not especially comfortable with math!)

As stated earlier in this chapter, a formula can contain cell references, mathematical operators, values, text, or functions. There are numerous ways to insert a function: from the Edit group on the Home menu; from a function library on the Formulas ribbon; or using the Insert Function dialog box. There is also a Quick Function feature for those who just want a quick glance at some standard calculations in their worksheet.

AutoSum Button Menu

A few functions are used so frequently in Excel that they are available right from the Home ribbon. The AutoSum button and menu are on the Editing group of the Home ribbon (pictured here) as well as on the Formulas ribbon.

TIP *If you have a small monitor, you may not see the AutoSum button label, so look for the sigma (Σ) symbol.*

Functions on the AutoSum button menu include the following:

- **Sum** Produces the sum of the arguments. For example, the formula =SUM(D5:D25) adds all of the numbers within that cell range.
- **Average** Returns the average (arithmetic mean) of the arguments. For example, the formula =AVERAGE(D5:D25) returns the average of the numbers contained within that cell range.
- **Count Numbers** Counts the number of cells that contain numbers. Using Figure 7-1 as an example, if a formula stated =COUNT(B3:E5), the result would be 12 since all 12 of those cells contain numbers. Change the formula to =COUNT(A1:E5) and the result would be 15 since 15 of those cells contain numbers.
- **Max** Returns the maximum value in a list of arguments. Using Figure 7-1 as an example, if a formula stated =MAX(D3:D5), the result would be $1,125.25 since that is the largest number in that range.
- **Min** Returns the minimum value in a list of arguments. Using Figure 7-1 as an example, if a formula stated =MIN(D3:D5), the result would be $800.00 since that is the smallest number in that range.

Writing a Formula Using the AutoSum Button

1. Select the cell where you want to place the formula.
2. In the Editing group on the Home ribbon, or on the Formulas ribbon, click the AutoSum button. The equal sign, along with the SUM function, will appear in the cell and Excel will make a suggestion as to which cells you want to sum based on the selected cell.
3. Do one of the following:
   - Press ENTER to accept the suggested cell range for the formula.
   - Type (or click and drag to select) a different range if necessary and then press ENTER.

Writing a Formula Using Other Functions on the AutoSum Button Menu

1. Select the cell where you want to place the formula.

2. In the Editing group on the Home ribbon, or on the Formulas ribbon, click the down arrow on the right side of the AutoSum button.

3. Choose a function from the AutoSum button menu. The equal sign, along with the function name, will appear in the cell and Excel will make a suggestion as to which cells you want to use in the formula based on the currently selected cell.

4. Do one of the following:

   • Press ENTER to accept the suggested cell range for the formula.

   • Type (or click and drag to select) a different range if necessary and then press ENTER.

Function Libraries

The Function Library group on the Formulas ribbon (pictured here) offers access to all of Excel's functions, arranged neatly into related categories. Clicking a library opens a menu of functions. Libraries include AutoSum (which contains the same options as the AutoSum button menu on the Home ribbon), Financial, Logical, Text, Date & Time, Lookup & Reference, and Math & Trig. Functions that don't fit into the existing libraries are listed in the More Functions library. The Recently Used library gives you your own library of favorite functions by displaying any functions you've recently used.

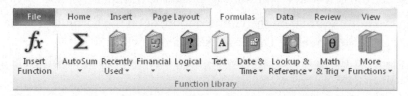

TIP *For a complete list of worksheet functions organized by category or alphabetically, search on "list of worksheet functions" in the Excel Help file.*

Writing a Formula Using a Function Library

1. Select the cell where you want to place the formula.

2. On the Formulas ribbon, click the desired library and select a function. An equal sign will appear in the cell and one or more dialog boxes may prompt you for additional information:

   • If the Select Arguments dialog box appears, Excel is prompting you to select an argument from the list supplied to complete the formula. (An argument is simply a value that provides necessary information for a function. Arguments may be cell references, text or numbers, or other formulas.) After selecting the argument, click OK to complete the formula.

   • If the Function Arguments dialog box (pictured here) appears, Excel is prompting you to specify additional information to complete the formula. Type a range into the fields provided or click Select Range to make the dialog box smaller so that you can then click and drag to select a range directly in the worksheet. If you are not certain what information to supply, click the Help On This Function link. After supplying the additional information, click OK to complete the formula.

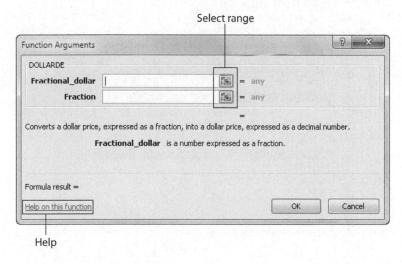

The Insert Function Dialog Box

The Insert Function dialog box, pictured in Figure 7-3, not only contains a complete list of all Excel functions, but allows you to search within that list as well. You can access the Insert Function dialog box in numerous ways:

- On the Formulas ribbon, click Insert Function.
- On the Home ribbon, choose More Functions from the AutoSum button menu.
- On the Formulas ribbon, choose Insert Formulas from any of the function library menus.

Writing a Formula Using the Insert Function

1. Select the cell where you want to place the formula.
2. On the Formulas ribbon, click Insert Function. The Insert Function dialog box appears (see Figure 7-3).
3. Do one of the following:
    - To search for a function, type a brief description of what you want to do in the Search for a function field (for example, "find the maximum number"), and then click Go.

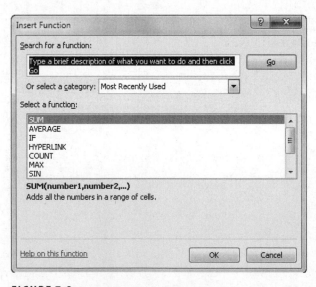

FIGURE 7-3 · Search for the exact function you need in the Insert Function dialog box.

- Choose a library from the Or Select A Category list. If you don't know which category to choose, select All to display a list of all functions.

- Choose a function from the Select A Function List, and click OK.

An equal sign will appear in the cell and one or more dialog boxes may prompt you for additional information:

- If the Select Arguments dialog box (pictured previously in this chapter) appears, select an argument from the list supplied to complete the formula. After selecting the argument, click OK to complete the formula.

- If the Function Arguments dialog box (pictured previously in this chapter) appears, specify additional information to complete the formula. Type a range into the fields provided, or click the Select Range button and then click and drag to select a range directly in the worksheet. After supplying the additional information, click OK to complete the formula.

TIP *Recently used functions can also be accessed in the Name Box of the Formula bar. Click in the cell where you want the formula, type an equal sign, and then click the drop-down button beside the Name box, where you can select a recently used function.*

Using Quick Functions

For a quick glance at some common calculations in a worksheet, select a group of cells and look at the status bar at the very bottom of the Excel window. Figure 7-4 shows two examples of Quick Functions in action.

In the worksheet on the left, cells A3 through A17 have been selected to obtain a quick count of how many names are in the list. As soon as the cells have been selected, the Count function in the status displays the number of names: 15.

In the worksheet on the right, cells B3 through D17 have been selected to obtain a quick sum of all donations. As soon as the cells have been selected, the SUM function in the status bar displays the total: $4,400.00. In addition, the Count function states that there are 45 numbers selected.

Right-clicking in the status bar displays a menu containing additional Quick Function options with their data showing in the menu, including Average, Minimum (the smallest number selected), and Maximum (the largest number selected). To add a Quick Function to the status bar, click the function name.

	A	B	C	D	E
1	Pennsylvania Donations By Name				
2		2008	2009	2010	
3	Edward Nugen	$ 100.00	$ 50.00	$ 225.00	
4	Darby Glande	$ 150.00	$ 50.00	$ 75.00	
5	Edward Kelle	$ 50.00	$ 100.00	$ 75.00	
6	Georgia Wallace	$ 225.00	$ 125.00	$ 125.00	
7	Erasmus Clefs	$ 75.00	$ 35.00	$ 35.00	
8	Edward Ketcheman	$ 75.00	$ 65.00	$ 100.00	
9	Lucille Loo	$ 125.00	$ 100.00	$ 150.00	
10	Thomas Rottenbury	$ 35.00	$ 125.00	$ 100.00	
11	Roger Deane	$ 65.00	$ 100.00	$ 75.00	
12	Iohn Harris	$ 150.00	$ 150.00	$ 100.00	
13	Frauncis Norris	$ 125.00	$ 50.00	$ 75.00	
14	Mathewe Lyne	$ 75.00	$ 25.00	$ 125.00	
15	Edward Kettell	$ 50.00	$ 75.00	$ 65.00	
16	Thomas Wisse	$ 75.00	$ 75.00	$ 150.00	
17	Robert Biscombe	$ 125.00	$ 75.00	$ 225.00	
18					

Donations by State / PA Donations by Name
Ready   Count: 15

	A	B	C	D	E
1	Pennsylvania Donations By Name				
2		2008	2009	2010	
3	Edward Nugen	$ 100.00	$ 50.00	$ 225.00	
4	Darby Glande	$ 150.00	$ 50.00	$ 75.00	
5	Edward Kelle	$ 50.00	$ 100.00	$ 75.00	
6	Georgia Wallace	$ 225.00	$ 125.00	$ 125.00	
7	Erasmus Clefs	$ 75.00	$ 35.00	$ 35.00	
8	Edward Ketcheman	$ 75.00	$ 65.00	$ 100.00	
9	Lucille Loo	$ 125.00	$ 100.00	$ 150.00	
10	Thomas Rottenbury	$ 35.00	$ 125.00	$ 100.00	
11	Roger Deane	$ 65.00	$ 100.00	$ 75.00	
12	Iohn Harris	$ 150.00	$ 150.00	$ 100.00	
13	Frauncis Norris	$ 125.00	$ 50.00	$ 75.00	
14	Mathewe Lyne	$ 75.00	$ 25.00	$ 125.00	
15	Edward Kettell	$ 50.00	$ 75.00	$ 65.00	
16	Thomas Wisse	$ 75.00	$ 75.00	$ 150.00	
17	Robert Biscombe	$ 125.00	$ 75.00	$ 225.00	
18					

Donations by State / PA Donations by Name
Ready   Average: $97.78   Count: 45   Sum: $4,400.00

FIGURE 7-4 · Excel 2010 Quick Function Status Bar offers basic worksheet details that reflect the cells selected.

Copying or Moving Formulas or Functions

When a formula is copied, cell references will change if relative cell references were used; cell references will not change if absolute cell references were used. When a formula is moved, cell references will not change regardless of the type of cell reference used.

Copying a Formula or Function Using Copy & Paste

1. Select the cell containing the formula to copy.
2. In the Clipboard group on the Home ribbon, click Copy.
3. Select the cell where you want the formula pasted.

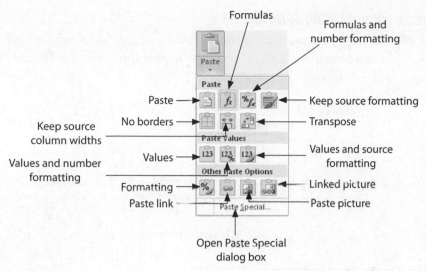

FIGURE 7-5 · The Paste menu in Excel 2010 offers numerous options when copying and pasting a formula.

4. Do one of the following:

- In the Clipboard group on the Home ribbon, click Paste to paste both the formula and cell formatting into the cell. (This is the default action for the Paste button.)

- For additional paste options, in the Clipboard group on the Home ribbon, click the Paste button menu, and then choose what you want to paste. For example, click the Formula button to paste only the formula and not the formatting. Figure 7-5 displays the Paste menu options that are available when copying a formula. Additional options are available in the Paste Special dialog box (click Paste Special in the menu). The button labels are self-explanatory, but you can learn more about these topics in the Excel Help file.

TIP   *The keyboard shortcut for the Copy command is CTRL-C. The keyboard shortcut for the Cut command is CTRL-X. The keyboard shortcut for the Paste command is CTRL-V.*

Copying a Formula Using AutoFill

A formula can be copied using the AutoFill handle. In the following illustration, for example, the formula in cell B6 could be copied into cells C6, D6, and E6 by dragging the Fill handle over those cells.

	A	B	C	D	E	F
1		Donations by State (in dollars)				
2		PA	NY	NJ	DE	
3	2008	$ 1,500.25	$2,200.50	$ 800.00	$2,300.00	
4	2009	$ 1,200.75	$1,800.00	$ 950.00	$1,900.50	
5	2010	$ 1,700.50	$2,800.25	$1,125.25	$2,600.75	
6		$ 4,401.50				
7						
8						

Drag fill handle to copy formula

Moving a Formula or Function

1. Select the cell containing the formula to move.

2. In the Clipboard group on the Home ribbon, click Cut.

3. Select the cell where you want the formula pasted.

4. In the Clipboard group on the Home ribbon, click Paste.

Working with Charts

A chart is a graphic representation of worksheet data. Well-designed and attractive charts can enhance business documents and sometimes convey data more effectively than paragraphs of text or a table of data. Figure 7-6 provides an example of a bar chart. Given the choice between looking at the data in table form as it exists in cells A2 through B5 and looking at the chart, many people would prefer the visual impact of the chart. Excel gives you the power to create visually impressive charts in just a few clicks.

Once created, a chart is dynamically linked to the data from which it was created. If data on the worksheet changes, the chart will be updated automatically. A chart can be embedded into the same worksheet as the data it depicts, or it can be placed on its own separate worksheet. After you create the chart, you can change its type, its formatting, or even the data it points to. You can add or remove labels, swap axis points, reposition the legend, and add or remove gridlines.

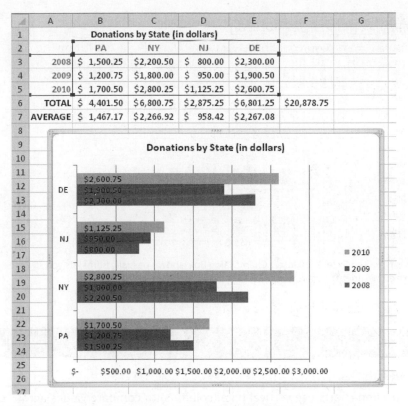

FIGURE 7-6 · Which would you rather look at: the data in cells A1 through E5, or the bar chart that represents the data in a more graphically appealing way?

Chart Types

Excel offers 11 different types of charts: column, line, pie, bar, area, X Y (scatter), stock, surface, doughnut, bubble, and radar. Each of these chart types offers two or more styles (or subtypes), including 2-D and 3-D designs. Figure 7-7 shows a portion of the Insert Chart dialog box, which should give you an idea of the variety of styles available. Table 7-2 describes these chart types in more detail.

TIP *For examples of each chart type, as well as tips on when to use each type, search on "available chart types" in Excel Help.*

Charting Data on a Worksheet

The data to be charted can be arranged in columns or rows; Excel will auto-matically determine the optimum way to display the data in the chosen

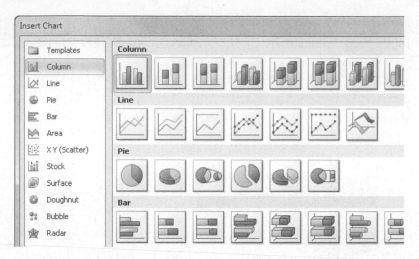

FIGURE 7-7 · The Excel 2010 Insert Chart Dialog Box (shown partially here) lets you choose from a variety of chart types.

TABLE 7-2   Excel 2010 Chart Types

Chart Type	Description
Column	Column charts use vertical bars (columns) to compare values across categories. In a column chart, categories usually occupy the horizontal axis, while values occupy the vertical axis.
Line	Line charts are especially good for showing trends in data over a continuous period of time. A line chart displays category data distributed evenly along the horizontal axis and value data distributed evenly along the vertical axis. Line charts should generally only be used where there is a specific period of time involved. These charts are perfect for displaying trends.
Pie	Pie charts emphasize the relationship between the whole and each part of that whole by showing data points as pieces of a pie. Pie charts are good for highlighting proportions within a single data series. Note that a pie chart won't work if a data series contains negative numbers or if more than one data point is zero. In addition, too many data points can make a pie chart difficult to read, so it's best to have fewer than seven or eight data points to plot.
Bar	Bar charts use horizontal bars to compare values across categories, and are especially useful for side-by-side comparison and spotting trends in a small number of discrete data points. They're a good alternative to line charts when you have only a few data points in a series.

TABLE 7-2 Excel 2010 Chart Types (*Continued*)

Chart Type	Description
Area	Area charts display graphically quantitative data, and are especially good for highlighting the amount of change over a period of time and the relationship of parts to a whole. Area charts are similar to line charts, but they display different colors in the areas below the lines, which can serve to make data stand out more graphically. The order of the data being charted can affect the clarity of the chart, as smaller values plotted in the back of an area chart can be hidden behind larger values.
X Y (Scatter)	X Y scatter charts are especially good for highlighting relationships between numeric values in multiple data series, for plotting two groups of numbers as a single series of *x y* coordinates, and for showing similarities between data sets as opposed to differences between data sets.
Stock	Stock charts are most often used for showing fluctuations in stock prices and displaying scientific data. For a stock chart to display properly, data needs to be organized in the correct order. (See the Help file for more information.)
Surface	A surface chart is ideally suited for finding the best possible combinations between two data sets. A surface chart will work when both categories and data series are numeric values.
Doughnut	A doughnut chart is similar to a pie chart in that it displays data points as pieces of a whole, but a doughnut chart can contain more than one data series. Note that doughnut charts can be a bit difficult to read and will not work for all data.
Bubble	A bubble chart displays a set of numeric values as circles that can be compared in terms of their size as well as their relative positions with respect to each numeric axis. (In this respect, they are loosely related to a scatter chart.) Bubble charts work best when *x* values are contained in the first column and corresponding *y* values are contained in adjacent columns.
Radar	Radar charts compare the aggregate values of several data series by drawing data points evenly spaced in a clockwise direction around the chart. The value of a point is represented by the distance from the center of the chart, where the center represents the minimum value, and the chart edge is the maximum value. Each data series is represented as one complete circuit of the chart.

chart type. If you are creating a pie chart, be sure to select only a single series. To create a pie chart based on the data in Figure 7-6, for example, you could either select a single state for all 3 years (e.g., B3:B5) or a single year for all four states (e.g., B3:E3).

Creating a Chart

1. In a worksheet, select a range of cells for the chart.

2. In the Charts group on the Insert ribbon, do one of the following:

   - Click a chart type button.

   - Click the Other Charts Button.

   - Click the Charts Dialog Box Launcher (located in the lower-right corner of the Charts group).

3. Choose a chart style. The chart will be embedded on the worksheet in its own window.

4. Reposition that chart by doing one of the following:

   - Click the chart and drag it anywhere within the worksheet.

   - On the Chart Tools Design ribbon, click Move Chart and choose whether you want the chart to be placed on a new or existing worksheet. (If you are placing the chart on its own worksheet, you can give the worksheet a name here as well.)

TIP *Want a quick way to embed a chart in a worksheet? Select data on the worksheet, and then use the ALT-F1 keyboard shortcut. A new chart (based on the default chart type, which is Column unless otherwise changed) is embedded in the worksheet instantly. Alternatively, to create a new chart on its own worksheet, select data and press the F11 key. You can change Excel's default chart type in the Insert Chart dialog box by selecting a chart type and then clicking the Set As Default Chart button.*

Chart Anatomy

If you don't know your X axis from your Y axis or your plot area from your legend, Figure 7-8 will help familiarize you with basic chart parts.

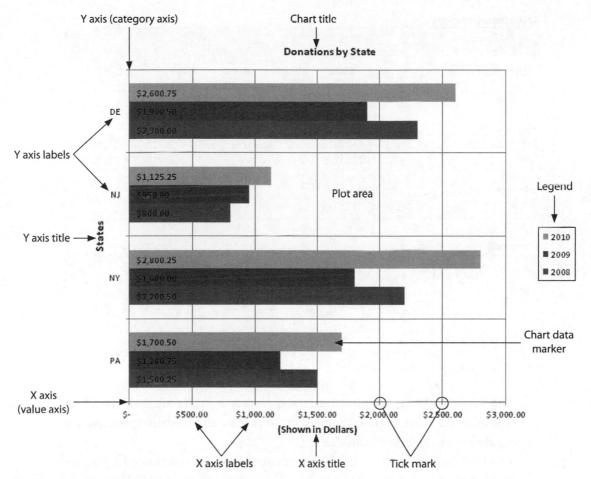

FIGURE 7-8 · Knowing what each part of a chart is called will help you work with charts more effectively.

Chart Formatting Basics

Selecting an existing chart activates the Chart Tools Design, Layout, and For-mat ribbons, pictured in Figure 7-9.

The Design ribbon lets you change chart types, switch rows and columns, change chart layouts and styles, or move a chart to another worksheet.

The Layout ribbon gives you control over specific chart parts, such as the chart title, axis titles, legend, data labels, and axes. From this ribbon you can also modify the plot area and chart background, or add other lines or bars, such as trend lines or error bars.

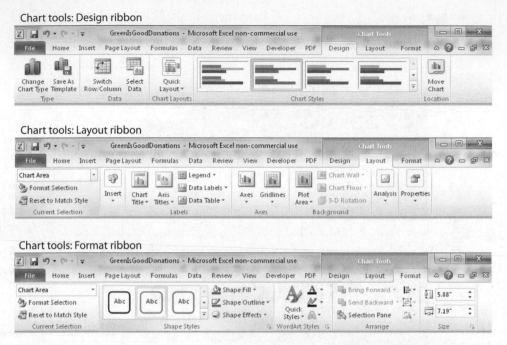

FIGURE 7-9 · Excel 2010 offers three ribbons that allow you to work with charts: the Design ribbon, the Layout ribbon, and the Format ribbon.

The Format ribbon lets you select and format specific areas of the chart; apply styles, fill color, outlines, and effects to shapes; add WordArt; arrange layers; and change the size of the chart.

The best way to learn about chart formatting options is to have fun experimenting with them! A few common formatting options are outlined here to get you started.

Changing the Chart Type

1. Select the chart.
2. On the Chart Tools Design ribbon, click the Change Chart Type button. The Change Chart Type dialog box appears.
3. Choose the new chart type and style.
4. Click OK.

Resizing a Chart

A chart is a graphic and, like other graphics in Office 2010, can be resized by selecting the chart area and then dragging the corner, top, bottom, left, or right center edges. (You are in the right spot for resizing when the cursor looks like a double-headed arrow.) To get more specific when sizing, do the following:

1. Select the chart area.
2. On the Chart Tools Format ribbon, in the Size group, do one of the following:
   - Type the desired size in the Shape Height and Shape Width fields.
   - Click the Sizes Dialog Box Launcher to open the Format Chart Area dialog box, where you can resize, rotate, or scale the chart from the Size tab.

TIP *When using the Shape Height and Shape Width fields, the maintain aspect ratio is off by default. If you want the chart to retain its aspect ratio when resizing, click the Sizes Dialog Box Launcher to open the Format Chart Area dialog box and select the Lock Aspect Ratio check box.*

Swapping Rows and Columns

As you read previously in this chapter, when you create a chart, Excel automatically determines the optimum way to display the data in the chosen chart type based on the way the data is organized in the worksheet. However, you have ultimate control over how your data is displayed. For example, in the following illustration, the chart on the left uses PA and NJ as the data points; swapping the rows and columns causes the years to be used as the data points instead, as shown in the chart on the right.

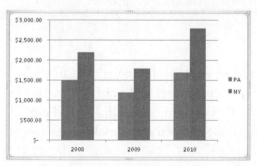 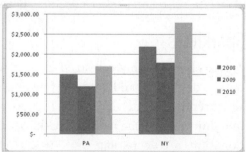

1. Select the chart.
2. On the Chart Tools Design ribbon, click the Switch Row/Column Button. The axis and legend are switched.

Changing Chart Styles

Changing a chart's style affects the colors, line styles, and effects in a chart.

1. Select the chart.
2. On the Chart Tools Design ribbon, choose a chart style from the Styles gallery.

Changing Chart Layout

Changing a chart's layout affects the plot area, legend, and labels in a chart.

1. Select the chart.
2. On the Chart Tools Design ribbon, choose a chart layout from the Layout gallery.

Adding a Chart Title

A chart title can be positioned as an overlay on the chart or above the chart.

1. Select the chart.
2. On the Chart Tools Layout ribbon, click Chart Title and choose the desired position.
3. Edit the chart title placeholder text as desired.

TIP   *Use the Font and Alignment groups on the Home ribbon to make changes to the formatting of a chart title. Click and drag the chart title to reposition it. To delete a chart title, select it and then press the DELETE or BACKSPACE key.*

Sparklines

A sparkline is a tiny cell-sized chart that can be embedded right next to the data it depicts. Sparklines help put numbers into context and can help you to spot trends or patterns quickly. In Figure 7-10, for example, the line sparklines in column E and the column sparklines in column F both make it obvious that donations are decreasing.

Adding a Sparkline

1. In a worksheet, select a range of cells for the sparkline. (To create Figure 7-10, cells B3 through D10 were selected.)

⬒	A	B	C	D	E	F
1	**Pennsylvania Donations By Name**					
2		2008	2009	2010		
3	Edward Nugen	$ 100.00	$ 50.00	$ 50.00		
4	Darby Glande	$ 150.00	$ 50.00	$ 25.00		
5	Edward Kelle	$ 50.00	$ 100.00	$ 75.00		
6	Georgia Wallace	$ 225.00	$ 100.00	$ 25.00		
7	Erasmus Clefs	$ 75.00	$ 35.00	$ 35.00		
8	Edward Ketcheman	$ 75.00	$ 65.00	$ 55.00		
9	Lucille Loo	$ 125.00	$ 100.00	$ 20.00		
10	Thomas Rottenbury	$ 35.00	$ 125.00	$ 100.00		

FIGURE 7-10 · Sparklines let you spot data trends at a glance.

2. On the Insert ribbon, in the Sparklines group, click a sparkline type button (Line, Column, or Win Loss). The Create Sparklines dialog box appears.

3. The data range you selected in step 1 should be displayed in the Data Range field. If the range is correct, move on to step 4. If the range is not correct, modify it by typing in the field or by clicking and dragging over the range in the worksheet. (Hint: Clicking the button on the right of the field will make the dialog box smaller. You can move the dialog box by clicking and dragging its title bar.)

4. In the Location Range field, enter the cell range representing where you want the sparklines to display. You can do this by manually typing the range or by clicking and dragging over the range in the worksheet. In Figure 7-10, cells E3:E10 were the location range for the sparklines in column E and cells F3:F10 were the location range for the sparklines in column F.

5. Click OK. The sparklines are added.

Deleting a Sparkline

1. Select the cells containing the sparklines you want to delete.

2. On the Sparkline Tools Design ribbon, click the Clear button.

3. Choose Clear Selected Sparklines (or Clear Selected Sparkline Groups if you have previously grouped the sparklines).

Formatting a Sparkline

Once they are on a worksheet, sparklines can be formatted in numerous ways: you can change the sparkline type; choose to show certain types of points within the sparkline (high, low, first, last, negative points, and markers); change the sparkline's color and weight; change marker colors; modify axis settings (plot data from right to left instead of the default left to right); and group or ungroup sparklines.

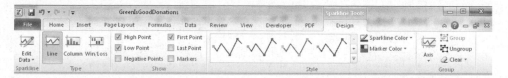

1. Select the sparklines you want to format.

2. On the Sparkline Tools Design ribbon, do one or more of the following as desired:

   • To change the sparkline type, click a new type in the Type group.

   • To show certain types of points along the sparkline, select the relevant check boxes in the Show group.

   • To change the sparkline style, select a style from the Style group.

   • To change the color of a sparkline, select a color from the Sparkline Color button menu in the Style group.

   • To change the weight of a line sparkline, click the Sparkline Color button and then choose a weight from the Weight menu.

   • To change marker colors, click the Marker Color button menu and choose colors for each of the types of markers you wish to change.

   • To make changes to the axis options, click the Axis drop-down button.

   • To group or ungroup sparklines, click the Group or Ungroup button.

Still Struggling

Remember to refer back to Chapter 2 for common program functionality, such as Backstage View (document properties and permissions, opening existing files and saving files); using undo and redo; working with the Office Clipboard (cut, copy, and paste); working with themes; and getting help.

Summary

In this chapter you learned about three features that help make Excel such a powerful business tool: formulas, functions, and charts. You learned how to write a formula and how to incorporate functions into a formula. You also learned how to use Excel's charting feature to bring your data to life. In Chapter 8 you will explore page layout and printing options in Excel 2010.

QUIZ

1. True or False: An Excel formula must begin with an equal sign.
   A. True
   B. False

2. Which of the following elements can a formula contain?
   A. Cell references
   B. Mathematical operators
   C. Values
   D. Functions
   E. All of the above

3. A function is a(n) _____ , built-in _____ . (Fill in the blanks using the following choices.)
   A. automatic
   B. systematic
   C. predefined
   D. operator
   E. formula

4. Which of the following is not a function available on the AutoSum button menu?
   A. Aggregate
   B. SUM
   C. Average
   D. Max
   E. Min

5. True or False: You must have an excellent command of math to be able to use Excel.
   A. True
   B. False

6. Which of the following is not a standard chart type in Excel?
   A. Pie
   B. Column
   C. Histogram
   D. Bar
   E. Line

7. **True or False: When you copy a formula, cell references will change if you used absolute cell references; cell references will not change if you used relative cell references.**
   A. True
   B. False

8. **A _____ is a tiny, cell-sized _____ that can be embedded right next to the data it depicts. (Fill in the blanks using the following choices.)**
   A. gadget
   B. sparkline
   C. chart
   D. picture
   E. weight line

9. **Which of the following is not a sparkline type? (Choose all that apply.)**
   A. Trend
   B. Pie
   C. Column
   D. Scatter
   E. Win/Lose

10. **True or False: The Insert Function dialog box lets you search for a function by typing a description.**
    A. True
    B. False

chapter 8

Page Layout, Viewing, and Printing

This chapter provides an overview of Microsoft Excel 2010's page setup, document viewing, and printing options. Controlling margins, page orientation, and page size and being able to manipulate where page breaks are placed are all useful techniques for making worksheet pages look as professional as possible. You will learn how to make good use of Excel's view options as well as how to preview and print a worksheet.

CHAPTER OBJECTIVES

In this chapter, you will learn how to

- Set margins, page orientation, and page size
- Work with page breaks
- Navigate, add, delete, name, move, and copy worksheets
- Use Excel's worksheet views
- Show/hide gridlines and row and column headings
- Freeze panes
- Preview and print a worksheet

Worksheet Page Layout Options

The Page Layout ribbon (pictured here) is where the most frequently used page setup commands (such as margins, orientation, size, and print area) and worksheet option commands (such as showing, hiding, and printing gridlines and headings) are accessed. Additional page-related and sheet-related commands can be accessed in the Page Setup dialog box, which is available by clicking the Page Setup Dialog Box Launcher (located in the lower-right corner of the Page Setup group).

Working with Margins

Page margins refer to the space between the edge of the page and the body of the worksheet. Worksheet content is positioned in the body of the worksheet. Headers, footers, and page numbers are positioned within the margins of the worksheet.

Excel's default margins—referred to as Normal—are set to .75" for the top and bottom margins and .7" for the left and right margins. If you are trying to fit more content on a single page, you can decrease the size of the page margins to give the body of the document more space. You might, for example, change the margins to .25" all around. If you are using headers or footers in the worksheet, you will need to be careful about encroaching upon the space these page elements need. In this case, you may choose to only modify the left and right margins to .25" and leave the top and bottom at .75" so that the header or footer fits comfortably.

1. On the Page Layout ribbon, click Margins.

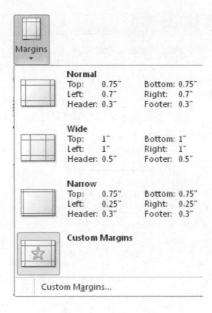

2. From the Margins menu, do one of the following:

- Choose one of the suggested margin settings (Normal, Wide, or Narrow).

- Choose Custom Margins to open the Page Setup dialog box. On the Margins tab (pictured in Figure 8-1), provide the desired custom margin settings in the Top, Bottom, Left, and Right fields, and then click OK.

Setting Page Orientation

Page orientation refers to whether the page is taller than it is wide (portrait) or wider than it is tall (landscape). Excel's default page orientation is set to landscape.

1. On the Page Layout ribbon, click Orientation.

2. Choose Portrait or Landscape.

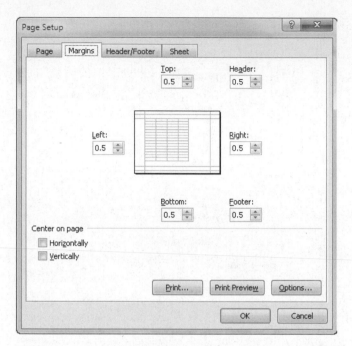

FIGURE 8-1 · The Excel 2010 Page Setup dialog box lets you control worksheet, page, and margin settings as well as header and footer settings.

Setting Page Size

Excel's default page size is set to 11" × 8.5"; however, a variety of other page sizes can be accommodated.

1. On the Page Layout ribbon, click Size.

2. From the Size menu, do one of the following:

   - Choose one of the suggested page sizes (A4, Legal, Executive, etc.).

   - Choose More Page Sizes to open the Page Setup dialog box. On the Page tab, type the desired custom margin settings in the Width and Height fields, and then click OK.

TIP *Check your printer user manual to see what page sizes the printer can accommodate and how to position the paper in the paper tray.*

Manipulating Page Breaks

As data is added to a worksheet, page breaks are automatically inserted in accordance with the page's margins and size. Sometimes a page breaks in an awkward location. For example, if an automatic page break happens in the middle of a group of related data that you would rather have displayed together on the same page, you might choose to insert a manual page break above the group to force it to display together on the next page.

In Excel, you must picture page breaks as happening both vertically (between columns) and horizontally (between rows).

Inserting a Page Break

1. Select the row below where you want a horizontal page break or the column to the right of where you want a vertical page break. For example, to place a horizontal page break between rows 50 and 51, select row 50; to place a vertical page break between columns F and G, select column G.

2. On the Page Layout ribbon, click Breaks.

3. From the Breaks menu, choose Insert Page Break. Page breaks appear as dashed lines between rows and columns, as pictured here.

	E	F	G	H	I
16	**Extra Payment**	**Total Payment**	**Principal**	**Interest**	**Ending Balan**
46	$ -	$ 1,434.53	$ 386.46	$ 1,048.07	$ 264,2
47	$ -	$ 1,434.53	$ 387.99	$ 1,046.54	$ 264,0
48	$ -	$ 1,434.53	$ 389.52	$ 1,045.01	$ 263,8
49	$ -	$ 1,434.53	$ 391.06	$ 1,043.47	$ 263,2
50	$ -	$ 1,434.53	$ 392.61	$ 1,041.92	$ 262,8
51	$ -	$ 1,434.53	$ 394.17	$ 1,040.36	$ 262,4
52	$ -	$ 1,434.53	$ 395.73	$ 1,038.80	$ 262,0
53	$ -	$ 1,434.53	$ 397.29	$ 1,037.24	$ 261,6
54	$ -	$ 1,434.53	$ 398.87	$ 1,035.66	$ 261,2
55	$ -	$ 1,434.53	$ 400.44	$ 1,034.09	$ 260,8
56	$ -	$ 1,434.53	$ 402.03	$ 1,032.50	$ 260,4

TIP *To preview page breaks, click the Page Break Preview button on the View ribbon.*

Deleting a Page Break

1. Select the row below a horizontal page break or the column to the right of a vertical page break. For example, to delete a horizontal page break between rows 50 and 51, select row 51; to delete a vertical page break between columns F and G, select column G.
2. On the Page Layout ribbon, click Breaks.
3. From the Breaks menu, choose Remove Page Break.

TIP   *Only a manual page break can be deleted using these instructions. The only way to get rid of an automatic page break is by inserting a manual page break where it will affect the desired change.*

Resetting All Page Breaks in a Worksheet

1. On the Page Layout ribbon, click Breaks.
2. From the Breaks menu, choose Reset All Page Breaks.

Working with Worksheets

As you may recall from Chapter 6, Excel provides three worksheets in each new workbook. You can add or delete worksheets as needed. Each worksheet appears on its own tab, as pictured here.

TIP   *Want to color-code your worksheet tabs? Right-click a tab and choose a color from the Tab Color menu.*

Navigating between Existing Worksheets

To move between worksheets, click a worksheet tab at the bottom of the Excel window. To scroll through available worksheets, use the navigation buttons to the left of the worksheet tabs. The outside two buttons will scroll to the first or last worksheet. The inside two buttons will scroll through worksheets one at a time.

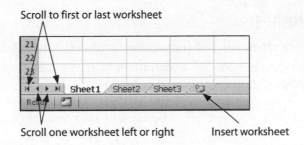

Scroll to first or last worksheet

Scroll one worksheet left or right   Insert worksheet

TIP *To view the next sheet in the workbook, press CTRL-PAGE DOWN. To view the previous sheet in the workbook, press CTRL-PAGE UP.*

Adding Worksheets

To insert a new worksheet, do one of the following:

- In the Cells group on the Home ribbon, click Insert and choose Sheet.
- Click the Insert Worksheet button (located to the right of the worksheet tabs at the bottom of the Excel window).
- Right-click an existing worksheet tab, and then choose Insert. On the General tab of the Insert dialog box click Worksheet and then click OK.
- Press SHIFT-F11.

TIP *To insert multiple worksheets, use CTRL-click to select multiple existing worksheet tabs and then right-click one of them. Choose Insert and on the General tab of the Insert dialog box click Worksheet and then click OK.*

Deleting Worksheets

To delete a worksheet, do one of the following:

- In the Cells group on the Home ribbon, click Delete and choose Sheet.
- Right-click an existing worksheet tab, and choose Delete.

TIP *To delete multiple worksheets, use CTRL-click to select multiple existing worksheet tabs, and then right-click one of them and choose Delete.*

Naming Worksheets

Excel worksheets are numbered consecutively: Sheet1, Sheet2, Sheet3, and so on. You can change the name of a worksheet to make it more meaningful. To rename a worksheet, do one of the following:

- Right-click a worksheet tab, choose Rename, and then type the new name.
- Double-click a worksheet tab, and then type a new name.

TIP   *Want your worksheet names to print? This can be accomplished by including the name in the header or footer of a worksheet. In the Text group of the Insert ribbon, click Header & Footer. This will display the header/footer areas on the worksheet. Click in the header/footer area where you want the worksheet name to display when printed (left, right, or center), and then click on the Sheet Name button on the Header & Footer Tools Design ribbon.*

Moving or Copying a Worksheet within the Same Workbook

1. Right-click the worksheet tab you want to move, and choose Move Or Copy. The Move Or Copy dialog box appears (pictured in Figure 8-2.)
2. In the Before Sheet area, click the worksheet you want to move or copy the worksheet in front of, or click (Move To End) to move/copy the worksheet to the last position.
3. Click OK.

FIGURE 8-2 · Use the Move or Copy dialog box to move or copy worksheets.

TIP   *To quickly move a worksheet, click its tab and drag it to its new location. As you drag, a page icon appears attached to the mouse pointer and a triangle appears where the worksheet will be moved to when the mouse is released. To quickly copy a worksheet, hold down the CTRL key, click the worksheet tab, and drag it to where you want the copied worksheet inserted. As you drag, a page icon with a plus sign on it appears attached to the mouse pointer and a triangle appears where the worksheet is moved to when the mouse is released.*

Moving or Copying a Worksheet to Another Workbook

To move or copy a worksheet to another workbook, both workbooks must be open.

1. Right-click the worksheet tab you want to move or copy, and choose Move Or Copy. The Move Or Copy dialog box appears (see Figure 8-2).
2. In the To Book drop-down list, choose the workbook where you want the worksheet to be placed.
3. In the Before Sheet list, click the worksheet you want to move/copy the worksheet in front of or click (Move To End) to move the worksheet to the last position.
4. Click OK.

TIP   *Note that calculations or charts based on worksheet data might become inaccurate if the worksheet is moved.*

Worksheet Navigation Tips

Navigating within a worksheet is fairly intuitive: click in a cell or use the arrow keys. However, if you would prefer not to use the mouse or have to press the arrow keys over and over, there are a few navigation tricks that are good to know, described in Table 8-1.

Working with Worksheets as a Group

Worksheets can be selected as a group so that you can apply certain features to all of them at once. Features that can be applied to a group of selected worksheets include setting print options, applying formats, unhiding rows and/or

TABLE 8-1 Worksheet Navigation Tips

To Move	Do This
To the first cell in the worksheet	CTRL–HOME
To the last cell in the worksheet (the lowest used row of the rightmost used column)	CTRL–END
To the edge of the current data region	CTRL–ARROW KEY
To the beginning of a row in a worksheet	HOME
One screen up or down	PAGE DOWN or PAGE UP
One screen left or right	ALT–PAGE DOWN or ALT–PAGE UP

columns, and typing text or formulas into the same cell address in all of the grouped sheets.

1. Click the first worksheet you want to group.

2. Do one of the following:

- To select worksheets that are adjacent, hold down the SHIFT key and click the last worksheet you want to group.

- To select worksheets that are not adjacent, hold down the CTRL key and click each of the worksheets you want to group.

TIP *To quickly group all of the worksheets in a workbook, right-click any worksheet tab and then choose Select All.*

Worksheet Viewing Options

The View ribbon (pictured here) is where commands related to viewing a document, such as layouts and zoom settings, are found.

- The Workbook Views group offers one-click access to each of Excel's view types: Normal, Page Layout, Page Break Preview, Custom, and Full Screen.
- The Show group lets you show or hide the ruler, gridlines, Formula bar, and column and row headings.
- The Zoom group allows you to modify the screen size of a document.
- The Window group lets you create new windows, arrange open windows, freeze panes, split a worksheet, and hide a worksheet.

Workbook Views

On the View ribbon, in the Workbook Views group, Excel offers five workbook views: Normal, Page Layout, Page Break Preview, Custom, and Full Screen. You can change views by clicking these buttons. In addition, Normal, Page Layout, and Page Break Preview buttons are available in the Excel status bar (located in the lower-right corner of the Excel window) as illustrated here.

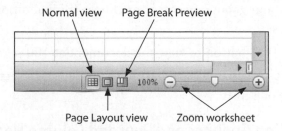

Normal

Normal is the default layout for Excel worksheets. Normal view presents the worksheet as one continual scrolling spreadsheet.

Page Layout

Excel's Page Layout view displays the worksheet as it would print: horizontal and vertical rulers are added to the row and column headings, and page margins, page breaks, and any headers or footers for the worksheet will display.

Page Break Preview

In this view, dashed lines indicate automatic page breaks (based on page size and margins) and solid lines indicate manually inserted page breaks. You can adjust page breaks by dragging them.

Full Screen

This view hides the ribbons, the Formula bar, and the status bar. Returning to Normal view reveals these items again.

Custom

A custom view is a named set of display settings (including column widths, row heights, hidden rows and columns, cell selections, filter settings, and window settings) and print settings (including print area, page settings, margins, headers and footers, and sheet settings) that can be applied to a workbook. You can learn more about creating and using custom views in the Excel Help file.

Zoom

The Zoom group on the View ribbon lets you control how a worksheet displays on screen.

- Click the Zoom button to open the Zoom dialog box, where you can customize your zoom percentage or choose from additional preset zoom percentages.
- Click the 100% button to view the document at 100 percent of its size.
- Click the Zoom To Selection button to display the selected cells as large as possible on screen.

Showing/Hiding Gridlines and Row and Column Headings

By default, gridlines and row and column headings display on-screen in a worksheet. However, these worksheet elements can be hidden if desired.

Showing/Hiding Gridlines

To show or hide gridlines in a worksheet, do one of the following:

- On the View ribbon (located in the Show group), select the Gridlines check box.
- On the Page Layout ribbon (located in the Sheet Options group), under the Gridlines heading, select the View check box.

A check mark in the check box indicates that the item will be displayed; no check mark in the check box means the item will be hidden.

Showing/Hiding Row and Column Headings

To show or hide row and column headings, do one of the following:

- On the View ribbon (located in the Show group), select the Headings check box.

- On the Page Layout ribbon (located in the Sheet Options group), in the Headings area, select the View check box.

A check mark in the check box indicates that the item will be displayed; no check mark in the check box means the item will be hidden.

Freezing Rows and/or Columns

In a large worksheet where row and/or column labels are positioned within the first few rows or columns, it can be challenging to scroll to the far reaches of the worksheet and still remember what those row and column labels were because they scroll out of sight. Excel's Freeze Panes feature solves this issue by letting you freeze the rows or columns containing the labels into place.

1. Select the row and/or column you want to freeze using the following guidelines:

   - To freeze rows, select the row below the row or rows that you want to keep visible when you scroll.

   - To freeze columns, select the column to the right of the column or columns that you want to keep visible when you scroll.

   - To freeze both rows and columns, click the cell below and to the right of the rows and columns that you want to keep visible when you scroll.

2. In the Window group on the View ribbon, choose Freeze Panes.

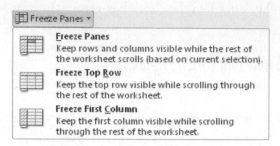

3. Do one of the following:

- Choose Freeze Top Row to freeze one row only.
- Choose Freeze First Column to freeze one column only.
- Choose Freeze Panes to freeze more than one row or column, or to freeze both rows and columns at the same time.

TIP   *To unfreeze panes, select the frozen row and/or column and in the Window group on the View ribbon, choose Freeze Panes, and then choose Unfreeze Panes. (Note that the Unfreeze Panes option will only be visible if the selected row and/ or column is frozen.)*

Printing and Previewing

The Print pane on the File ribbon (pictured in Figure 8-3) is where you will go to preview how a worksheet will print and to print a worksheet. Several page layout options are also available on this pane.

In addition to the Print command, the Print pane provides a preview of the printed worksheet, as well as page layout commands, such as paper orientation, page size, and margins. Here, you can also choose a specific printer if you have more than one, specify which pages in a document are to be printed, and, if your printer has duplex printing and/or collating features, set those options as well.

Previewing a Worksheet

1. Click the File ribbon.

2. Click Print. The worksheet preview is displayed on the right side of the Print pane.

Margins

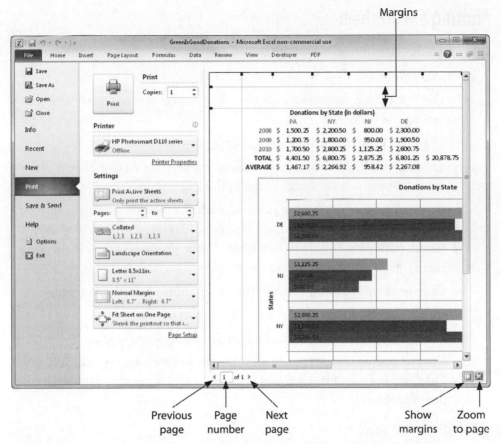

Previous page   Page number   Next page   Show margins   Zoom to page

FIGURE 8-3 • The Print Pane on the File Ribbon combines printing and previewing options.

- To navigate between pages in the preview, use the Previous Page and Next Page buttons at the bottom-left corner of the Preview pane, or type a number in the Page Number field.

- To zoom the preview screen, use the Zoom To Page button at the bottom-right corner of the Preview pane. To return to single-page view, click the Zoom To Page button again.

- To view page margins, click the Show Margins button at the bottom-right corner of the Preview pane. To hide margins, click the Show Margins Button again.

Printing a Worksheet

1. Click the File ribbon.
2. Click Print.
3. In the Print pane (pictured in Figure 8-3), make any necessary changes, including the following:
   - Choose a printer from the Printer drop-down menu.
   - Specify which worksheet to print from in the Print Active Sheets drop-down menu, or type a page range in the Pages field.
   - If your printer has duplex printing and/or collating features, specify those options in the Print One Sided and Collated drop-down menus (these options will only be available if your printer is capable of using them).
   - Change the page orientation in the Orientation drop-down menu.
   - Change the page size in the Size drop-down menu.
   - Change the page margins in the Margins drop-down menu.
   - Choose scaling options (such as Fit Sheet On One Page, Fit All Columns On One Page, or Fit All Rows On One Page) from the Scaling drop-down menu.
4. Click Print.

TIP *To quickly access the Print pane on the File ribbon, press* CTRL-P.

Printing Gridlines

By default, gridlines do not print. However, you can choose to print the gridlines if desired. To print gridlines, do one of the following:

- On the View ribbon (located in the Show group), select the Gridlines check box. The Gridlines check box is a toggle switch: placing a check mark in the check box indicates that the gridlines will print; no check mark in the check box means the gridlines will not print.
- On the Page Layout ribbon (located in the Sheet Options group), under the Gridlines heading, select the View check box. The Gridlines check box is a toggle switch: placing a check mark in the check box indicates that the gridlines will print; no check mark in the check box means the headings will not print.

Printing Row and Column Headings

By default, row and column headings do not print. You can choose to print these headings if desired. To print row and column headings, do one of the following:

- On the View ribbon (located in the Show group), select the Headings check box. The Headings check box is a toggle switch: placing a check mark in the check box indicates that the headings will print; no check mark in the check box means the headings will not print.

- On the Page Layout ribbon (located in the Sheet Options group), under the Headings area, select the View check box. The Headings check box is a toggle switch: placing a check mark in the check box indicates that the headings will print; no check mark in the check box means the headings will not print.

Still Struggling

Remember to refer back to Chapter 2 for common program functionality, such as Backstage View (document properties and permissions, opening existing files, and saving files); using undo and redo; working with the Office Clipboard (cut, copy, and paste); working with themes; and getting help.

Summary

In this chapter you learned about Microsoft Excel 2010's page setup, document viewing, and printing options. You learned how to control margins, change page orientation and page size, and manipulate where page breaks are placed. You also explored Excel's views and printing options. In Chapter 9 you will get started with Office 2010's presentation program: PowerPoint.

QUIZ

1. **True or False: Gridlines are always included when printing.**
    A. True
    B. False

2. **Which of the following is/are not a workbook view in Excel?**
    A. Page Layout
    B. Normal
    C. Full Screen
    D. Outline
    E. Page Break Preview

3. **As data is added to a worksheet, page breaks are automatically inserted in accordance with the page's _____ and _____ . (Fill in the blanks using the following choices.)**
    A. orientation
    B. margins
    C. theme
    D. print titles
    E. page size

4. **Which of the following is not on the Page Layout ribbon?**
    A. Margins
    B. Orientation
    C. Picture
    D. Size
    E. Print area

5. **True or False: Excel worksheet tabs can be color-coded.**
    A. True
    B. False

6. **Which of the following zoom views displays selected cells as large as possible?**
    A. 100%
    B. Zoom To Selection
    C. One Page
    D. Two Pages
    E. None of the above

7. **Which of the following statements is/are true? (Choose all that apply.)**
   A. Excel gridlines print by default.
   B. Excel gridlines do not print by default.
   C. Excel gridlines display on-screen by default.
   D. Excel gridlines do not display on-screen by default.
   E. All of the above

8. **A(n) _____ page orientation refers to when the page is wider than it is tall; _____ page orientation refers to when a page is taller than it is wide (Fill in the blanks using the following choices.)**
   A. landscape
   B. narrow
   C. portrait
   D. even
   E. letter

9. **Which of the following is not an option on the Print pane?**
   A. Orientation
   B. Margins
   C. Scaling
   D. Print titles
   E. Printer

10. **True or False: The View ribbon is where the most frequently used page-related commands, such as margins, orientation, and size, are accessed.**
    A. True
    B. False

Part IV

Microsoft PowerPoint

chapter 9

Getting Started with PowerPoint

This chapter gets you started using Microsoft PowerPoint 2010. You'll create a new presentation, learn how to add and delete slides, and learn how to navigate between slides. You'll add slide content and become familiar with text and paragraph formatting. You will learn to add slide notes for use by the presenter, and you will also be introduced to PowerPoint's spelling checker to help ensure typo-free presentations.

CHAPTER OBJECTIVES

In this chapter, you will learn how to

- Create a new presentation (from scratch or from a template)
- Add and delete slides and navigate within a presentation
- Work with text formatting (adding, deleting, and formatting)
- Work with paragraph formatting (alignment, indenting, bullets, and numbering)
- Add speaker notes to a presentation
- Correct spelling errors in a presentation

Building a New Presentation

As you learned in Chapter 2, launching PowerPoint presents you with a new, blank presentation in which you can immediately begin working. You can also use the New command on the File ribbon to create a new presentation in PowerPoint. Doing so displays the New pane, which gives you the option of starting with a completely blank presentation, starting with an available template, or starting with a template from the Microsoft Office website.

Creating a New Presentation in PowerPoint

1. Click the File ribbon.
2. Choose New.
3. Do one of the following:
   - To start with a blank document, click Blank (located under the Available Templates heading).
   - To start with a template, navigate to and select the desired template under the Available Templates or Office.com Templates headings.
4. Click the Create button.

Working with a Blank Presentation

A blank presentation gives you the opportunity to build a presentation completely from scratch, offering you a great deal of creative latitude. You can design your own slide backgrounds (colors, pictures, lines, shapes, etc.) and choose your own fonts, styles, and colors.

A new, blank presentation is always based on a default template named Normal.potx. The Normal.potx template's master slides can be modified to suit your preferences. You will learn more about working with master slides in Chapter 10.

In the default template, a title slide will always appear as the first slide in the presentation. The title slide (pictured in Figure 9-1) provides two placeholders for text: title and subhead. The title slide can be changed to a different type of slide if needed using the Layout drop-down menu on the Home ribbon, which will be covered later in this chapter.

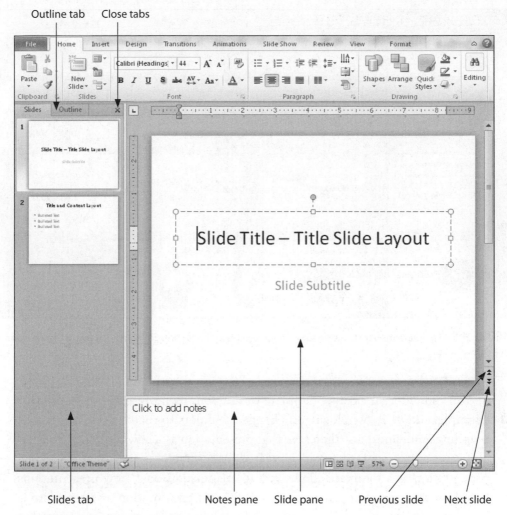

FIGURE 9-1 · PowerPoint 2010 Normal View is the default view when you launch the program.

Working with a Template

You may recall from Chapter 2 that a template is a preformatted presentation layout that serves as the basis for a brand-new presentation. In addition to being preformatted, most templates include text placeholders that can be modified to suit your needs. Figure 9-2 shows the Training template (in Slide Sorter view) available from the Sample Templates list. Note that the suggested text is there as a guide to get you started quickly; it can (and should) be modified to suit the presentation you are developing.

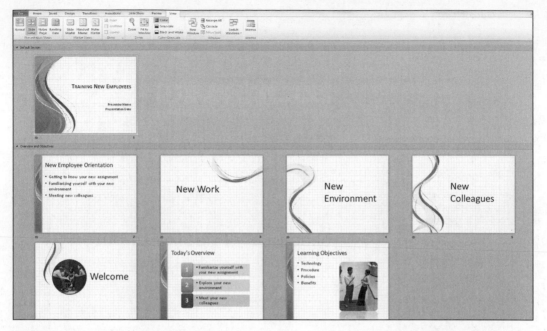

FIGURE 9-2 · Sample templates, such as the Training template shown here, offer a quick way to get started on a presentation.

You can tailor an existing template to suit your own presentation needs (for example, add your own logo and change the colors to match your company's branding guidelines) and then save that presentation as a new template. You can also save any presentation you've created from scratch as a template. Saving a presentation as a template allows you to create additional, new presentations based on that template. One benefit of saving a presentation as a template is that you are protecting the presentation from being easily overwritten. The first time you save a presentation that is based on a template, the Save As dialog box will open (even if you chose the Save command). This reminds you to give the file a unique name and save it in a specific location where you can find it again.

TIP   *A PowerPoint document has a .pptx file extension. A PowerPoint template has a .potx file extension.*

Saving a Document as a Template

1. On the File ribbon, click Save As.

2. From the Save As Type drop-down list, choose PowerPoint Template. The default file folder location for Office 2010 templates will be selected automatically.

3. Type a unique name in the File Name field.

4. Click Save.

TIP *If you make modifications to a template and want to save the revised template as a template instead of a document, use the Save As command on the File ribbon. From the Save As Type drop-down list, choose PowerPoint Template, and save the document in the same location using the same name. This will overwrite the old version of the template with the revised version. If you do not want to rewrite the old version of the template with the revised version, provide the file with a unique name.*

Still Struggling

Confused about the difference between a theme and a template? A theme is a designer-coordinated collection of fonts, color combinations, table formats, and graphic concepts. A template is a preformatted presentation that serves as the basis for a brand-new presentation. A template can use a theme as its basis, but it will also contain other elements such as placeholders and suggested text.

PowerPoint Normal View

By default, the PowerPoint window opens in Normal view (pictured in Figure 9-3). Normal view offers four resizable panes:

- **Slide pane** (top-right area of the screen): Displays the current slide
- **Notes pane** (bottom-right area of the screen): Displays presenter notes (if present)
- **Slides tab** (left side of screen; click Slides): Displays thumbnails of all slides
- **Outline tab** (left side of screen; click Outline): Displays the presentation text in outline form

To resize a Normal view pane, position the mouse pointer on the edge of a pane, and then click and drag. For example, to resize the Notes pane, point to the top edge of the pane (you are in the right spot when the cursor resembles a double-headed arrow), and then click and drag up to increase the pane's height, or drag down to decrease the pane's height. To resize the Slides tab pane, point to the right edge of the pane (again, look for the double-headed arrow), and then click and drag to the right to increase the width of the pane, or drag to the left to decrease the width of the pane.

TIP *Need more screen real estate? Hide the Slides and Outline tabs by clicking in the close box (X) in the top-right corner of the pane area. To bring them back into view, click Normal on the View ribbon.*

You will be learning about other PowerPoint views in Chapter 11.

Navigating in Normal View

To move between slides in Normal view, do one of the following:

- Click the Previous Slide and Next Slide buttons (located in the lower-right corner of the Slide pane).
- Click a slide in the Slides tab.
- Press the PAGE UP and PAGE DOWN keys on the keyboard.
- Press the UP ARROW and DOWN ARROW keys on the keyboard.

TIP *To quickly move to the very first slide in the presentation, press the HOME key on the keyboard. To quickly move to the very last slide in the presentation, press the END key on the keyboard.*

Working with Slides

Whether you start with a blank canvas or a template, working with slides is easy. You can add, delete, or modify slides as needed and choose specific slide layouts as required for your presentation.

The Slides group (pictured here to the right) on the Home ribbon provides most of the commands you will need to work with slides.

Exploring Slide Layouts

PowerPoint slide layouts delineate the formatting, positioning, and content placeholders for each slide element. Content placeholders exist for text (titles, body text, bulleted lists), tables, charts, graphics (pictures, clip art, SmartArt), movies, and sounds. Layouts also include the slide background as well as theme colors, fonts, and effects.

The Layout button menu (pictured here) on the Home ribbon showcases nine built-in slide layouts: Title Slide, Title and Content, Section Header, Two Content, Comparison, Title Only, Blank, Content with Caption, and Picture with Caption.

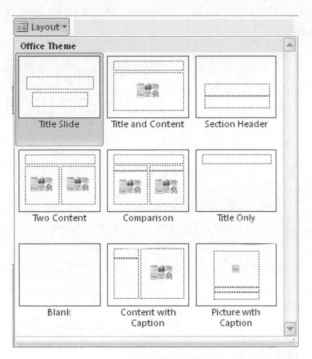

TIP *If the standard layouts don't meet your presentation's needs, you can create custom layouts. For more information on creating custom layouts, search for the "what is a slide layout" article in PowerPoint Help, and then scroll down to "Create a Custom Layout."*

Adding a New Slide

1. Click the Home ribbon.

2. In the Slides group, do one of the following:

   - To insert a new Title And Content layout slide, click the top half of the New Slide button.

   - To select from a list of layouts, click the bottom half of the New Slide button to display the New Slide button menu (pictured here), and then click the type of slide you wish to add. Alternatively, to quickly add a slide that uses the same layout as an existing slide in your presentation, right-click the slide in the Slides tab, and then choose New Slide from the menu.

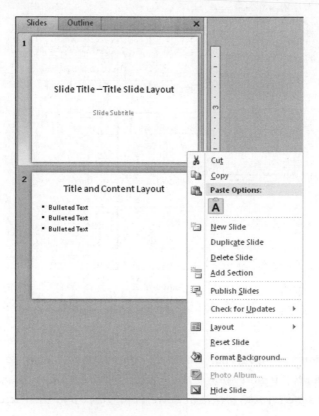

Deleting a Slide

To delete a slide, do one of the following:

- In the Slides tab, select the slide you want to delete, and then press the DELETE or BACKSPACE key.
- In the Slides tab, right-click the slide you want to delete, and choose Delete Slide from the menu.

Changing a Slide's Layout

To change a slide's layout, do one of the following:

- In the Slides tab, select the slide you want to change, and then choose a different layout from the Layout button menu (located on the Home ribbon).
- In the Slides tab, right-click the slide you want to change, choose Layout, and then select a layout from the Layout submenu.

Duplicating Slides

To duplicate an existing slide, do one of the following:

- In the Slides tab, right-click the slide you want to duplicate, and choose Duplicate Slide (the duplicate slide appears directly below the selected slide).
- In the Slides tab, select the slide(s) you want to duplicate, and then, on the Home ribbon, click the bottom half of the New Slide menu and choose Duplicate Selected Slides (the duplicate slide appears directly below the selected slide).
- In the Slides tab, right-click the slide you want to duplicate, and choose Copy. Then right-click the slide you want the copied slide to be positioned after, and choose Paste

TIP *Alternatively, you can use the Copy and Paste buttons on the Home ribbon or the copy and paste keyboard shortcuts to duplicate a slide. The keyboard shortcut for the Copy command is CTRL-C. The keyboard shortcut for the Paste command is CTRL-V.*

Reordering Slides in Normal View

In Normal view, slides can be repositioned by using the Cut and Paste commands or by dragging. In Chapter 11, you will learn how to reorder slides in Slide Sorter view.

- In the Slides tab, click and drag a slide into a new position (the solid line indicates where the slide will be positioned when you release the mouse).
- In the Slides tab, right-click the slide you want to move, and choose Cut. Then right-click the slide you want the cut slide to be positioned after, and choose Paste

TIP   *Alternatively, you can use the Cut and Paste buttons on the Home ribbon or the Cut and Paste keyboard shortcuts to move a slide. The keyboard shortcut for the Cut command is CTRL-X. The keyboard shortcut for the Paste command is CTRL-V.*

Changing Slide Orientation

Slide orientation refers to whether the page is taller than it is wide (portrait) or wider than it is tall (landscape). PowerPoint's default page orientation is set to landscape.

1. On the Design ribbon, click Orientation.
2. Choose Portrait or Landscape.

Working with Text

To add text to a PowerPoint slide, simply click in a placeholder and start typing. For example, in the title slide pictured in Figure 9-1, you would click where it says "Click to add title" and then type your presentation's title. Then you could click where it says "Click to add subtitle" and type your presentation's subtitle (or the name of the presenter or company—whatever suits the presentation you are creating).

In a PowerPoint placeholder, text will automatically wrap to the next line when you've run out of space in the current line, just like it does in Word. As you type, you can use the BACKSPACE key to delete in a backward direction and the DELETE key to delete in a forward direction. If the text becomes too lengthy for the placeholder, the text will simply spill over the placeholder's edges.

You can always fix this issue later by changing the size of the text or moving and/or resizing the placeholder text box.

Selecting Text

To format, cut, or copy text, you must select (or highlight) it first. In the following illustration the title text is selected and the subtitle text is not selected. Note that the placeholder borders show when text in the placeholder is selected.

TABLE 9-1 Popular Text Selection Methods

To select...	Do this:
Any amount of text	Click and drag with your mouse pointer.
A single word	Double-click in the middle of the word.
All of the text in the placeholder	Click in the placeholder and then use the CTRL-A keyboard shortcut. OR Triple-click in the placeholder.
To select a placeholder	Click anywhere in the placeholder and then press the ESC key.
To select multiple placeholders	Select the first placeholder and then hold down the CTRL key and click the next placeholder.

There are numerous ways to select text in a presentation. Table 9-1 lists some of the most popular methods.

TIP   *To format all of the text in a placeholder, you can select just the placeholder instead of clicking and dragging to highlight the text within the placeholder. To format all of the text in multiple placeholders, you can select the placeholders one at a time using the CTRL key as described in Table 9-1.*

Deleting Text in a Placeholder

In addition to using the BACKSPACE and DELETE keys to delete individual characters while you are typing, you can select larger chunks for deletion. To delete text within a placeholder, you have two choices:

- To delete a portion of the text in a placeholder, click in the placeholder, select the text you wish to delete, and press the BACKSPACE or DELETE key.

- To delete all of the text in a placeholder, click in the placeholder, press the ESC key, and then press the BACKSPACE or DELETE key.

Deleting a Placeholder

1. Click in the placeholder you want to delete, and press ESC.
2. Press the BACKSPACE or DELETE key to delete the text in the placeholder. The default text for the placeholder will take its place, if applicable (e.g., *Click to add title*).

3. Once again, click in the placeholder you want to delete, and press ESC.

4. Press the BACKSPACE or DELETE key to delete the placeholder.

Formatting Text

The Font group on the Home ribbon offers many ways to format text in PowerPoint, including font, size, style, and color modifications.

Changing Font, Size, Style, and Color

As you may recall from Chapter 3, a font can be loosely defined as a complete character set (a–z, plus numbers and symbols) of a particular typeface, such as Arial or Times Roman. The creative use of fonts, along with size, style, and color choices, can add personality to a document and enhance readability when used properly. Font, Size, Style, and Color menus can all be found on the Font group of the Home ribbon (pictured in Figure 9-3).

1. Select the text you wish to format.

2. From the Home ribbon, choose a font from the Font drop-down list.

3. From the Home ribbon, choose a size from the Size drop-down list, type a size in the Size field, or use the Increase Size and Decrease Size buttons to change the font size.

4. From the Home ribbon, choose bold, italic, underline, shadow, or strikethrough effects by clicking the appropriate buttons.

5. From the Home ribbon, choose a color from the Color button menu.

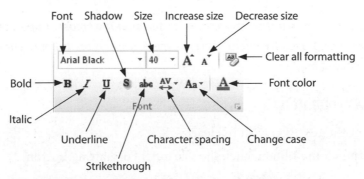

FIGURE 9-3 • The PowerPoint 2010 Font group on the Home ribbon provides all the tools you need to format text, including font, size, style, and color.

TIP *If you enjoy using keyboard shortcuts, you can resize text using the keyboard instead of the mouse. To increase the size of selected text, use the CTRL-SHIFT-> keyboard shortcut. To decrease the size of selected text, use the CTRL-SHIFT-< keyboard shortcut. (Watch the Size field on the Home ribbon as you do this to see the size increase or decrease.) Keyboard shortcuts can also be used to modify the style of selected text. To make text bold, press CTRL-B; to make it italic, press CTRL-I; and to add an underline, press CTRL-U.*

Changing Text Case

If you accidentally typed an entire line in all caps or an entire paragraph of text in all lowercase, you can use the Change Case command to fix the error instead of having to retype the text.

1. Select the text that needs the case changed.
2. On the Home ribbon, click the Change Case button, and choose the appropriate case for the text.
   - Sentence case capitalizes the first letter in every sentence.
   - Lowercase changes all of the selected text to lowercase letters.
   - Uppercase changes all of the selected text to capital letters.
   - Capitalize Each Word capitalizes every word in the selection.
   - Toggle Case changes uppercase letters to lowercase letters and vice versa.

TIP *The keyboard shortcut SHIFT-F3 cycles through lowercase, uppercase, and sentence case. Select the text, and press SHIFT-F3 one or more times to change the case to your liking.*

Clearing All Formatting

1. Select the text you wish to clear.
2. On the Home ribbon, click the Clear All Formatting button.

Paragraph Formatting

Most paragraph formatting commands can be found on the Paragraph group on the Home ribbon (pictured in Figure 9-4). Paragraph formatting options apply

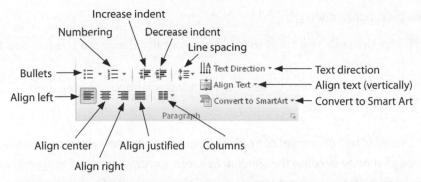

FIGURE 9-4 · The PowerPoint 2010 Paragraph group on the Home ribbon provides all the tools you need to format paragraphs, including bullets and numbering, indenting, line spacing, and alignment.

to entire paragraphs (as opposed to one or more words within a paragraph). You can select one or more paragraphs and then apply the formatting, or simply have the cursor anywhere in a single paragraph before applying the formatting. You can also choose your formatting options before you begin typing.

Changing Alignment

Values in placeholders or text boxes can be aligned horizontally (between the left and right edges) as well as vertically (between the top and bottom edges). The Paragraph group on the Home ribbon offers one-click access to the alignment options used most often (pictured in Figure 9-4).

Horizontal alignment options include the following:

- Left (aligned to the left margin of the placeholder/text box, producing a ragged right edge)
- Centered (centered between the left and right margins of the placeholder/text box)
- Right (aligned to the right margin of the placeholder/text box, producing a ragged left edge)
- Justified (aligned to both the left and right sides with no ragged edge)

Vertical alignment options include the following:

- Top (floats to the top of the placeholder or text box)
- Middle (centered between the top and bottom edges of the placeholder or text box)
- Bottom (floats to the bottom of the placeholder or text box)

Aligning Text Horizontally

1. Select the cells you want to align horizontally (between the left and right edges of the cell).
2. From the Alignment group on the Home ribbon, choose Left, Center, Right, or Justified.

TIP *Justified text alignment can cause unattractive rivers of white space running through a page because the spacing between words is adjusted to spread out between the margins. For this reason, it is infrequently used.*

Aligning Text Vertically

1. Select the cells you want to align vertically (between the top and bottom edges of the cell).
2. From the Alignment group on the Home ribbon, choose Top Align, Middle Align, or Bottom Align.

Aligned with top of text box   Aligned with middle of text box   Aligned with bottom of text box

Indenting Text

Indenting a line of text by pressing the SPACEBAR over and over is not considered a good practice. (The size of the space will change with the size of the font, which can make for non-uniform spacing.) Instead, use the Increase Indent and Decrease Indent buttons on the Home ribbon. This will help ensure that all of your indents are uniform.

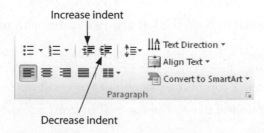

Increase indent

Decrease indent

1. Select the line(s) you want to indent.

2. Do one of the following:

   • Click the Increase Indent button to push the text away from the left margin.

   • Click the Decrease Indent button to push the text closer to the left margin.

Setting a First-Line Indent   To indent only the first line of one or more paragraphs, you can simply press the TAB key in front of each paragraph as you are typing, or you can use the First Line Indent setting in the Paragraph dialog box (described here).

1. Select the paragraph(s) in which you want the first line indented.

2. Click the Paragraph Dialog Box Launcher (located in the lower-right corner of the Paragraph group).

3. In the Paragraph dialog box (pictured in Figure 9-5), under the Indentation heading, choose First Line from the Special drop-down list.

4. Modify the indent width in the By field. You can type a number directly in the field or use the up and down arrows to change the number.

5. Click OK.

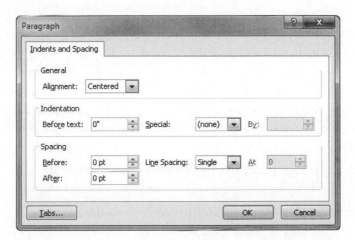

FIGURE 9-5 • The Indents and Spacing tab in the Paragraph Dialog Box gives you control over margin indents and line spacing.

Setting Line and Paragraph Spacing

Line spacing is the spacing between each line in a paragraph. Paragraph spacing is the extra spacing before and/or after paragraphs. The following illustration shows an example of line spacing and paragraph spacing. The paragraphs on the left side of the slide use single line spacing (1.0) with no extra spacing between paragraphs (or bullet points in this case). The paragraphs on the right side of the slide use 1.5 line spacing and have an extra 12 points of space between paragraphs. Extra line spacing and paragraph spacing can make dense text easier to read. Compare the two mission statements in the following illustration.

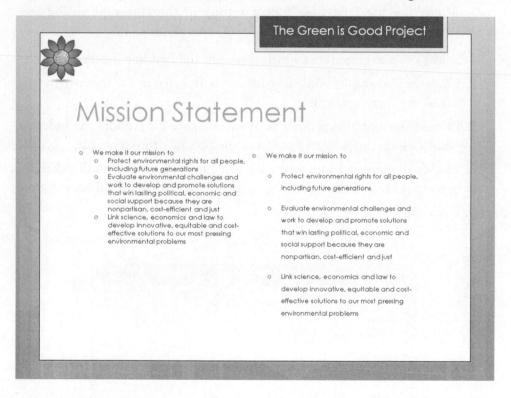

1. Select the paragraph(s) or bullet points you want to format.

2. Click the Line Spacing button in the Paragraph group, located on the Home ribbon. A drop-down menu of options appears (pictured here).

3. To modify line spacing, choose from the line spacing settings at the top of the menu or select Line Spacing Options to open the Paragraph dialog box (see Figure 9-5).

4. To modify paragraph spacing, open the Paragraph dialog box by clicking the Paragraph Dialog Box Launcher at the lower-right corner of the Paragraph Group or by choosing Line Spacing Options from the Line Spacing button menu), and adjust the spacing in the Spacing Before and Spacing After fields.

5. Click OK.

Working with Bullets and Numbering

By default, most content placeholders in PowerPoint incorporate bullet points. As in Microsoft Word, text using bullet points is formatted with a hanging indent so that the text wraps neatly within the confines of the indented bullet point. Using the Bullets button on the Home ribbon, you can choose to toggle the bullet points off or change the bullet point style. You can use the Numbering button on the Home ribbon to switch the bullet points to numbers as needed for your presentation. Of course, both buttons can be used to add bullets or numbers to plain text as well.

The Bullets and Numbering buttons on the Home ribbon are both split buttons. Clicking the left side of the button assigns the default bullet point or numbering style to the selected text. Clicking the right side of the button produces a drop-down list of alternative bullet points or numbering schemes (pictured in Figure 9-6).

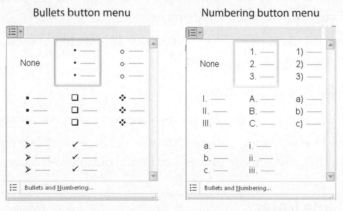

FIGURE 9-6 · PowerPoint 2010 Bullets and Numbering Button Menus lets you add bullets or numbers with a single click.

Adding Bullet Points to Plain Text

1. Select the lines(s) where you want to add bullets.
2. Do one of the following:
   - Click the left side of the Bullets button to format the paragraph using the currently selected bullet type.
   - Click the right side of the Bullets button to choose a bullet from the Bullet library.

Changing Bullet Points to Numbers

1. Select the bulleted line(s) where you want to switch from bullet points to numbers.
2. Do one of the following:
   - Click the left side of the Numbering button to format the paragraph using the currently selected numbering style.
   - Click the right side of the Numbering button to choose a numbering scheme from the Numbering library.

Numbering Plain Text

1. Select the lines(s) where you want to add numbers.
2. Do one of the following:
   - Click left side of the Numbering button to format the paragraph using the currently selected numbering style.
   - Click the right side of the Numbering button to choose a numbering scheme from the Numbering library.

Removing Bullet Points or Numbering

1. Select the lines(s) where you want to remove bullets or numbering.
2. On the Home ribbon, click the left side of the Bullets button to remove bullets; click the left side of the Numbering button to remove numbering.

Working with Slide Notes

In Normal view, the Notes pane that runs along the bottom of the slide provides a space for you to add slide notes. Slide notes can contain formatted text only (no graphics). These notes, which do not display during a slide show, are typically used by the person giving the presentation to augment the talking points for each slide.

As you will learn in Chapter 11, notes can be printed. You will also explore the use of Notes view in Chapter 11.

Adding Notes

1. Select a slide.
2. Click in the Notes pane.
3. Type your notes.
4. If desired, format your notes using the formatting buttons on the Home ribbon.

Deleting Notes

1. Select a slide.
2. In the Notes pane, select the text you wish to delete.
3. Press the BACKSPACE or DELETE key on the keyboard.

Proofing a Presentation

As you work in a presentation, spelling is checked automatically. When a spelling error is found, the word in question has a squiggly red underline (as shown in the first two bullet points on the slide in the following illustration).

Correcting Spelling Errors

1. Right-click the misspelled word.

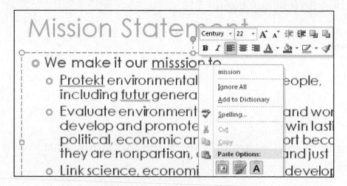

2. Choose the correct spelling from the drop-down menu.

Still Struggling

PowerPoint's spelling checker flags words in your document that are not in its dictionary. Sometimes words are highlighted that are not necessarily misspelled, for example, obscure technical terms or proper names with unusual spellings. You can add these words to PowerPoint's dictionary so that they will no longer be flagged. Simply right-click a word and choose Add To Dictionary from the drop-down menu.

Changing Proofing Settings

Options for proofing can be set on the Proofing tab of the File ribbon (pictured in Figure 9-7).

1. Click the File ribbon.

2. Choose Options.

3. Click Proofing.

4. Check or uncheck settings as desired under the When Correcting Spelling In PowerPoint heading. For example, if you do not want spelling to be checked as you type, clear the Check Spelling As You Type check box.

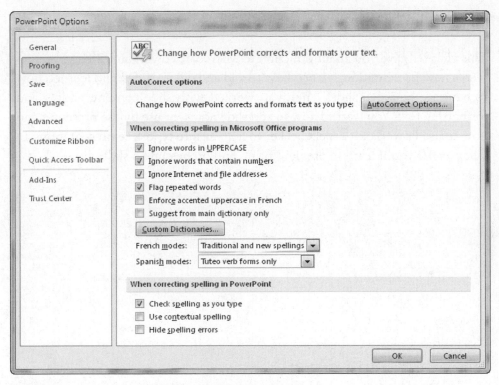

FIGURE 9-7 • PowerPoint 2010 Options Dialog Box (Proofing)

Still Struggling

Remember to refer back to Chapter 2 for common program functionality, such as Backstage View (document properties and permissions, opening existing files, and saving files), using undo and redo, working with the Office Clipboard (cut, copy, and paste), working with themes, and getting help.

Summary

This chapter gave you an introduction to Microsoft PowerPoint 2010. You created a new presentation, learned how to add and delete slides, and learned how to navigate between slides. Then you worked with slide content, adding and formatting text. You learned how to add slide notes for use by the presenter and how to use PowerPoint's spellchecker to help ensure typo-free presentations. In Chapter 10 you'll learn to preview, print, and orchestrate a slide show.

QUIZ

1. **True or False: PowerPoint's default page orientation is set to portrait.**
   A. True
   B. False

2. **What pane appears in Normal view?**
   A. Slide
   B. Outline tab
   C. Slide tab
   D. Notes
   E. All of the above

3. **In Normal view, the _____ that runs along the bottom of the slide provides a space for you to add _____ . (Fill in the blanks using the following choices.)**
   A. Outline pane
   B. slide graphics
   C. Notes pane
   D. Slides pane
   E. slide notes

4. **Which view does a presentation open in by default?**
   A. Notes
   B. Normal
   C. Slide Sorter
   D. Reading
   E. None of the above

5. **True or False: You can tailor an existing template to suit your own presentation needs (for example, add your own logo and change the colors to match your company's branding guidelines) and then save that presentation as a new template.**
   A. True
   B. False

6. **Which of the following is not one of PowerPoint's default slide layouts?**
   A. Title Slide
   B. Title And Content
   C. Notes Page
   D. Two Content
   E. Comparison

7. True or False: In a PowerPoint placeholder, text will automatically wrap to the next line when you've run out of space in the current line, just like it does in Word.
   A. True
   B. False

8. _____ is the spacing between each line in a paragraph. _____ is the extra spacing before and/or after paragraphs. (Fill in the blanks using the following choices.)
   A. Bullet spacing
   B. Paragraph spacing
   C. Number spacing
   D. Line spacing
   E. Graphic spacing

9. Which ribbon offers options for modifying PowerPoint's proofing settings?
   A. File
   B. Home
   C. View
   D. Design
   E. Transitions

10. True or False: Notes from the Notes pane cannot be printed.
    A. True
    B. False

chapter 10

Viewing and Printing Presentations and Working with Slide Masters

This chapter provides an overview of Microsoft PowerPoint 2010's viewing and printing options and slide masters. You will explore PowerPoint's view options and learn to print slides, notes pages, audience handouts, and outlines for a presentation. You will also become familiar with the timesaving benefits of using PowerPoint slide masters.

CHAPTER OBJECTIVES

In this chapter, you will learn how to

- Use the various views available on the View ribbon
- Print slides, notes pages, handouts, and outlines
- Work in slide master views

Viewing and Printing a Presentation

The View ribbon (pictured here) is where presentation viewing–related commands are found. PowerPoint's views can be used for editing, printing, or delivering a presentation.

- The Presentation Views group gives you one-click access to each of PowerPoint's view types: Normal (default), Slide Sorter, Notes Page, and Reading View.
- The Master Views group lets you work with slide, handout, and notes masters.
- The Show group lets you show or hide the ruler, gridlines, and guides.
- The Zoom group allows you to modify the screen size of a document.
- The Color/Grayscale group gives you easy access to ink-saving printing options.

Presentation views can also be accessed from the buttons on the lower-right corner of the window, as pictured below.

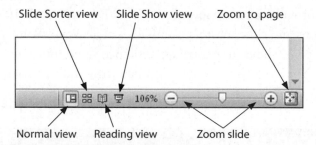

The Print pane on the File ribbon (pictured in Figure 10-1) is where you will go to preview how a document will print and to print a document. Several page layout options are also available on this pane.

Exploring PowerPoint View Options

As mentioned, PowerPoint offers four main presentation views: Normal, Slide Sorter, Notes Page, and Reading. (Master view will be discussed elsewhere in this chapter; Slide Show view is discussed in Chapter 12.) To change to a presentation view, click the View ribbon, and then click the desired layout in the Presentation Views group. Each presentation view is described in detail in the following sections.

Normal View

As you may remember from Chapter 9, PowerPoint's default view is Normal view (pictured in Figure 10-1). Normal view offers four resizable panes: the Slide pane, Notes pane, Slides tab, and Outline tab.

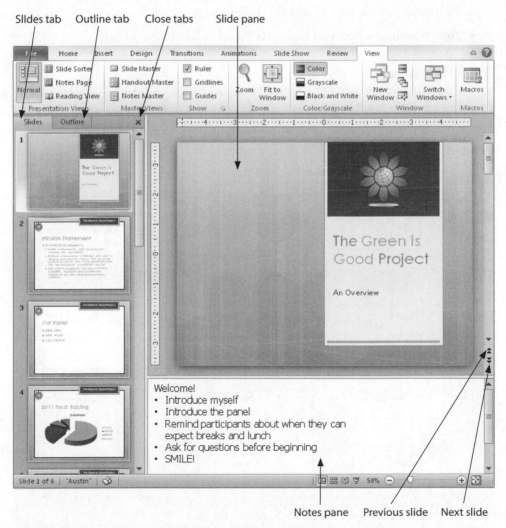

FIGURE 10-1 · Normal view is in the default view for PowerPoint.

TIP   *For more information on Normal view, such as navigating slides and resizing panes, refer to Chapter 9.*

Slide Sorter View

Slide Sorter view (shown in Figure 10-2) displays your presentation slides as thumbnails (small pictures), making it easy for you to change the slide order. In Slide Show view, you can do the following:

- Quickly rearrange slides (just click a slide and drag it to a new position)
- Delete slides (right-click a slide and choose Delete)
- Rehearse a presentation and set slide timing
- Add transitions between slides (covered in Chapter 11)

Notes Page View

Notes Page view (shown in Figure 10-3) lets you create and print speaker notes for a presentation. In Chapter 9, you learned to work with notes in Normal view as well. Notes are hidden from view during a slide show, but can be printed.

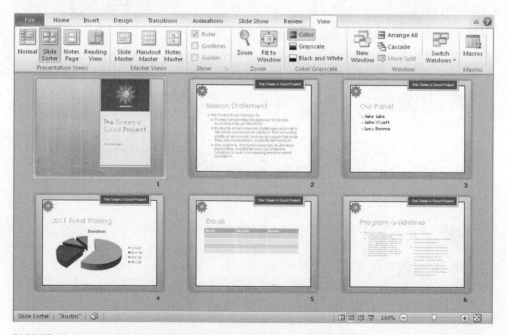

FIGURE 10-2 · Slide Sorter view displays a thumbnail version of each slide.

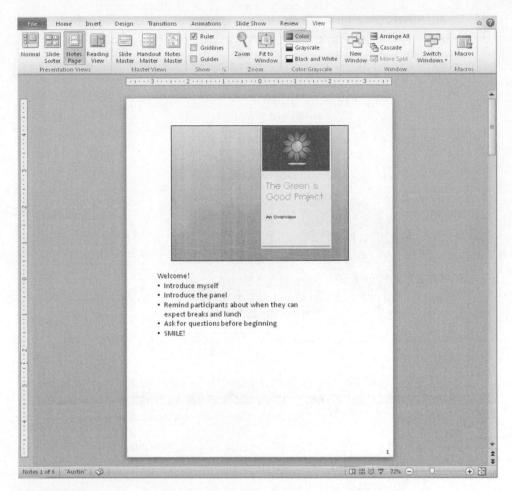

FIGURE 10-3 · Notes view provides space for adding speaker notes to a presentation.

TIP   *Notes can consist of text only; the Notes area cannot contain graphics, tables, or charts.*

Reading View

Reading view (pictured in Figure 10-4) displays the presentation for maximum ease of reading. The ribbons, status bar, and taskbar are all hidden. In Reading view, navigation arrows are available in the lower right corner of the status bar.

TIP   *Press the ESC key to return to the previous view.*

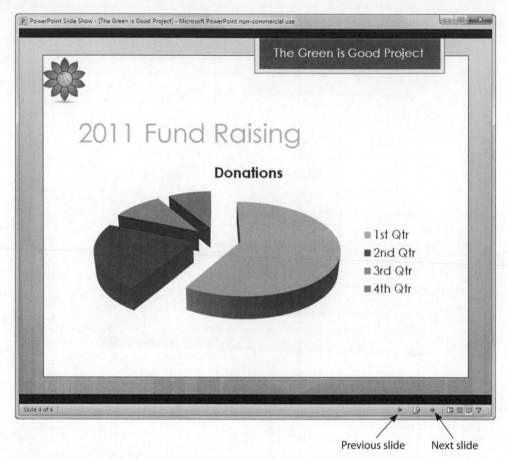

Previous slide   Next slide

FIGURE 10-4 · Reading view offers an uncluttered preview of a presentation.

Zoom

The Zoom group on the View ribbon (pictured here) lets you control how a document displays on screen.

- Click the Zoom button to open the Zoom dialog box, where you can customize your zoom percentage or choose from additional preset zoom percentages.
- Click the Fit To Window button to fit one entire slide in the window.

Still Struggling

PowerPoint opens in Normal view by default. Normal view displays the Slides pane, Notes pane, Slides tab, and Outline tab. You can have PowerPoint open in a different view by default if desired, such as Outline Only, Notes Page, Slide Sorter, or variations on Normal view.

On the File ribbon, click Options and then click Advanced. Under the Display heading, choose a view from the Open All Documents Using This View list (pictured here), and then click OK.

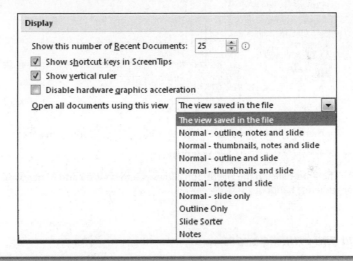

Printing a Presentation

PowerPoint allows you to print slides (one on a page), notes pages (with the slide on the top half of the page and the notes on the bottom of the page), and handouts (multiple slides per page).

The Print pane on the File ribbon (pictured in Figure 10-5) provides a preview of the printed document, a few printing options, and the Print button. Here, you can also choose a specific printer, specify which slides in a presentation are to be printed, and, if your printer has duplex printing and/or collating features, set those options as well.

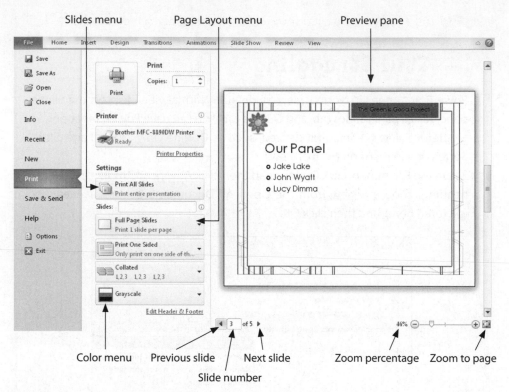

FIGURE 10-5 · The Print pane on the File ribbon allows you to preview and print your presentation, notes pages, or audience handouts.

Previewing and Printing Slides

1. Select the slides you wish to print. If you are printing the entire presentation, you can skip this step.

2. Click the File ribbon.

3. Click Print.

4. Under the Settings heading, click the Page Layout menu (pictured in Figure 10-6).

5. Choose Full Page Slides from the Page Layout menu.

6. Under the Settings heading, click the Slides menu and choose one of the following:

   • **Print All Slides** (to print every slide in the presentation)

   • **Print Selection** (to print only the slides you selected in step 1)

- **Print Current Slide** (to print only the currently selected slide)
- **Custom Range** (to print a specific range of slides)

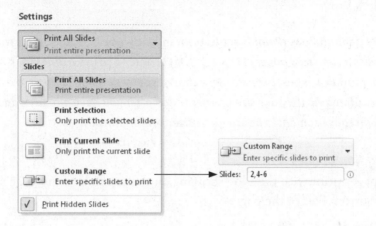

7. If you are printing a custom range, add the slide numbers in the Slides field (as pictured here). Use a hyphen to indicate a range of slides (e.g., 4-6); use commas to separate individual slide numbers (e.g., 3, 4, 7, 9).

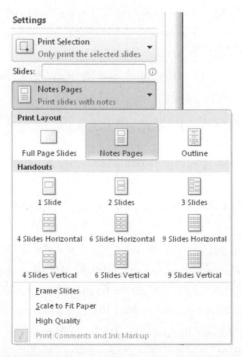

FIGURE 10-6 • Page Layout Printing Options are offered on the Print tab of the File ribbon.

8. Preview what will print using the navigation arrows at the bottom of the Preview pane.

9. Click Print.

TIP *By default, PowerPoint is set to print in landscape orientation on standard business letter-sized paper (11″ × 8.5″). If you intend to use a different size page or orientation, it is best to make these changes before adding content to a presentation. Changing the page size or orientation after you have already added content can cause content to be scaled (resized) automatically.*

Printing Notes Pages

Notes pages print with the slide showing on the top half of the page and notes on the bottom half of the page.

1. Select the slides for which you wish to print the notes pages. If you are printing notes pages for the entire presentation, you can skip this step.

2. Click the File ribbon.

3. Click Print.

4. Under the Settings heading, click the Page Layout menu (pictured in Figure 10-6).

5. Choose Notes Pages from the Page Layout menu.

6. Under the Settings heading, click the Slides menu, and choose one of the following:

   • **Print All Slides** (to print notes pages for every slide in the presentation)

   • **Print Selection** (to print notes pages only for the slides you selected in step 1)

   • **Print Current Slide** (to print notes page for the currently selected slide only)

   • **Custom Range** (to print notes pages for a specific range of slides)

7. If you are printing a custom range, add the slide numbers in the Slides field (as pictured earlier). Use a hyphen to indicate a range of slides (e.g., 4-6); use commas to separate individual slide numbers (e.g., 3, 4, 7, 9).

8. Preview what you will print using the navigation arrows at the bottom of the Preview pane.

- To navigate between pages in the preview, use the Previous Page and Next Page buttons at the bottom-left corner of the Preview pane, or type a number in the Page Number field.

- To zoom the preview screen, use the Decrease Zoom and Increase Zoom buttons at the bottom-right corner of the Preview pane, or drag the zoom indicator on the line between the buttons. To return to single-page view, click the Zoom To Page button.

9. Click Print.

Printing Handouts

The handouts options lets you print multiple (two, four, six, or nine) slides per page. The illustration here, for example, shows a handout page containing six slides. Handouts do not include slide notes.

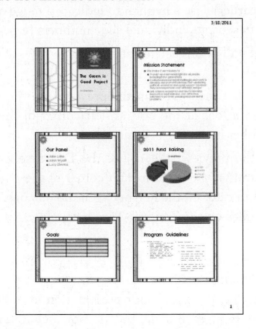

1. Select the slides for which you wish to print the handout pages. If you are printing handout pages for the entire presentation, you can skip this step.

2. Click the File ribbon.

3. Click Print.

4. Under the Settings heading, click the Page Layout menu (pictured in Figure 10-6).

5. Choose a layout from the Page Layout menu (two, four, six, or nine slides per page).

6. Under the Settings heading, click the Slides menu, and choose one of the following:

   • **Print All Slides** (to print handout pages for every slide in the presentation)

   • **Print Selection** (to print handout pages only for the slides you selected in step 1)

   • **Print Current Slide** (to print handout pages for the currently selected slide only)

   • **Custom Range** (to print handout pages for a specific range of slides)

7. If you are printing a custom range, add the slide numbers in the Slides field (as pictured earlier). Use a hyphen to indicate a range of slides (e.g., 4-6); use commas to separate individual slide numbers (e.g., 3, 4, 7, 9).

8. Preview what will print using the navigation arrows at the bottom of the Preview pane.

   • To navigate between pages in the preview, use the Previous Page and Next Page buttons at the bottom-left corner of the Preview pane or type a number in the Page Number field.

   • To zoom the preview screen, use the Decrease Zoom and Increase Zoom Buttons at the bottom-right corner of the preview pane or drag the zoom indicator on the line between the buttons. To return to single page view click on the Zoom to Page button

9. Click Print.

Printing a Presentation Outline

The outline option lets you print your presentation in outline form. Outline pages contain text from each slide, but do not include graphics, tables, or charts.

TIP *You cannot print an outline for selected slides only. Outline view displays all slides.*

1. Click the File ribbon.
2. Click Print.

3. Under the Settings heading, click the Page Layout menu (pictured in Figure 10-6).

4. Choose Outline.

5. Preview what will print using the navigation arrows at the bottom of the Preview pane.

   - To navigate between pages in the preview, use the Previous Page and Next Page Buttons at the bottom-left corner of the Preview pane or type a number in the Page Number field.

   - To zoom the preview screen, use the Decrease Zoom and Increase Zoom buttons at the bottom-right corner of the Preview pane, or drag the zoom indicator on the line between the buttons. To return to single-page view, click the Zoom To Page button.

6. Click Print.

Working with Master Views

Until now, you've probably used the default formatting parameters (background, color, fonts, effects, placeholder sizes, and positioning) that came standard in whatever template you were using (default or custom). When different formatting was needed, you've most likely manually formatted one slide at a time as you developed the presentation. For larger slide presentations, manually formatting slides one at a time can be time-consuming. Formatting slides manually can also lead to inconsistencies within the presentation. For example, perhaps you've copied and pasted a company logo in the same spot on every slide in a presentation. A few days later, right before the meeting, you add a few key slides and completely forget to copy the logo on the new slides. Inconsistencies like this are noticed and can make a presentation seem unprofessional.

PowerPoint's master view feature offers you the time-saving option of being able to make formatting changes to a set of masters that can then be applied throughout the presentation. There are master views for slides, handouts, and notes. Every presentation contains at least one slide master and multiple layouts. Using the logo example, you would place the company logo onto a master slide. Each time you create a new slide based on that master, the logo (and everything else pertaining to that master) will automatically appear.

TIP   *It is possible to create multiple slide masters within a presentation. This allows you to mix and match themes and styles within the same presentation (which typically is not a great idea, but sometimes needs to be done to accommodate certain design goals). If you are interesting in learning more about this, search on "multiple slide masters" in PowerPoint Help.*

Working in Slide Master View

1. Click the View ribbon.
2. In the Master Views group, click Slide Master. Slide Master view is pictured in Figure 10-7.

TIP   *To exit Slide Master view, click the red Close Master View button on the Slide Master ribbon, or click Normal on the View ribbon.*

Slide Masters and Layouts

In Slide Master view, the topmost slide in the left margin is the slide master. Each of the layouts indented below the master has a unique appearance and a unique name, yet all of these layouts have inherited their "good looks" (color scheme, fonts, effects, etc.) from the slide master at the top.

Figure 10-7 shows a modified version of the Austin template (one of the standard templates available in PowerPoint 2010) in Master view. Underneath the slide master are four supporting layouts that offer a slightly different twist on the slide master. In this case, each of the layouts uses the same color scheme and fonts but has a different assortment of text and graphics placeholders. The second layout under the slide master is the currently selected layout, so it also appears in the main Slide pane. One layout in a presentation usually will be intended for use as a title slide, another might be completely blank except for a heading at the top, another might provide for positioning content in two columns, and so on. The names of these layouts will correspond to the names of the layouts listed in both the Layout menu and the New Slide menu on the Home ribbon. You likely will not use all of the layouts offered, but they're there in case you need them.

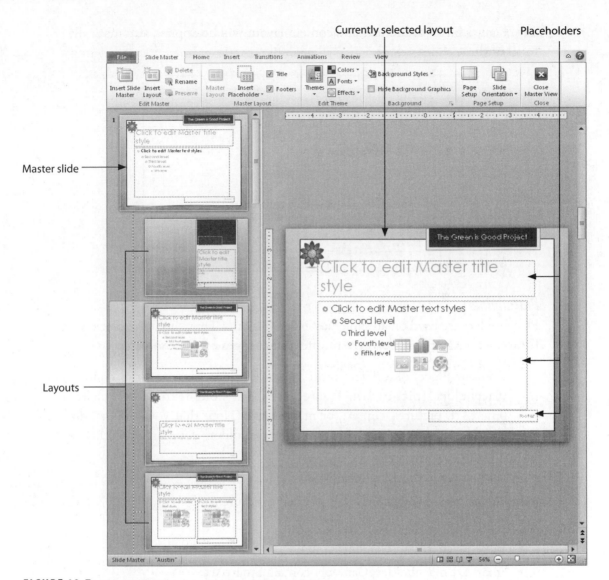

FIGURE 10-7 · Slide Master View lets you choose from multiple layouts.

If you point to a layout (without clicking), a tooltip will display its name. In addition, the tooltip will identify which slides (if any) are currently using that layout. In the following illustration, you can see that the Title And Content layout is being used by slides 2 through 7 in this presentation. That means that any changes made to the title and content layout will be applied automatically to all of those slides.

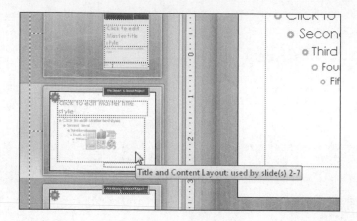

Placeholders

Placeholders are used on all slide masters and layouts. They "hold the place" for future text or graphics. PowerPoint offers eight types of placeholders:

- **Content placeholder**: The most versatile of placeholders, the content placeholder (pictured in Figure 10-8) can hold text, tables, charts, SmartArt, pictures, clip art, or media clips. (Note that you cannot "mix and match" these items in a single placeholder; you can only choose one.)
- **Text placeholder**: Can only contain text.
- **Picture placeholder**: Can only contain a picture.
- **Chart placeholder**: Can only contain a chart.
- **Table placeholder**: Can only contain a table.
- **SmartArt placeholder**: Can only contain SmartArt.
- **Media Clip placeholder**: Can only contain media.
- **Clip Art placeholder**: Can only contain clip art.

When you are in Slide Master view, placeholders look slightly different than when you are in Normal view. The top half of Figure 10-8, for example, shows the Content placeholder in Slide Master view; the bottom half shows that same placeholder in Normal view. Note that in Slide Master view, all five indent levels are displayed so you can modify their formatting if needed.

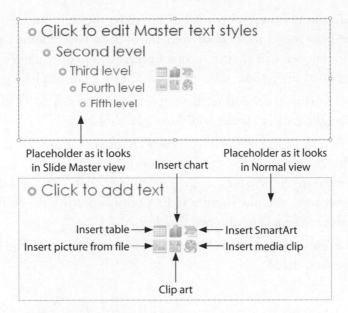

FIGURE 10-8 · PowerPoint 2010 provides a variety of placeholders for slide objects. Placeholders look different in Slide Master view than they do in Normal view.

Modifying an Existing Slide Master or Slide Master Layout

To modify an existing slide master or a slide master layout, you must first be in Slide Master view.

1. Click the View ribbon.

2. In the Master Views group, click Slide Master.

3. Do one of the following:

   • To make a formatting change that will affect all of the layouts (changing the title font and/or color, choosing a different theme, etc.), click the slide master.

   • To make a formatting change that only affects a specific layout (for example, the title slide), click that layout.

4. Using options on the Slide Master ribbon, format the slide master or layout as you wish, keeping in mind the following:

   • Use options in the Edit Theme group to choose a different theme or variation on a theme (colors, fonts, effects).

   • Use options in the Background group to either hide or modify the background (hiding the background is not an option for the slide master):

- To modify the background of the slide, click the Background Styles button menu and choose from one of the related theme backgrounds in the menu, or choose Format Background to open the Format Background dialog box, where you can create a custom background.
- Use options in the Master Layout group to show/hide Title or Footers placeholders or to insert additional placeholders:
    - To add a placeholder to a layout, choose one from the Insert Placeholder button menu (pictured here) on the Slide Master ribbon (located in the Master Layout group), and then click and drag where you want the placeholder to be positioned on the slide (in essence, you are "drawing" the placeholder).
5. On the View ribbon, click Normal to view the effects of the formatting changes you made.

Still Struggling

Wondering why a slide's formatting is not updating after you've modified the master on which it is based? Manual formatting changes override master formatting. Therefore, if you have manually formatted a slide prior to modifying the master the slide is based on, the manually formatted slide may not reflect subsequent formatting changes made to the master. This is easily remedied by resetting the layout for the affected slide.

1. Click the slide you wish to reset.
2. On the Home ribbon, choose the appropriate layout from the Layout menu.
3. Also on the Home ribbon, click the Reset button.

Creating a Custom Layout in Master View

The Slide Master ribbon (pictured here) provides the tools needed to create a new layout in Master view. (This ribbon is available only in Slide Master view.)

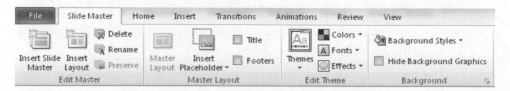

1. Click the View ribbon.

2. In the Master Views group, click Slide Master.

3. On the Slide Master ribbon, in the Edit Master group, click Insert Layout. A new layout titled "Custom Layout Layout" will be added to the bottom of the list of layouts.

4. Right-click the new custom layout, and choose Rename.

5. Give the new layout a unique name, and click OK.

6. Format the layout as you wish, keeping in mind the following:

   - Use options in the Edit Theme group to choose a different theme or variation on a theme (colors, fonts, effects).

   - Use options in the Background group to either hide or modify the background:

     - To modify the background of the slide, click the Background Styles button menu, and choose from one of the related theme backgrounds in the menu, or choose Format Background to open the Format Background dialog box, where you can create a custom background.

     - To delete an existing placeholder on the layout, click it and press the DELETE or BACKSPACE key.

   - Use options in the Master Layout group to show/hide Title or Footers placeholders or to insert additional placeholders:

     - To add a placeholder to a layout, choose one from the Insert Placeholder button menu (pictured here) on the Slide Master ribbon (located on the Master Layout group), and then click and drag where you want the placeholder to be positioned on the slide (in essence, you are "drawing" the placeholder).

7. Make any other desired formatting changes.

8. Click the Close Master View button to return to Normal view, and then test your new layout by creating a new slide based on it or by applying it to an existing slide.

Deleting a Slide Master Layout

1. Click the View ribbon.

2. In the Master Views group, click Slide Master.

3. Right-click the layout you wish to delete, and choose Delete.

TIP   *The Title Slide layout and the Title And Content layout cannot be deleted.*

Working in Handout Master View

As you may recall from earlier in this chapter, PowerPoint's handout feature lets you print multiple slides per page for use as audience "take-aways." In the Handout Master view you can

- Modify, move, resize, or format headers and footers
- Add a background
- Set handout page orientation separate from slide orientation (landscape or portrait)
- Set the number of slides that you want to appear on each page (two, four, six, or nine)

Changes made to a handout master do not apply to the slide master or notes master. However, changes will appear in a printed outline.

TIP   *The slide placeholders on a handout master cannot be resized.*

1. Click the View ribbon.

2. In the Master Views group, click Handout Master. Handout Master view is pictured in Figure 10-9.

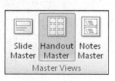

TIP   *To exit Handout Master view, click the red Close Master View button on the Handout Master ribbon, or click Normal on the View ribbon.*

Modifying the Handout Master

1. Click the View ribbon.

2. In the Master Views group, click Handout Master.

3. Type text in the header and footer placeholders. This text will appear on every page of the handout.

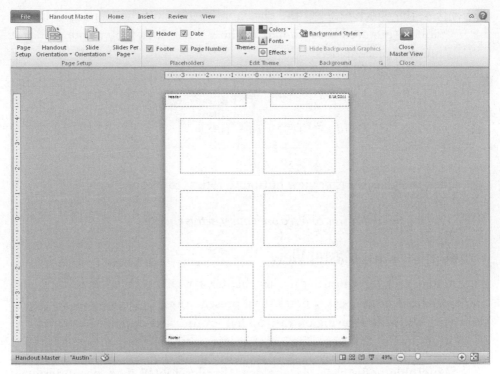

FIGURE 10-9 • Handout Master View lets you modify elements of your audience handouts.

4. Modify the date and page number placeholders if needed.

5. Format the handout master as you wish, keeping in mind the following:

   • Use options in the Edit Theme group to choose a different theme or variation on a theme (colors, fonts, effects).

   • Use options in the Background group to either hide or modify the background:

     • To modify the background of the slide, click the Background Styles button menu, and choose from one of the related theme backgrounds in the menu, or choose Format Background to open the Format Background dialog box, where you can create a custom background.

   • Use commands in the Page Setup group of the Handout Master ribbon (pictured here) to modify the handout orientation, slide orientation, and number of slides per page.

- Use the check boxes in the Placeholders group of the Handout Master ribbon (pictured here) to hide or show the header, footer, date, or page number placeholders.

6. Click the Close Master view button to return to Normal view.

TIP *Printing handouts was covered previously in this chapter.*

Working in Notes Master View

As you may recall from earlier in this chapter, PowerPoint's notes feature lets you create and print speaker notes for a presentation. By default, notes pages print with the slide showing on the top half of the page and speaker notes on the bottom half of the page. The Notes Master view lets you

- Show/hide notes page placeholders (header, footer, date, page number, slide image, and/or body)
- Modify, move, resize, or format headers and footers
- Add a background
- Set notes page orientation separate from slide orientation (landscape or portrait)

Changes made to the notes master do not apply to the slide master or handout master.

1. Click the View ribbon.
2. In the Master Views group, click Notes Master (pictured here). Notes Master view is pictured in Figure 10-9.

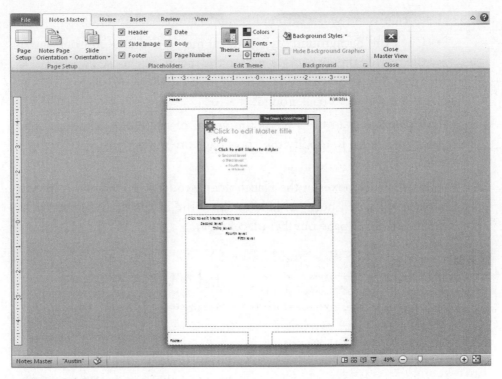

FIGURE 10-10 • Notes Master View lets you format your speaker notes.

TIP *To exit Notes Master view, click the red Close Master View button on the Notes Master ribbon, or click Normal on the View ribbon.*

Modifying the Notes Master

1. Click the View ribbon.
2. In the Master Views group, click Notes Master.
3. Type text in the header and footer placeholders. This text will appear on every notes page.
4. Modify the date and page number placeholders if needed.
5. Format the notes master as you wish, keeping in mind the following:
   - Use options in the Edit Theme group to choose a different theme or variation on a theme (colors, fonts, effects).

- Use options in the Background group to add a background:
  - Click the Background Styles button menu, and choose from one of the related theme backgrounds in the menu, or choose Format Background to open the Format Background dialog box, where you can create a custom background.
- Use commands in the Page Setup group of the Notes Master ribbon (pictured here) to modify the notes page orientation and slide orientation.
- Use the check boxes in the Placeholders group of the Handout Master ribbon (pictured here) to hide or show the header, footer, date, slide image, body, or page number placeholders.

6. Click the Close Master View button to return to Normal view.

TIP   *Printing notes pages was covered previously in this chapter.*

Summary

This chapter provided an overview of Microsoft PowerPoint 2010's viewing and printing options. You explored PowerPoint's view options and learned to print slides, notes pages, handouts, and outlines. You also became familiar with the time-saving benefits of slide masters. In Chapter 11 you'll start adding a bit of pizazz to your PowerPoint presentations, including tables, graphics, and multimedia.

QUIZ

1. **True or False: PowerPoint's notes feature lets you create and print handouts for a presentation.**
    A. True
    B. False

2. **Which of the following is a document view in PowerPoint?**
    A. Notes Pages
    B. Reading
    C. Slide Sorter
    D. Normal
    E. All of the above

3. **Which of the following is an option on the Print pane located on the File ribbon?**
    A. Orientation
    B. Printer
    C. Margin
    D. Breaks
    E. Watermark

4. **PowerPoint's _____ feature offers you the time-saving option of being able to make formatting changes to a set of masters that can then be applied throughout the presentation. (Fill in the blank using the following choices.)**
    A. Slide Show view
    B. Custom slide show
    C. Master view
    D. Placeholders view
    E. Zoom

5. **Which of the following cannot be printed in PowerPoint 2010?**
    A. Slides
    B. Handouts
    C. Animations
    D. Graphics
    E. Notes

6. **True or False: In Reading view, which displays the presentation for maximum ease of reading, the ribbons, status bar, and taskbar are all hidden.**
    A. True
    B. False

7. **What type of content can the multipurpose content placeholder hold?**
   A. Text
   B. SmartArt
   C. Media
   D. Tables
   E. All of the above

8. **The _____ provides the tools needed to create a new layout in Master view. (Fill in the blank using the following choices.)**
   A. Handout Master ribbon
   B. Home ribbon
   C. View ribbon
   D. Slide Master ribbon
   E. Notes Master ribbon

9. **Which of the following is not a type of placeholder?**
   A. Content
   B. Text
   C. Handout
   D. Picture
   E. Chart

10. **True or False: PowerPoint opens in Normal view by default, but you can change this setting if desired.**
    A. True
    B. False

chapter **11**

Adding Pizzazz to a Presentation

This chapter shows you how to make your presentations more engaging by incorporating graphics, tables, charts, and multimedia. You will also learn how to animate text and graphics in a presentation and to use transitions between slides to create visual interest.

CHAPTER OBJECTIVES

In this chapter, you will learn how to

- Add graphics and tables to a presentation
- Use slide transitions
- Animate text and graphics
- Incorporate multimedia into a presentation

Inserting and Working with Graphics

You can add a variety of graphic elements to a PowerPoint Presentation, including clip art (Office-supplied artwork provided for decorative purposes), pictures (photographs or other artwork you own), shapes (rectangles, circles, banners, and more that are drawn using tools provided in Office), SmartArt (visual representation of information), and tables.

Inserting and working with graphics works basically the same across all of the Office applications, so what you've learned previously in this book applies to PowerPoint as well. Clip art and pictures were covered in Chapter 4. Charts were covered in Chapter 7. Shapes, WordArt, and SmartArt are covered in this chapter.

Working with Shapes

PowerPoint offers dozens of shape tools that you can use to add graphic elements to your slides, including lines, basic geometric shapes, arrows, equation shapes, flowchart shapes, stars, banners, and callouts. After a shape has been placed on a slide, it can be modified with Quick Styles and other effects. Text can be added to some shapes as well. Figure 11-1 shows a piece of clip art (the cartoon character), a callout (the text balloon near the cartoon character), and five additional shapes used to create a simple graphic. Each of the shapes was drawn individually and then formatted and positioned after the text was added.

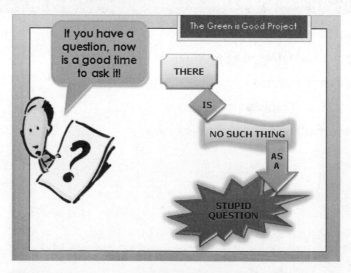

FIGURE 11-1 · PowerPoint shapes add visual interest to slides.

TIP *In Chapter 4, you learned numerous techniques for working with graphics, including sizing, rotating, and positioning. Since shapes are also graphics, these techniques will also work with the shapes you create in PowerPoint.*

Adding a Shape

Shapes can be added from the Drawing group on the Home ribbon or from the Illustrations group on the Insert ribbon (pictured in Figure 11-2). The Shapes Gallery menu organizes shapes into nine categories: Lines, Rectangles, Basic Shapes, Block Arrows, Equation Shapes, Flowchart, Stars and Banners, Callouts, Action Buttons, and Recently Used Shapes (which can include shapes from any of the other categories). When you are on the Home ribbon, the recently used

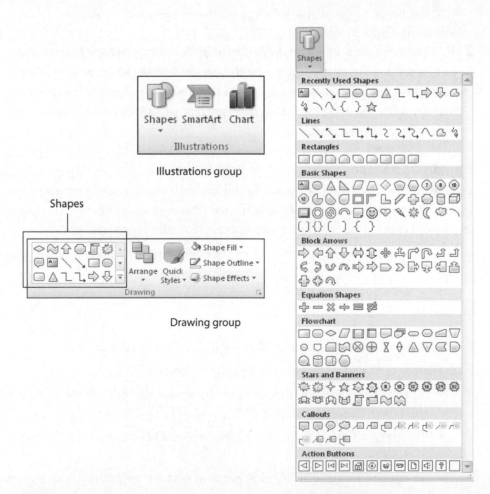

FIGURE 11-2 · The PowerPoint Shapes menu offers a wide variety of shapes.

shapes appear right on the ribbon so that you can choose one without having to display a menu.

1. Select the slide where the graphic will be placed.

2. Click a shape in the Shapes menu. The Shapes menu can be accessed from either the Drawing group on the Home ribbon or from the Illustrations group on the Insert ribbon.

3. On the slide, click and drag to draw the shape. When the mouse is released, the shape will be placed on the slide. By default, the shape will match the presentation's theme with regard to color and effects.

4. Adjust the size of the shape by selecting it and then clicking and dragging the shape's edges.

5. To add text to the shape, select it and begin typing.

TIP   *Hold down the SHIFT key on the keyboard while drawing a shape to constrain its proportions. For example, if you hold down the SHIFT key while using the Oval Shape tool, you will be able to easily draw a perfect circle; if you hold down the SHIFT key while you using the Rectangle Shape tool, you will be able to easily constraint it to be a perfect square.*

Formatting a Shape

Formatting options for shapes are found on both the Drawing group on the Home ribbon and the Drawing Tools Format ribbon (pictured here). The Drawing Tools Format ribbon offers more options than the Home ribbon.

1. Select a shape and click the Drawing Tools Format ribbon.

2. Format the shape, keeping in mind the following:

   • To change one shape into another shape, use the Edit Shape button in the Insert Shapes group.

   • To apply a Quick Style to a shape, make a selection from the Shape Styles gallery.

   • To fill the shape with a color, pattern, texture, or picture, use the options in the Shape Fill button menu.

- To change the shape's outline color, style, or width, use the options in the Shape Outline button menu.
- To apply shape effects (shadow, reflections, glow, and so on), use options in the Shape Effects button menu.

Layering Shapes and Other Graphics

When combining multiple shapes, it is sometimes necessary to control which shapes overlap other shapes or graphics. The following illustration showcases this concept. Layering shapes is accomplished by selecting a shape and then using the Order Objects commands on the Drawing Tools Format ribbon:

- **Bring To front** places a shape in the topmost layer.
- **Send To back** places a shape in the backmost layer.
- **Bring Forward** brings a shape forward one layer.
- **Send backward** places a shape one layer back.

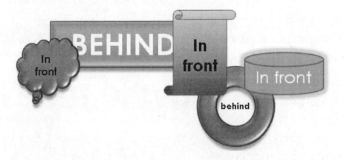

1. Select a shape and then click the Drawing Tools Format ribbon.
2. Click the Format ribbon.
3. Select a layering option under the Order Objects heading.

TIP *You can also access the Order Objects commands by right-clicking an object and choosing Bring To Front or Send To Back.*

Deleting a Shape

1. Select the shape(s) you want to delete.
2. Press the BACKSPACE or DELETE key on the keyboard.

Working with WordArt

Office 2010's WordArt gallery provides you with a toolbox of special decorative effects that can help you create attention-grabbing artistic text. Using the WordArt text-styling feature, you can stretch, skew, or rotate text; design text to fit a preset shape; or add a gradient fill to text. WordArt text can be edited at any time. Figure 11-3 displays just a few of the WordArt options available.

TIP   *In Word and PowerPoint, you can convert existing text into WordArt.*

Adding WordArt

WordArt can be inserted from either the Text group on the Insert ribbon or the WordArt Styles group on the Drawing Tools Format ribbon.

1. Select the slide where the WordArt will be placed, and then click the Insert ribbon.

FIGURE 11-3 • WordArt lets you add interest to text on a slide.

2. Click the Insert WordArt button, and choose a style from the menu (pictured here). As soon as you click a style, a WordArt placeholder with the words "Your text here" (in the chosen style) appears on the slide.

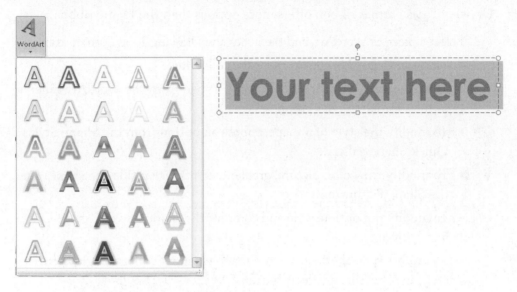

3. Type your text.

4. Resize the text as necessary. You can do this in either of two ways:

   • Change the font size of the text on the Home ribbon.

   • Select the WordArt object, and then click and drag a sizing handle to resize.

5. Position the WordArt on the slide by selecting it and then dragging it by an edge (drag anywhere except on the resizing handles).

Formatting Existing Text as WordArt

1. Select the text you wish to format as WordArt, and then click the Drawing Tools Format ribbon.

2. Choose a style from the WordArt Styles gallery.

3. Resize the text as necessary. You can do this in either of two ways:

   • Change the font size of the text on the Home ribbon.

   • Select the WordArt object, and then click and drag a sizing handle to resize.

4. Position the WordArt on the slide by selecting it and then dragging it by an edge (drag anywhere except on the resizing handles).

Modifying WordArt

WordArt can be formatted using both the Drawing group on the Home ribbon and the Drawing Tools Format ribbon (pictured previously in this chapter). The Drawing Tools Format ribbon offers more options than the Home ribbon.

1. Select a piece of WordArt, and then click the Drawing Tools Format ribbon.
2. Format the shape, keeping in mind the following:
   - To change the WordArt style, choose a style from the WordArt gallery in the WordArt Styles group.
   - To modify the style of a shape, choose an option from the Shape Styles Quick Shape gallery.
   - To modify the color, picture, gradient, or texture inside the shape, use the Shape Fill button.
   - To modify the outline style and color for the shape, use the Shape Outline button.
   - To modify special effects for the shape (shadow, reflection glow, edges, etc.), use the Shape Effects button.

Deleting WordArt

1. Select the WordArt you want to delete.
2. Press the BACKSPACE or DELETE key on the keyboard.

Working with SmartArt

SmartArt is a graphic that combines shapes, text placeholders, and lines. SmartArt automatically coordinates with a presentation's theme (colors, effects, and font); however, it can be manually formatted if changes are desired. SmartArt can take a boring, plain-vanilla text slide and jazz it up a bit to add visual interest. It can also help illuminate relationships between text with more clarity than plain text. For example, the slides on the left side of Figure 11-4 are standard text slides—use too many of these in a presentation, and your audience will be snoring sooner than you'd like! The two slides on the right side of Figure 11-4 use SmartArt and are much more pleasing to the eye—and only took mere seconds to create!

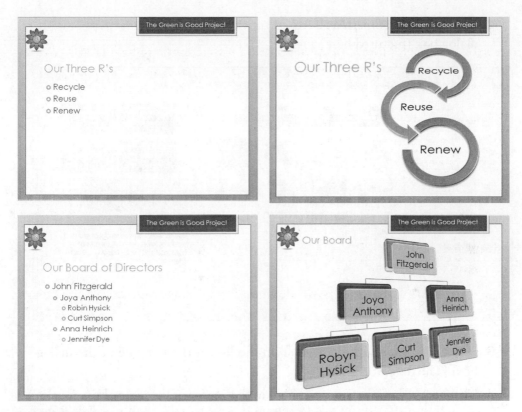

FIGURE 11-4 • SmartArt lets you turn plain text into WOW!

PowerPoint organizes SmartArt into eight categories: List, Process, Cycle, Hierarchy, Relationship, Matrix, Pyramid, and Picture. While each category's name points you toward using it for a specific type of information (for example, using the hierarchy category for an organization chart), don't be afraid to think outside of these labels and experiment!

Adding SmartArt

SmartArt can be inserted from the Text group on the Insert ribbon and modified on the WordArt Styles group on the Drawing Tools Format ribbon.

1. Select the slide where the SmartArt will be placed, and then click the Insert ribbon.

2. Click the Insert SmartArt button to open the Choose A SmartArt Graphic dialog box (pictured here).

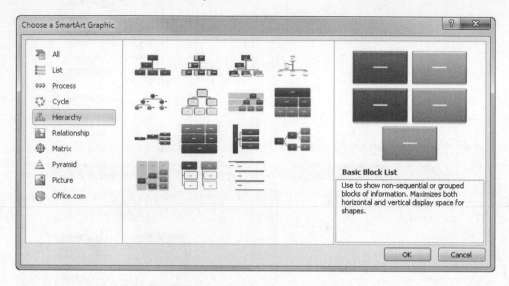

3. Select a category of SmartArt from the list on the left side of the dialog box. (The default is All).

4. Choose a style from those pictured in the center of the dialog box. A brief overview of the selected style will display in the lower-right corner of the dialog box.

5. Click OK.

6. Resize the SmartArt graphic by selecting it and then dragging a sizing handle.

7. Position the SmartArt on the slide by selecting it and then dragging it by an edge (anywhere except on the resizing handles).

8. Add text to the SmartArt text placeholders as needed. (Click in a placeholder and type.)

Modifying SmartArt

SmartArt is formatted using the SmartArt Tools Design ribbon, pictured near the top of Figure 11-5. You can modify text in SmartArt either directly in each shape (click in the shape and type) or by clicking the left edge the SmartArt to display the Type Your Text Here window (also pictured in Figure 11-5), which lets you modify text in outline form.

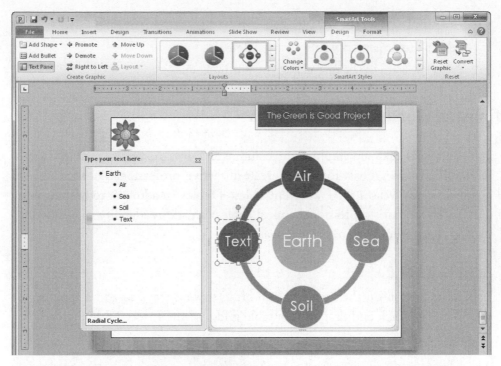

FIGURE 11-5 · The SmartArt Tools Design ribbon offers a variety of tools that let you customize SmartArt.

1. Select the SmartArt graphic you want to modify, and then click the SmartArt Tools Design ribbon.

2. Format the graphic, keeping in mind the following:

   • To change the layout of the SmartArt graphic, make a selection from the Layouts gallery.

   • To change the style of the SmartArt graphic, use the SmartArt Styles gallery.

   • To delete a shape within the SmartArt graphic, select the shape and then press the BACKSPACE or DELETE key on the keyboard.

   • Use the buttons in the Create Graphic group to add a shape, bullet, or text pane as well as to promote and demote or move a shape (up, down, right, or left).

TIP *To return the SmartArt graphic to its original form, click the Reset Graphic button in the Reset group.*

Deleting SmartArt

1. Select the SmartArt you want to delete.
2. Press the BACKSPACE or DELETE key on the keyboard.

Inserting and Working with Tables

Tables organize text and graphics into columns and rows. As you learned in Chapter 4, Office makes it easy for you to create attractive, professional-looking tables. Figure 11-6 showcases three different styles of tables. In addition to helping enhance a document's professional appeal, tables can add readability to a slide by making dense information easier to grasp.

Adding a Table

The Table button on the Insert ribbon offers several ways to add a table to a slide. You can click and drag on the table grid, use the Insert Table dialog box

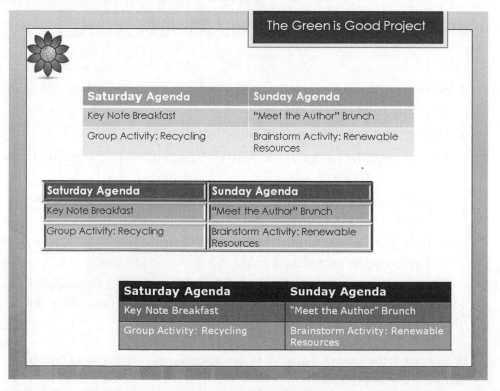

FIGURE 11-6 · PowerPoint 2010 offers a diverse array of table formats.

or draw a table one cell at a time. You can even create an Excel spreadsheet in a presentation if you wish. Adding a table using the table grid is described below.

Using the Table Button Menu Grid

Use Word's Table button menu grid to quickly create a basic table. The following illustration shows the Table button menu grid with a 3 × 3 table chosen.

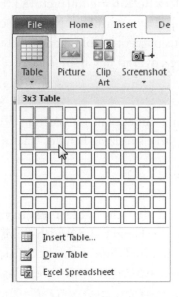

1. Position the cursor where you want the table to be placed.

2. From the Insert ribbon, choose Table.

3. Use the grid at the top of the menu to choose the number of rows and columns you want your table to have, and then click. (You are limited to a ten-row, eight-column table using the grid. To create a larger table, use the Insert Table command instead.)

4. Add text and formatting to the table to suit your needs.

TIP *If you would prefer to use a dialog box approach to creating a table rather than clicking and dragging the Table button grid, choose Insert Table from the Table button menu. Complete the Number Of Columns and Number Of Rows fields, and click OK.*

Modifying a Table's Layout

Even after a table has been created, it can still be modified. You can add or delete rows and columns, resize row height or column width, or resize the entire table.

Selecting in a Table

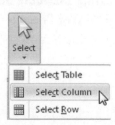

Modifying a table usually requires that you select a portion of the table first. The Select button menu (pictured to the right) on the Table Tools Layout ribbon provides commands for selecting various parts of a table. Additional table selection techniques were covered in Chapter 4.

Resizing a Table

Resize a table by specifying dimensions on the Table Tools Layout ribbon or by clicking and dragging the table's resizing handles (pictured in Figure 11-7).

1. Click in the table.
2. Do one of the following:
   - Select the table and view the Table Tools Layout ribbon. Type the desired table size in the Height and Width fields in the Table Size group (pictured in Figure 11-8). Select the Lock Aspect Ratio check box to maintain the table's aspect ratio while resizing.

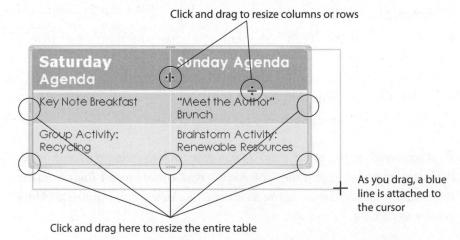

FIGURE 11-7 · Resizing a table is as easy as clicking and dragging on an edge.

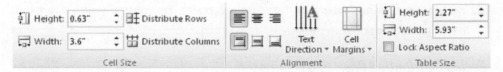

FIGURE 11-8 · The PowerPoint Table Tools Layout ribbon lets you modify cell size, alignment, and table size.

- Click and drag one of the resizing handle near the center or corner edges of the selected table (pictured in Figure 11-7). As you drag, a light blue line represents the new size and shape of the table. Drag outward to make the table larger; drag inward to make the table smaller.

TIP *Hold down the SHIFT key while dragging to retain the table's current aspect ratio.*

Changing Row Height or Column Width

Resize a row or column on the Table Tools Layout ribbon or by clicking and dragging the row or column edges (pictured in Figure 11-7).

1. Click in the row you want to resize, and then do one of the following:
   - View the Table Tools Layout ribbon and, in the Cell Size group (pictured in Figure 11-8), type the desired row height in the Height field.
   - Position the mouse pointer on the bottom edge of the row you want to resize. You are in the correct place when the cursor resembles a double-headed arrow pointing up and down (pictured in Figure 11-7). Drag up to decrease the row height; drag down to increase the row height.
2. Click in the column you want to resize, and then do one of the following:
   - View the Table Tools Layout ribbon and, in the Cell Size group (pictured in Figure 11-8), type the desired column width in the Width field.
   - Position the mouse pointer on the right edge of the column you want to resize. You are in the correct place when the cursor resembles a double-headed arrow pointing left and right (pictured in Figure 11-7). Drag to the left to make the column smaller; drag to the right to make the column wider.

TIP *Double-clicking instead of dragging will resize the column width or row height to suit the text it contains.*

Evenly Distributing Rows and Columns

PowerPoint makes it easy for you to quickly distribute the height of rows or the width of columns to fill out the table size.

1. Click anywhere in the table.
2. Do one or both of the following:
   - To evenly distribute all rows in the table, click the Distribute Rows button in the Cell Size group on the Table Tools Layout ribbon.
   - To evenly distribute all columns in the table, click the Distribute Columns button in the Cell Size group on the Table Tools Layout ribbon.

Deleting Rows and Columns

1. Select the row or column you want to delete.
2. Do one of the following:
   - Right-click the selected row or column, and choose Delete Rows or Delete Columns.
   - On the Table Tools Layout ribbon (pictured in Figure 11-9), click the Delete button (located in the Rows & Columns group), and then choose Delete Rows or Delete Columns.

Adding Rows and Columns

1. Select a row or column adjacent to where you want to add a new row or column.
2. Do one of the following:
   - Right-click the selected row or column, and choose from among the following:
     - Insert | Insert Columns To The Left
     - Insert | Insert Columns To The Right
     - Insert | Insert Rows Above
     - Insert | Insert Rows Below
   - On the Table Tools Layout ribbon, in the Rows & Columns group, click the appropriate Insert button (pictured in the previous illustration).

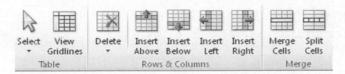

FIGURE 11-9 · The PowerPoint Table Tools Layout ribbon gives you total control of your tables.

TIP   *Select multiple rows or columns to add multiple rows or columns. For example, if you select two rows and choose Insert Rows Above, two rows will be added above the selected two rows.*

Merging or Splitting Cells

Merging two or more cells together is typically done to visually center text over, under, or next to a group of rows or columns. In the following illustration, the bottom two cells in row 4 have been merged together.

Saturday Agenda	Sunday Agenda	
Key Note Breakfast	"Meet the Author" Brunch	
Group Activity: Recycling Demo	Group A: Brainstorm Activity – Renewable Resources	Group B: Brainstorm Activity – Global Swarming
Cocktails & Dinner		

Cell split into two columns and one row

Two columns merged into one

Splitting a cell is done to evenly break up a cell into one or more rows or columns. In the previous illustration, one cell in row 3 has been split into two columns to accommodate two different group activities.

1. Select the cells you wish to merge or the cell you wish to split.

2. To merge, click the Merge Cells button in the Merge group on the Table Tools Layout ribbon. To split, click the Split Cells button.

TIP   *To quickly merge two or more cells, select the cells, right-click in one of them, and choose Merge Cells from the menu. To quickly split a cell, right-click in the cell and choose Split Cells from the menu.*

Modifying a Table's Design

The Table Tools Design ribbon (pictured here) contains numerous tools for modifying a table's design.

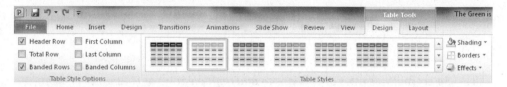

Working with Table Styles, Cell Shading, Borders, and Effects

When you create a table, a combination of formatting options (color combinations, fonts, effects) based on the presentation's theme is automatically applied to the table. The Table Styles gallery on the Table Tools Design ribbon offers single-click variations on the theme.

1. Click anywhere in the table, and click in the Table Tools Design ribbon.

2. In the Table Styles group, do one or more of the following:

   - Select a style from the Table Styles gallery.

   - To fill one or more cells with a different color background, select one or more cells in the table, and then choose a color from the Shading button.

   - To add borders, select one or more cells in the table, then click the Borders button, and choose the type of borders you want to use.

   - To add cell effects (such as bevels, shadows, and reflections), select one or more cells in the table, and then click the Effects button. Choose the desired effects from the Bevels, Shadows, and Effects submenus.

Working with Slide Transitions

Slide transitions are animated segues between slides. For example, slides can fade to black or dissolve as you move between them. This is an easy (and quick!) way to add visual interest to a presentation. In addition to choosing from a few dozen transition styles, you can control their speed, add sound, and even customize certain transition properties. The Transitions ribbon (pictured here) is where slide transitions are added and modified.

Adding Transitions Between Slides

To add transitions between slides you must first select one or more slides. You can apply transitions to one slide at a time if you wish, but for a presentation with a large number of slides, this would be time-consuming. To add transitions to all slides at once, it's useful to work in Slide Sorter view.

TIP *A little goes a long way with slide transitions! Using a completely different transition for every single slide in a presentation can become disorienting for an audience. If you want to mix it up a bit, try using a single transition style, but mixing up the transition effect options every few slides. For example, use the Wipe transition throughout, but have the slides wipe in different directions every now and then. This keeps things "fresh" but doesn't visually overwhelm the audience.*

1. Click the View ribbon, and choose Slide Sorter View. (Note that transitions can be added from Normal view if you prefer.)
2. Select the slide(s) you want to add transitions to. (To select all of the slides, use the CTRL-A keyboard shortcut.)
3. Click the Transitions ribbon.
4. Choose a transition from the Transitions To This Slide gallery.
5. Preview the slide presentation in Slide Show view.

Setting Transition Timing

The Duration field on the Transitions ribbon lets you set the length of a transition in seconds.

1. Select the slide(s) you wish to modify, and then click the Transitions ribbon.
2. In the Timing group, type the desired transition length in the Duration field. If you want the duration to be the same for all of the slides in a presentation, click the Apply To All button in the Timing group.
3. Preview the presentation in Slide Show view to get the full effect.

Setting Transition Effects

Most (but not all) transition types have special effects that can be set. For example, the effect options for the Shape transition let you choose between a circle, diamond, and plus sign shape as well as whether the transition moves inward or outward.

1. Select the slide(s) you wish to modify, and then click the Transitions ribbon.
2. In the Transitions To This Slide group, click the Effect Options button.
3. Choose an effect.
4. The effect will preview in Slide Sorter view, but you can preview the slide presentation in Slide Show view to get the full effect.

Removing a Transition

1. Select the slide(s) you want to remove transitions from, and then click the Transitions ribbon.
2. Choose None in the Transitions To This Slide gallery.

Animating Text and Graphics

Any object in PowerPoint, including text, can be animated. For example, you can have text appear one line at a time, bring graphics in when prompted, and play a sound clip when an object appears. Animation can be useful for keeping an audience engaged, bringing focus to important content and controlling the flow of a presentation. PowerPoint offers four types of animation effects, which can be used on their own or in combination with one another (see Table 11-1).

Animating an Object

The Animation Ribbon (pictured here) is used to add and control animations in a PowerPoint presentation. To select an animation, use either the Animation gallery on the Animation group or the Add Animation button on the Advanced Animations menu (the same choices are available in either group).

TABLE 11-1 PowerPoint 2010 Animation Effects	
Animation Effect	**Description**
Entrance Effect	Used to have an object make a grand entrance onto the slide (for example, dissolve gradually into focus, fly onto the slide from an edge, or grow and turn)
Exit Effect	Used to make an object leave the slide (for example, fly off of the slide, disappear from view, or bounce off the slide)
Emphasis Effect	Used to call attention to an object (for example, shrink or grow in size, change color, or teeter on its center)
Motion Path	Used to give an object movement on a slide (for example, move up or down, left or right, or in a pattern)

1. Select the object or text that you want to animate.

2. Choose an animation style from the Animation gallery or from the Add Animation button menu. The object or text will have a numbered label attached to it indicating its order within all of the animations on that slide. (The label does not print and only shows in Normal view.) Use the Reorder Animation buttons to modify the animation order if needed.

TIP *If you do not see a particular entrance, exit, emphasis, or motion path animation effect, click More Entrance Effects, More Emphasis Effects, More Exit Effects, or More Motion Paths.*

Modifying Animation Timing

An animation's start, duration, or delay timing can be set on the Timing group of the Animations ribbon.

1. Select the object or text that you want to modify.

2. Click the arrow to the right of the Start menu, and select when you want the animation to begin: On Click, With Previous or After Previous.

3. To specify the length of an animation, type a number in the Duration field.

4. To create a delay between the end of one animation and the start of another, type the number of seconds in the Delay field.

Adding Multimedia to a Presentation

Adding multimedia files—video and/or audio—to a presentation can help keep an audience engaged and break up the monotony of a long presentation. Adding multimedia is also a useful engagement technique for kiosk presentations (an unmanned, looping presentation).

TIP *A little goes a long way with multimedia! Putting a video on every single slide can make for a disengaging experience. Likewise, adding audio (such as audience applause or canned laughter) on every single slide can quickly become tedious. Used sparingly and effectively, however, multimedia files can help keep your audience glued to their seats. Be certain to add video or audio where it makes sense for your content—in other words, don't just insert a multimedia file "because you can!"*

Inserting Video

1. Select the slide where you wish to add the video, and then click the Insert ribbon.

2. In the Media group, click Video. The Video button menu opens (pictured here).

3. Choose the type of video you are inserting, keeping the following in mind:

- If you are inserting a video from a file, the Insert Video dialog box opens, allowing you to navigate to the video you wish to insert. Select the video and click Insert.

- If you are inserting a video from a website, you will need to have the author's permission, as well as the necessary coding (called the "embed code") from the website so that you can paste it into the Insert Video From Web Site dialog box. Read more about embedding videos in the PowerPoint Help file by searching on "embed video." Note that you can also choose to *link* to a video on the Web as well, which would require an Internet connection during a presentation. Read more about this in the Help file by searching on "Link to a video file on a web site."

- If you are inserting a clip art video, the Clip Art pane will open to allow you to search for a video by keyword. When you find the video you want, click it to insert it.

4. Resize the inserted video by clicking and dragging any one of its eight re-sizing handles. (Be aware that resizing a video may negatively affect resolu-tion as well as change a video's natural aspect ratio.)

5. Reposition the video on the slide by clicking in the middle of it (not on a handle) and dragging it to a new location.

6. Use the playback controls attached to the bottom of the inserted video to play or pause the video and to adjust the volume.

Still Struggling

Wondering what type of video and audio formats will work in PowerPoint? Com-patible video formats include Adobe Flash Media (.swf), Windows Media File (.asf), Windows Video File (.avi), Movie File (.mpeg or .mpg), and Windows Media Video File (.wmv). If the Apple QuickTime Player is installed, you can also use QuickTime video formats (.mp4, .mov, and .qt).

Compatible audio formats include AIFF Audio File (.aiff), AU Audio File (.au), MIDI File (.mid or .midi), MP3 Audio File (.mp3), Windows Audio File (.wav), and Windows Media Audio File (.wma). Advanced Audio Coding (.aac) is compatible if the necessary codec (a program that encodes and decodes digital media, such as Apple's QuickTime Player) is installed.

Formatting the Video

The Video Tools Format ribbon (pictured here) provides numerous options for formatting the video window and adjusting the video. This ribbon is visible only when a video is selected.

Modifying the Video Window Style

1. Select the video and click the Video Tools Format ribbon.

2. Format the video window, keeping in mind the following:

   • To apply a Quick Style to a video window, make a selection from the Video Styles gallery.

   • To change the shape of the video window, use the options in the Video Shape button menu.

   • To add or modify the border of the video window, use the options in the Video Border button menu.

   • To apply special effects to the video window (shadow, reflections, glow, etc.), use the options in the Video Effects button menu.

TIP   *To learn how to adjust video brightness and contrast, recolor a video, or use a single frame from a video as the poster frame, search on "adjust video" in PowerPoint Help.*

Working with Video Playback Options

The Video Tools Playback ribbon (pictured here) provides numerous options for controlling video playback during a presentation. This ribbon is visible only when a video is selected.

Editing a Video The Editing group on the Video Tools Playback ribbon lets you set fade in/fade out details for the video as well as trim (shorten) a video.

1. Select the video and then click the Video Tools Playback ribbon.

2. In the Editing group, provide the fade-in and/or fade-out durations in the Fade In and Fade Out fields (type a number in the field or use the up/down arrows).

3. Click Trim Video to open the Trim Video dialog box (pictured here).

4. Use the playback controls to view the video. Move the green handle in the playback progress bar to where you want the video to begin. Move the red handle to where you want the video to stop.

5. Click OK.

Modifying Video Options The Video Options group on the Video Tools Playback ribbon offers five different playback options:

- Start (you can start the video by clicking the Play button, or start it automatically as soon as the slide appears)
- Play Full Screen

- Hide While Not Playing
- Loop Until Stopped (good for a kiosk presentation)
- Rewind After Playing (so it's all set to go for the next presentation)

Inserting Audio

1. Go to the slide where you wish to add audio, and then click the Insert ribbon.

2. In the Media group, click Audio. The Audio button menu opens (pictured here).

3. Choose the type of audio you are inserting, keeping the following in mind:

   - If you are inserting audio from a file, the Insert Audio dialog box opens, allowing you to navigate to the sound file you wish to insert. Select the file and click Insert.

   - If you are inserting clip art audio, the Clip Art pane will open to allow you to search for a clip by keyword. When you find the audio file you want, click it to insert it.

   - If you are recording your own audio, you will need to have a microphone. When you choose Record Audio, the Record Sound dialog box opens (pictured here). Click the Record button (the red dot) to begin recording. Click the Stop button (the black rectangle) to stop recording. Click the Play button (the triangle) to listen to the recording. Click OK to close the dialog box.

4. The audio clip appears on the slide as an image of a speaker with playback controls underneath. Resize the inserted audio icon by clicking and dragging any one of its eight resizing handles.

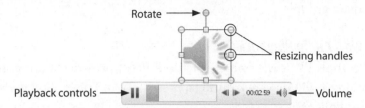

5. Reposition the audio icon on the slide by clicking in the middle of it (not on a handle) and dragging it to a new location.

6. Use the playback controls attached to the bottom of the inserted video to play or pause the video and to adjust the volume.

Formatting the Audio

The Audio Tools Format ribbon (pictured here) provides numerous options for formatting the audio icon and adjusting the audio. This ribbon is visible only when an audio icon is selected.

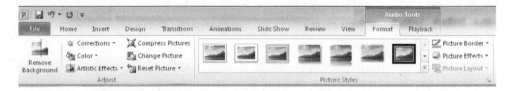

Modifying the Audio Icon Style

1. Select the audio icon, and click the Audio Tools Format ribbon.

2. Format the audio icon, keeping in mind the following:

   - To select a different picture, click the Change Picture button and navigate to and select the image you want to use.

   - To apply a Quick Style to the audio icon, make a selection from the Picture Styles gallery.

   - To add or modify the border of the audio icon, use the options in the Picture Border button menu.

- To apply special effects to the audio icon (shadow, reflections, glow, etc.), use the options in the Picture Effects button menu.

- To recolor the audio icon or apply artistic effects, use the options in the Adjust group.

Working with Audio Playback Options

The Audio Tools Playback ribbon (pictured here) provides numerous options for controlling audio playback during a presentation. This ribbon is visible only when an audio icon is selected.

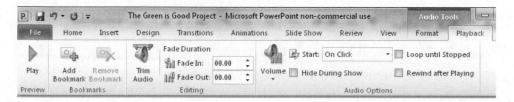

Editing an Audio Clip The Editing group on the Audio Tools Playback ribbon lets you set fade-in/fade-out details for the audio clip as well as trim (shorten) it.

1. Select the audio icon, and click the Audio Tools Playback ribbon.

2. In the Editing group, provide the fade-in and/or fade-out durations in the Fade In and Fade Out fields (type a number in the field or use the up/down arrows).

3. Click Trim Audio to open the Trim Audio dialog box (pictured here).

4. Use the playback controls to listen to the audio clip. Move the green handle in the playback progress bar to where you want the clip to begin. Move the red handle to where you want the clip to stop.

5. Click OK.

Modifying Audio Options The Audio Options group on the Audio Tools Playback ribbon offers four different playback options:

- Start (you can start the audio by clicking the Play button, or start it automatically as soon as the slide appears)
- Hide During Show
- Loop Until Stopped (good for a kiosk presentation)
- Rewind After Playing (so it's all set to go for the next presentation)

Still Struggling

Remember to refer back to Chapter 2 for common program functionality, such as Backstage View (document properties and permissions, opening existing files, and saving files); using undo and redo; working with the Office Clipboard (cut, copy, and paste); working with themes; and getting help.

Summary

In this chapter you learned how to make presentations more engaging by incorporating graphics, tables, and multimedia. You also learned how to animate text and graphics in a presentation and to use transitions between slides to create visual interest. In Chapter 12 you will learn how to orchestrate a slide show.

QUIZ

1. True or False: In PowerPoint, existing text can be converted into WordArt.
   A. True
   B. False

2. Which of the following shapes is available in PowerPoint?
   A. Block arrows
   B. Stars
   C. Equation shapes
   D. Flow chart
   E. All of the above

3. The _____ on the _____ ribbon lets you set fade-in/fade-out details for the audio clip as well as trim (shorten) it. (Fill in the blanks using the following choices.)
   A. Audio Tools Playback
   B. Audio Options
   C. Editing group
   D. Adjust group
   E. Audio Tools Format

4. Which of the following is not a type of SmartArt?
   A. Cycle
   B. Process
   C. Picture
   D. Stars
   E. Relationship

5. True or False: The Video Tools Playback ribbon is visible only when a video is selected.
   A. True
   B. False

6. Which of the following describes WordArt?
   A. A graphic that combines shapes, text placeholders, and lines
   B. Organizes text and graphics into columns and rows
   C. A text-styling feature
   D. Animated text
   E. None of the above

7. **Which of the following is a PowerPoint animation effect?**
    A. Entrance
    B. Exit
    C. Emphasis
    D. Motion path
    E. All of the above

8. **The start, duration, or delay timing for an animation can be set on the _____ of the _____ ribbon. (Fill in the blanks using the following choices.)**
    A. Animations
    B. Format
    C. Advanced Animations group
    D. Timing group
    E. Playback

9. **Which of the following modifications can be made to a table after you have created it?**
    A. Add or delete rows
    B. Add or delete columns
    C. Resize row height or column width
    D. Resize the entire table
    E. All of the above

10. **True or False: Any object in PowerPoint, including text, can be animated.**
    A. True
    B. False

chapter 12

Orchestrating a Slide Show

This chapter teaches you how to orchestrate a slide show. You will learn how to work in Slide Show view and how to create a custom presentation based on an existing presentation. You will also discover the numerous options Power-Point gives you for setting up a presentation.

CHAPTER OBJECTIVES

In this chapter, you will learn how to

- View a presentation in Slide Show view
- Create and run a custom slide show
- Set up a slide show
- Rehearse and record a slide show

Delivering a Slide Show Presentation

Ready to deliver a presentation? PowerPoint's Slide Show ribbon (pictured here) provides all of the tools you will need.

The Start Slide Show group lets you view a presentation in Slide Show view, broadcast a presentation over the Internet, and create a custom show.

The Set Up group lets you access the Set Up Slide Show dialog box, where you can choose a show type and set show options, such as how to advance slides and whether or not to loop a presentation. The Set Up group also lets you hide slides; rehearse timings; record a slide show; and choose whether or not to play narrations, use timings, or show media controls. The Monitors group lets you change your monitor's resolution and/or use PowerPoint's Presenter View feature.

Working in Slide Show View

Slide Show view displays a presentation in full-screen mode exactly as an audience will see it, with all graphics, timings, movies, animated effects, and transitions.

Viewing a Slide Show Presentation in Slide Show View

1. View the Slide Show ribbon.
2. Do one of the following:
   - In the Start Slide Show group, click From Beginning to begin viewing the slides from the first slide.
   - In the Start Slide Show group, click From Current Slide to begin viewing from the current slide.
3. To navigate between slides, do any of the following:
   - To move to the next slide, click the mouse or press the RIGHT ARROW, DOWN ARROW, or PAGE DOWN keys on the keyboard.
   - To move to the previous slide, press the LEFT ARROW, UP ARROW, or PAGE UP keys on the keyboard.

- When the final slide is reached, the screen turns black and you can either click the mouse or press the ESC key to exit.
- During the slide show, there are four almost transparent buttons near the bottom-left corner of the screen (pictured in Figure 12-1). The buttons offer additional controls for a presentation, including a pen that you can use to draw on a slide, as well as a menu of options that let you navigate to a specific slide, switch to a blank black or white screen, or end the presentation.

TIP *PowerPoint provides a laser pointer to use during a presentation. While in Slide Show view, hold down the CTRL key and then click and drag anywhere on the screen to display the laser pointer.*

Still Struggling

PowerPoint's Presenter View feature lets you view a presentation with notes on one monitor while delivering the presentation through another monitor (without notes) for an audience. Two monitors are needed to use this feature. To learn more about Presenter View, search on "presenter view" in PowerPoint Help.

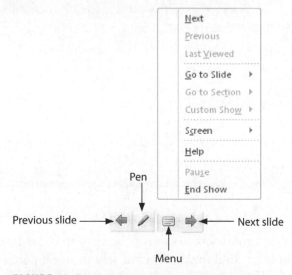

FIGURE 12-1 · Slide show controls can be found in the bottom-left corner of the screen in Slide Show view.

TIP   *To begin a slide show from the first slide in the deck, use the F5 keyboard shortcut.*

Working with Custom Slide Shows

PowerPoint's Custom Slide Show feature allows you to make alternative versions of a presentation by choosing which slides appear and which are hidden and/or customizing the order of a slide presentation. For example, assume you are giving a series of presentations about company benefits to various groups of employees. Your presentation has 20 slides in it. Several of these slides do not pertain to employees in a specific division of the company. You can use the Custom Slide Show option to create a version of the presentation for the employees in that division.

Creating a Custom Slide Show

1. View the Slide Show ribbon.
2. In the Start Slide Show group, click Custom Slide Show, and choose Custom Shows. The Custom Shows dialog box opens.
3. In the Custom Shows dialog box, click New. The Define Custom Show dialog box opens (pictured here).

4. Type a name for the custom show in the Slide Show Name field.
5. Select the slides you want to use for the custom show from the Slides In Presentation list. (Hold down the CTRL key to select nonadjacent slides.)
6. Click the Add button to add the slides to the Slides In Custom Show list.

7. To reorder slides in the custom slide show, click a slide, and then use the up or down arrow keys to reposition the slide in the list.

8. Click OK to close the Define Custom Show dialog box.

9. In the Custom Shows dialog box, click Show to preview the custom show or click Close to close the dialog box.

Running a Custom Slide Show

1. View the Slide Show ribbon.

2. In the Start Slide Show group, click Custom Slide Show, and choose Custom Shows. The Custom Shows dialog box opens.

3. In the Custom Shows dialog box, select the custom show you wish to run.

4. Click Show.

TIP   *You can set a custom show as the default show in the Set Up Slide Show dialog box. On the Slide Show ribbon, click Set Up Slide Show. Under the Show Slides heading, click the Custom Show option, and select a custom show from the drop-down list. Click OK. If you ever want to remove this show as the default, click the All option or choose a different custom show.*

Setting Up a Slide Show Presentation

Use the Set Up group on the Slide Show ribbon (pictured here) to modify a presentation. In the Set Up Show dialog box (pictured in Figure 12-2), you can select a show type as well as various show options, such as how to advance slides and whether or not to loop a presentation. You can also hide slides; rehearse timings; record a slide show; and choose whether or not to play narrations, use timings, or show media controls.

TABLE 12-1 Slide Show Types in PowerPoint 2010

Show Type	Description
Presented by a speaker (full screen)	Displays full screen with no navigation buttons showing on the screen; the presenter controls the slide show using the mouse or keyboard.
Browsed by an individual (window)	Displays full screen in a window similar to Reading view, with navigation buttons at the lower-right corner of the window. If timings are used, the slides will progress according to the timings; however, the user can also navigate freely through the slides.
Browsed at a kiosk (full screen)	Displays full screen with no navigation buttons showing on the screen. The show is controlled by the timings. If this show type is selected, the Loop Continuously Until 'Esc' option under the Show Options heading will be automatically selected.

Selecting a Show Type

PowerPoint offers three show type options, as described in Table 12-1.

1. View the Slide Show ribbon.
2. In the Set Up group, click Set Up Slide Show.
3. Choose a show type under the Show Type heading.
4. Click OK.

Options for Advancing Slides

By default, if timings are present, PowerPoint slides will advance according to the timings. You can control this in the Set Up Show dialog box (see Figure 12-2).

1. View the Slide Show ribbon.
2. In the Set Up group, click Set Up Slide Show.
3. Under the Advance Slides heading, choose Manually or Using Timings, If Present.
4. Click OK.

TIP *Note that the options under the Advance Slides heading can also be controlled by selecting or deselecting the Use Timings check box on the Slide Show ribbon.*

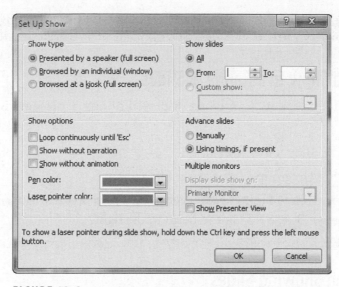

FIGURE 12-2 · The Set Up Show dialog box lets you control how slides advance during a presentation, among other things.

Selecting Show Options

PowerPoint offers several additional playback options, as described in Table 12-2.

1. View the Slide Show ribbon.
2. In the Set Up group, click Set Up Slide Show.

TABLE 12-2 Slide Show Options in PowerPoint 2010	
Show Option	**Description**
Loop Continuously Until 'Esc'	This option is used when delivering a presentation at an unmanned kiosk, letting a presentation play over and over again, stopping only when the ESC key is pressed. This option is automatically selected if the Show type is set to Browsed At Kiosk.
Show Without Narration	Suppresses any voiceover narration recorded in the presentation. Note that this feature can also be controlled by selecting or deselecting the Play Narrations check box on the Slide Show ribbon.
Show Without Animation	Suppresses any animations in the presentation.
Pen Color	Allows you to choose a pen color for the Slide Show view pen (see Figure 12–1).
Laser Pointer Color	Allows you to choose a laser pointer color.

3. Choose one or more options under the Show Options heading.

4. Click OK.

Limiting a Show to a Range of Slides

Hiding a slide keeps it from being displayed during a presentation in Slide Show view.

1. View the Slide Show ribbon.

2. In the Set Up group, click Set Up Slide Show.

3. Under the Show Slides heading, click the From down arrow and type the slide range (3, 4, 8-13) in the fields to the right.

4. Click OK.

Hiding and Showing Slides

Hiding a slide keeps it from being displayed during a presentation in Slide Show view. The slide will still be visible in all other views.

1. Select the slide(s) you wish to hide or show. (Select multiple slides in the Slides tab by holding down the CTRL key and clicking each slide.)

2. View the Slide Show ribbon.

3. In the Set Up group, click Hide Slide.

Rehearsing Timings

If you will be giving a live presentation in front of an audience, you will probably want to rehearse a few times to make sure that everything flows smoothly and that the timing is appropriate. PowerPoint's Rehearse Timings option helps you get ready by keeping track of the time as you rehearse.

1. View the Slide Show ribbon.

2. In the Set Up group, click Rehearse Timings. The presentation begins and recording controls (pictured here) appear in the top-left corner.

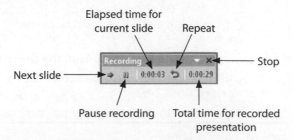

3. Begin rehearsing, switching slides as necessary and proceeding at your normal pace. Use the recording controls to pause if necessary (which will stop the timer from progressing). When the presentation is done, an alert window opens letting you know the total time of the show and asking if you want to keep the slide timings to use when you view the slide show.

4. Click Yes to save the timings, or click No to discard the timings.

Recording a Slide Show

PowerPoint's Record Slide Show feature makes it easy to create a self-contained representation of a presentation, including narration, animations, and timing of slide changes. Your computer must have a microphone to record voiceover narration and speakers to be able to listen to a recorded presentation.

1. View the Slide Show ribbon.

2. In the Set Up group, click Record Slide Show, and choose one of the following:

   • To being recording from the first slide, choose Start Recording From The Beginning.

   • To begin recording from the current slide, choose Start Recording From Current Slide.

3. In the Record Slide Show dialog box (pictured here), select which features you want to include. (For example, if you do not want to record a voiceover narration, deselect the Narrations And Laser Pointer check box.)

4. Give your presentation, keeping the following in mind:

   • While you are recording, use the recording controls (shown earlier) to control and monitor the recording. You can pause at any time and then resume recording, as well as repeat a slide or stop recording.

   • If you are recording a voiceover narration, speak clearly and do not rush.

- If the presentation contains animations, click to build the slide just as you would when giving a live presentation.

- Move from slide to slide just as you would when giving a live presentation (long pauses will be recorded if you are recording the slide and animation timings).

5. To view the recorded presentation, click the From Beginning or From Current Slide buttons in the Start Slide Show group.

    - If you make a mistake on one slide, you do not have to re-record the entire presentation to fix it. Instead, select the slide and then choose Start Recording From Current Slide from the Record Slide Show button menu. Record that one slide, and then click the Stop button in the recording controls to stop recording.

6. Save the presentation:

    - You can save a copy of the recorded presentation as a PowerPoint slide show to share with others without giving them the actual PowerPoint file. This would allow those who do not own the PowerPoint program to view a presentation. From the File ribbon, choose Save As. In the Save As dialog box, type a name for the presentation in the File Name field, and choose PowerPoint Show from the Save As File Type list. The file is saved with a .pps extension, which allows others to view the presentation but not edit it.

    - To delete the timing and/or narration from a presentation, choose Clear from the Record Slide Show button menu (located on the Slide Show ribbon).

TIP   *For more professional results when recording a presentation, prepare a script for the presentation in advance of recording. Add the script to each slide's notes page and then print the notes pages to refer to as you give the presentation.*

Still Struggling

Need to accommodate both a local and remote audience? PowerPoint 2010 allows you to broadcast a presentation over the Internet to a remote audience. This means that while you are giving your presentation to a local audience, others (to whom you have sent the link via e-mail) are able to follow along on their web browser. To be able to use this feature, you must have a network service available to host the presentation. Some organizations may have the ability to host a show via their own SharePoint server using Microsoft Office Web Apps. If your organization utilizes SharePoint, check with your network administrator to determine whether you can use the network to host a PowerPoint presentation and also whether there are any file size restrictions that might affect your ability to stream a presentation.

For those who do not have access to an internal SharePoint server, another option is the PowerPoint Broadcast Service, which is open to those with a Windows Live ID. (A Windows Live ID is an e-mail address and password that is used to sign in to all Windows Live services. You can learn more about this service at www.passport.net.) To learn more about Presenter View, search on "broadcast" in PowerPoint Help.

Summary

This chapter provided an overview of how to orchestrate a slide show. You learned how to work in Slide Show view and how to create a custom presentation based on an existing presentation. You also discovered the many options PowerPoint offers for setting up and delivering a presentation. In Chapter 13 you'll begin exploring Outlook.

QUIZ

1. **True or False: If you made a mistake while recording a presentation, you must record the entire presentation again.**

    A. True

    B. False

2. **Which group on the Slide Show ribbon lets you view a presentation in Slide Show view, broadcast a presentation over the Internet, and create a custom show?**

    A. Monitors

    B. Set Up

    C. Start Slide Show

    D. View

    E. None of the above

3. **Which of the following options on PowerPoint's Slide Show ribbon lets you keep a slide from showing during a presentation?**

    A. Broadcast Slide Show

    B. Set Up Slide Show

    C. From Beginning

    D. Hide Slide

    E. Rehearse Timings

4. **PowerPoint's _____ option helps you get ready by keeping track of the _____ for you as you rehearse. (Fill in the blanks using the following choices.)**

    A. Broadcast Slide Show

    B. Time

    C. Set Up Slide Show

    D. Bandwidth

    E. Rehearse Timings

5. **Which PowerPoint feature makes it easy to create a self-contained representation of your presentation, including narration, animations, and timing of slide changes?**

    A. Record Slide Show

    B. Rehearse Timings

    C. Custom Slide Show

    D. Presenter View

    E. Slide Sorter View

6. **True or False: If the Browsed At A Kiosk (Full Screen) show type is selected, the Loop Continuously Until Esc option under the Show Options heading will be automatically selected.**

   A. True
   B. False

7. **Which of the following is an option for setting up a slide show?**

   A. Loop Continuously Until 'Esc'
   B. Show Without Narration
   C. Show Without Animation
   D. Pen Color
   E. All of the above

8. **Which of the following is not an option on the Slide Show ribbon?**

   A. Slide Sorter View
   B. Set Up Slide Show
   C. From Beginning
   D. From Current Slide
   E. Rehearse Timings

9. **PowerPoint's _____ feature allows you to make alternative versions of a presentation by choosing which slides appear and which are hidden and/or customizing the order of a slide presentation (Fill in the blank using the following choices.)**

   A. Rehearse Timings
   B. Slide Sorter View
   C. Custom Slide Show
   D. Record Slide Show
   E. None of the above

10. **True or False: By default, if timings are present, PowerPoint slides will advance according to the timings; however, you can control this in the Set Up Show dialog box.**

    A. True
    B. False

Part V

Microsoft Outlook

chapter 13

Getting Started with Outlook

As you learned in Chapter 1, Outlook is a full-featured personal information management (PIM) program that provides e-mail, scheduling (calendar), contact management (address book), and task tracking capabilities. This chapter gets you started using Outlook for e-mail. You will learn how to set up an e-mail account and how to send, format, read, reply to, and forward e-mail. You will also learn how to attach a file to an e-mail, create an e-mail signature, and organize your Outlook Inbox. Finally, you will get a brief introduction to the Outlook Social Connector, which lets you use Outlook to connect to your personal and business social networks.

CHAPTER OBJECTIVES

In this chapter, you will learn how to

- Set up an e-mail account
- Work with e-mail (send, read, reply, forward, delete)
- Create an e-mail signature
- Organize the Outlook Inbox
- Use the Outlook Social Connector

Setting Up an E-mail Account

To send and receive e-mail messages in Outlook, you must add and configure an e-mail account. Outlook supports both Post Office Protocol (POP3) and Internet Message Access Protocol (IMAP) as a means of transferring e-mail messages from a server.

If you were using a previous version of Outlook on your computer, account settings may be automatically imported from that previous version, so you may not have to set up an e-mail account.

If you are installing Outlook for the first time, the Auto Account Setup wizard will walk you through the process of configuring e-mail account settings. You will be prompted for your name, e-mail address, and password. If an e-mail account cannot be automatically configured, you will have to add the missing information manually, as described later in this section.

Still Struggling

Wondering what the difference is between POP3 and IMAP? The main difference between the two protocols is that POP3 is a one-way operation: you connect to a mail server, download all your new messages, and then disconnect. POP deletes mail from the server once it has been downloaded by you, although you can opt to leave copies of messages on the server. There is no two-way synchronization between the mail server and whatever devices you download your e-mail onto (smart phone, laptop, iPad, etc.). This means that if you check e-mail on a different device later, e-mail that was previously downloaded from the server (and therefore deleted) will not be downloaded as new mail. Most personal e-mail systems use POP3 protocols.

IMAP provides a more flexible two-way operation, in that it synchronizes between the server and whatever device(s) you use to access your e-mail. So if you read an e-mail on your smart phone, it is also marked as having been read on the server. This means that when you check e-mail on your laptop later, it will be marked as having been read there as well. Likewise, any messages you move or delete will be updated across all devices. Most businesses use IMAP protocols.

TIP   *If you work in a company that has an e-mail administrator or IT support department, contact them to obtain the information needed to set up an e-mail account. If you work from home or in a small business, contact your Internet service provider (ISP) for the necessary information. (You can usually find the information you need on an ISP's website, in either a FAQ or on its support page.)*

Adding an E-mail Account

1. On the Info tab, located on the File ribbon, click Add Account. The Add New Account dialog box opens (pictured in Figure 13-1).

2. Complete the following fields on the first page of the Auto Account Setup dialog box:

   - Your Name
   - E-mail Address (including the domain)
   - Password
   - Retype Password

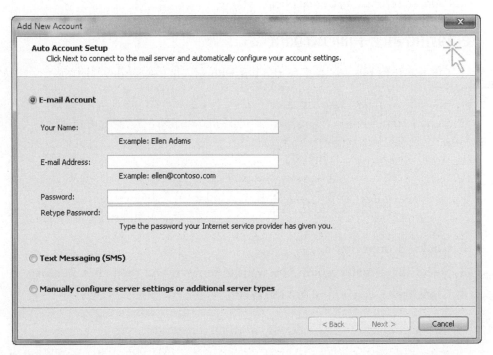

FIGURE 13-1: The Add New Account dialog box is where you begin the e-mail configuration process.

NOTE *If your e-mail address is with hotmail.com or msn.com, you need to use the Microsoft Outlook Connector for Windows Live Hotmail to add the account. For additional information, search on "Hotmail" in Outlook Help. In addition, if your computer is connected to a Microsoft Exchange network domain, your e-mail address is entered automatically and the password field does not appear because Outlook will use your network password.*

3. Click Next. The setup process can take a few minutes. In the meantime, a progress indicator will appear during configuration.

4. If everything goes well, the account will be set up and you can click Finish to close the Auto Account Setup dialog box and then exit and restart Outlook.

TIP *If the first attempt to configure an account fails, you will be prompted to try a second time using an unencrypted connection to the mail server. If prompted to do so, click Next to continue. If the second attempt also fails, you will have to configure your server settings manually. For additional information, search on "advanced settings" in Outlook Help.*

Removing an E-mail Account

1. On the Info tab, located on the File ribbon, click Account Settings.

2. Click Account Settings.

3. Select the e-mail account you want to remove, and then click Remove.

4. Click Yes to confirm or No to cancel.

Modifying E-mail Account Settings

There are numerous reasons why you may need to make changes to an existing e-mail account: if your ISP password changes, if your mail server or the security settings change, or if you just want to customize certain settings, such as how your name displays to others. The type of account you have dictates the type of changes you can make. For example, if you are using an Exchange account, only the server administrator would be able to change how your name displays to others.

1. On the File ribbon, click the Info tab.

2. Click Account Settings.

3. Select the e-mail account to modify, and then click Change. The Change Account dialog box opens.

4. Make changes as necessary, keeping the following in mind:

   - Click Test Account Settings to send a test e-mail to your account.

   - Click More Settings to open the Internet E-mail Settings dialog box, where you can modify advanced settings, such as specifying port numbers, server message copy setting, return e-mail address, outgoing server information, and connection details.

   - Click Next to continue (if Test Account Settings By Clicking The Next button is selected, clicking Next will also send a test e-mail to your account).

5. Click Close if you are in the Test Account Settings dialog box, or click Finish if you are in the Change Account dialog box.

Understanding the Outlook Profile

The first time you run Outlook, a profile named "Outlook" is automatically created. This profile contains e-mail configuration information, data files (.pst), and information about where e-mail messages are saved. As you add or change e-mail addresses or include additional Outlook data files, the profile is updated.

Outlook profiles are stored in the Windows registry and contain account information, such as user name, display name, e-mail server name, Internet service provider (ISP), and account password. The profile also contains details on where e-mail is delivered and saved. Typically, data is delivered and saved either on the e-mail server or in the Outlook data file (.pst) on your computer.

(Note that some accounts, such as Microsoft Exchange Server accounts, might use an offline Outlook data file (.ost). This data includes rules, messages, contacts, calendars, notes, tasks, journals, search folders, and other settings.)

Most people need only a single profile, but it is possible to create multiple profiles on the same computer—for example, if you share a computer with others, or if you want to have one profile for work and another for personal use.

Modifying a Profile

1. Exit Outlook.

2. Click the Start button, and choose Control Panel.

3. In the Control Panel menu, click Mail. The Mail Setup dialog box (pictured in the following illustration) opens.

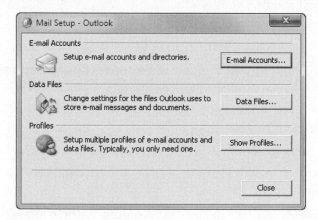

4. Do one or more of the following as needed:

   • To add, repair, change, or move an e-mail account, click E-mail Accounts.

   • To add or modify Outlook data storage options, click Data Files.

   • To view, add, delete, or modify profiles, click Show Profiles.

5. Click Close.

Outlook E-mail Primer

Outlook offers a powerful set of tools for you to create, work with, and organize your e-mail. The E-mail window (pictured in Figure 13-2) lets you view and navigate the e-mail Inbox and other folders. If the Reading pane is displayed,

Home ribbon

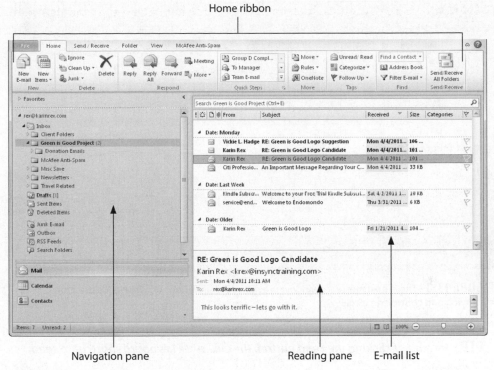

FIGURE 13-2 • The Mail View window gives you total control over all e-mail functions.

you can read e-mail in this view as well. The Home ribbon lets you work with e-mail, including creating a new e-mail, replying or forwarding an e-mail, deleting e-mail and more. The Send/Receive, Folder, and View ribbons offer additional e-mail options.

Writing and Sending an E-mail

1. In Outlook E-mail view, click New E-mail on the Home ribbon. A new, blank e-mail message (pictured in Figure 13-3) opens.

2. Type an e-mail address in the To field. If you have multiple addresses, separate each address with a semicolon (;). To send a copy of the e-mail to another recipient, type the address in the Cc field.

3. Type a meaningful yet succinct title for the e-mail in the Subject field.

4. Type your message in the e-mail message area below the headings.

5. Click Send.

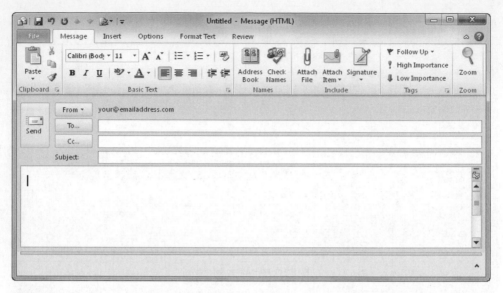

FIGURE 13-3 • The e-mail message window provides several ribbons of commands used for modifying and controlling e-mail.

TIP   *Instead of clicking the Send button, the* CTRL-ENTER *keyboard shortcut to send an e-mail.*

Formatting an E-mail

E-mail formatting options are available in both the Basic Text group of the Message ribbon (see Figure 13-4), as well as on the Format Text ribbon (pictured in Figure 13-5). The Basic Text group on the Message ribbon provides

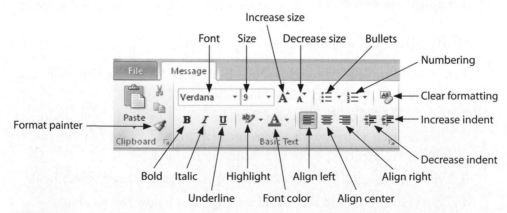

FIGURE 13-4 • The Basic Text Group on the Message Ribbon contains commands for formatting e-mail text.

FIGURE 13-5 • The Format Text Ribbon provides tools for working with text and paragraphs as well as the Clipboard.

fewer formatting options than the Format Text ribbon. The Format Text ribbon provides the same rich set of formatting options as the Microsoft Word Home ribbon, including bullets, numbering, and styles.

Changing Font, Size, Style, and Color

As you may recall from Chapter 3, a font can be loosely defined as a complete character set (a–z, plus numbers and symbols) of a particular typeface, such as Arial or Times Roman. The creative use of fonts, along with size, style, and color choices, can add personality to an e-mail message and enhance readability when used properly.

1. Select the text you wish to format.
2. View the Message ribbon or the Format Text ribbon.
3. Format the text, keeping the following in mind:
   - Choose a font from the Font drop-down list.
   - Choose a size from the Size drop-down list, type a size in the Size field, or use the Increase Size and Decrease Size buttons to change the font size.
   - Choose bold, italic, or underline by clicking the Bold, Italic, or Underline button, respectively (note that additional styles are available on the Format Text ribbon).
   - Choose a highlight color from the Highlight button menu.
   - To clear all formatting, click the Clear Formatting button.

TIP   *If you enjoy using keyboard shortcuts, you can format text using the keyboard instead of the buttons on the Message ribbon. To increase the size of selected text, use the CTRL-SHIFT-> keyboard shortcut. To decrease the size of selected text, use the CTRL-SHIFT-< keyboard shortcut. Keyboard shortcuts can also be used to modify the style of selected text. Press CTRL-B to make text bold, CTRL-I to make it italic, and CTRL-U to add an underline.*

Using Styles

1. Select the text you wish to format.
2. View the Format Text ribbon.
3. Choose a style from the Styles gallery.

Aligning and Indenting Text

1. Select the text you wish to format.
2. View the Message ribbon or the Format Text ribbon.
3. Format the text, keeping the following in mind:
   - Use the Align Left, Align Center, or Align Right buttons to align paragraphs of text within the e-mail message window.
   - Use the Increase Indent button to move text closer to the right side of the e-mail message window.
   - Use the Decrease Indent button to move text closer to the left side of the e-mail message window.

Adding Bullets and Numbering

1. Select the text you wish to format.
2. View the Format Text ribbon.
3. Format the text, keeping the following in mind:
   - Use the Bullets button to add bullets to the selected text.
   - Use the Numbering button to number the selected paragraphs.

Attaching a File to an E-mail

1. With the e-mail message open, click the Message ribbon.
2. In the Include Group (pictured here), click Attach File.

3. In the Insert File dialog box, navigate to the folder containing the file you wish to attach, and select it.

4. Click Insert. Inserted documents appear in the Attached field of the e-mail (pictured here).

5. To insert additional files, repeat steps 2 through 4.

6. Click Send.

TIP *You can drag a file into an open e-mail document to attach it. This requires that you have both the e-mail message window and the document folder window visible on screen (as pictured here). Click and drag the file you wish to attach to the e-mail directly into the body of the e-mail, and release.*

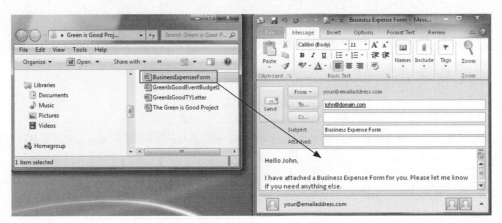

Reading and Replying to an E-mail

New, unread messages in the E-mail List (pictured in Figure 13-2) appear in bold text. By contrast, read messages are in plain text. To open a message in its own window, double-click it. Opening a message will mark it as having been read.

Using the Reading Pane

The Reading pane (pictured here) lets you preview a message just by clicking it. The Reading pane can be resized by positioning the mouse pointer on the line separating the E-mail List and the Reading pane and then clicking and dragging (the mouse pointer looks like a double-headed arrow when you are in the right place).

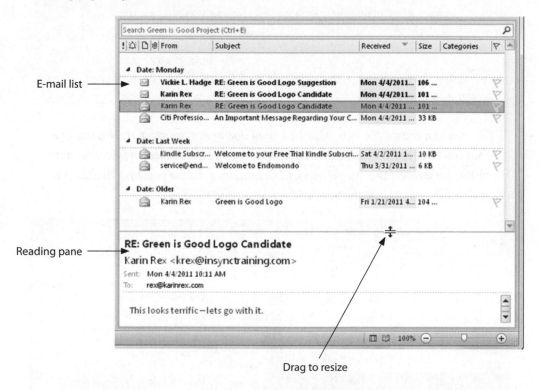

The Reading pane can be toggled on or off or repositioned on the View ribbon. In the Layout group, click Reading Pane, and then click Right to position the pane on the right side of the window, Bottom to position the pane at the bottom of the window, or Off to hide the pane completely.

If active, the Reading pane (pictured in Figure 13-2) displays the selected e-mail message's content. That message will be marked as having been read when you select a different e-mail message to read.

TIP   *You can control when a message is marked as having been read when viewed in the Reading pane. On the File ribbon, click Options and then click Mail. Scroll down and click the Reading pane button. In the Reading Pane dialog box (pictured here), use the available options to set your preferences. For example, if you want Outlook to wait 45 seconds before marking a message as having been read, select the Mark items As Read When Viewed In The Reading Pane check box, and then type **45** in the Wait field. Click OK to close the dialog box and save your settings.*

Replying to an E-mail

To reply to an e-mail, use either the Reply or Reply All buttons in the Respond group (pictured here). The Respond Group appears on both the Home ribbon (so you can reply to messages while reading them in the Reading pane) and the Message ribbon (so you can reply to a message when reading it in a separate window).

1. Open the e-mail message in a separate window or select it in the E-mail List.
2. Click the Reply button to reply to the person who sent the e-mail. Click Reply All if you also want to reply to everybody else who received the e-mail. An e-mail message window will open with the To and Subject fields already completed for you.
3. Type any additional e-mail addresses in the To field, separating each address with a semicolon. To send a copy of the e-mail to another recipient, type the address in the Cc field.
4. Type a reply in the e-mail message area below the headings.
5. Click Send.

Viewing and Downloading an E-mail Attachment

E-mails containing attachments display a small paper clip icon in the Attachments column of the E-mail List (pictured here).

Attachments

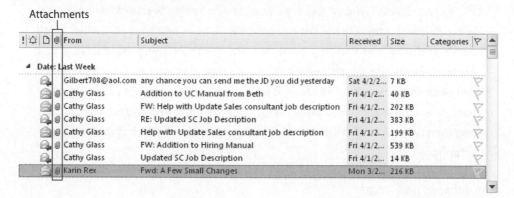

1. Open the e-mail message in a separate window or select it in the E-mail List. The attachment(s) will appear just under the message heading.

2. Do one of the following:

   • To preview an attached document in the e-mail window, click it. (Not all attachments can be previewed before downloading.)

   • To open an attached document, double-click it (you will be prompted to either open or save the document).

   • To download a single attachment, right-click it and choose Save As. In the Save As dialog box, navigate to the folder where you would like the downloaded file to be stored, and then click Save.

   • To download multiple attachments, right-click one of them and choose Save All Attachments. In the Save All Attachments dialog box, select all of the attachments you want to download. In the Save As dialog box, navigate to the appropriate folder, and then click Save.

Forwarding an E-mail

Forwarding an e-mail means you are sending an existing e-mail to another person. When you forward an e-mail, both the text of the e-mail and any attachments are included.

1. Open the e-mail message in a separate window or select it in the E-mail List.

2. In the Respond group, click the Forward button. A new e-mail window will open, containing a copy of the e-mail.

3. Type an e-mail address in the To field. If you have multiple addresses, separate each address with a semicolon. To send a copy of the e-mail to another recipient, type the address in the Cc field.

4. Modify the Subject line if needed.

5. Add a message in the message area, if needed.

6. Click Send.

Deleting an E-mail

1. Select one or more messages in the E-mail List.

2. Do one of the following:

   • Click the Delete button (the red X).

   • Press the DELETE key on the keyboard.

   • Right-click a selected e-mail, and choose delete from the menu.

TIP *Accidentally deleted an e-mail? Use the CTRL-Z keyboard shortcut to undo the deletion.*

Working with an E-mail Signature

An e-mail signature is a snippet of information that can be automatically or manually inserted at the bottom of an e-mail. Typically, a signature contains your name, title, company name, and contact information. In Outlook, a signature can also include links and graphics. Two examples are shown here.

Karin Rex
215-393-7640
rex@karinrex.com
WRITER | DEVELOPER | TRAINER | GEEK!
Owner, Geeky Girl, LLC
www.geekygirlonline.com

Jennifer Hofmann
InSync Training, LLC
(O) 203-468-8322
(F) 775-522-2740
jennifer@insynctraining.com
New York Time Zone

Click Here to Follow Us!

twitter

Synchronous
Learning
Expert

You may create as many e-mail signatures as needed. For example, you might have one signature for work, another for personal use, and another for school.

Creating an E-mail Signature

1. In Outlook, create a new e-mail message.

2. In the Include group on the Message ribbon, click Signature and then choose Signatures from the menu. The Signatures And Stationery dialog box opens (pictured in Figure 13-6).

3. Click New. The New Signature dialog box opens.

4. Type a name for your signature in the field provided, and then click OK.

5. In the large field at the bottom of the dialog box, type and format your signature. (You can always adjust it later if necessary.) Keep in mind the following:

   • Use the buttons above the signature field to format text as bold, italic, or underline, to choose a font and size, and to align text in the signature.

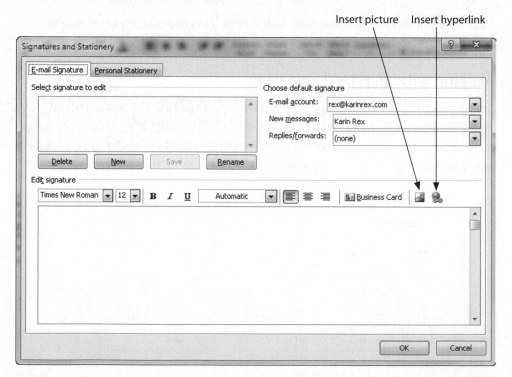

FIGURE 13-6 · Signatures are a great way to personalize your e-mails and provide additional contact information.

- Use the Insert Picture button to add a graphic to the signature.
- Use the Insert Hyperlink button to add a link to the signature.

6. If you have more than one e-mail account, choose which e-mail account you want to use this signature with from the E-mail Account drop-down list.

7. If you have created more than one signature, choose the signature you want automatically inserted into all new e-mails from the New Messages drop-down list. To insert signatures manually, choose None.

8. To include a signature in your replies and forwarded messages, choose a signature from the Replies (Forwards) drop-down menu.

9. Click OK.

TIP *The signature you just created won't automatically appear in the currently open e-mail message. You will have to insert the signature manually (or close the message if it is blank and create another new e-mail).*

Manually Inserting an E-mail Signature

If you did not choose a signature in the New Message drop-down list in the Signatures And Stationery dialog box, you will have to manually insert a signature into an e-mail.

1. Create or open the e-mail message where you want the signature.

2. In the Include group on the Message ribbon, click Signature. The Signature button menu appears, listing all of your signatures (an example is pictured here).

TIP *To remove a signature from an e-mail message, select the signature in the message body, and then press the DELETE or BACKSPACE key.*

Working in the Outlook Inbox and E-mail View

In Outlook's Mail view (pictured in Figure 13-7), folders (such as the Inbox, Sent Items, and Deleted Items folders, as well as any custom folders you create) are shown on the left side of the window in the navigation pane. E-mail in the currently selected folder is listed in the center of the window (in the E-mail List). The currently highlighted e-mail message is displayed in the Reading pane under the list of e-mails. The To-Do bar is shown on the right side of the window.

The E-mail View window is customizable, so your window may look different from Figure 13-7. The View ribbon (pictured here) lets you personalize E-mail view to suit your needs.

Modifying Outlook Mail View

1. In Outlook Mail view, click the View menu.

2. Modify Mail view, keeping the following in mind:

   • Select the Show As Conversations check box to display e-mail messages as threaded conversations (similar to how some discussion boards work). This keeps e-mails with the same subject line grouped together.

   • Use the Arrange By options to sort e-mail in different ways, for example, by name, date, or file size (note that you can also sort items in the E-mail List by clicking a column heading).

   • Click Reverse Sort to change the direction of a sort, for example, from Z–A instead of from A–Z or from oldest to newest instead of newest to oldest.

   • Control the layout of the window by using the navigation pane, Reading pane, and To-Do bar button menus (the People pane button is covered later in this chapter).

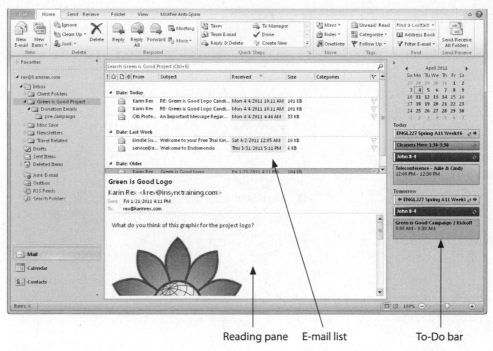

Reading pane   E-mail list   To-Do bar

FIGURE 13-7 • Outlook's Mail view lets you navigate through and read mail messages.

Outlook Folders

Outlook supplies several organizational folders for you by default:

- **Inbox**   Used for incoming e-mail
- **Drafts**   Used for e-mail you've started to create but have not yet sent
- **Sent Items**   Used for mail you have sent to others
- **Deleted Items**   Used for e-mail you have deleted from the E-mail List
- **Outbox**   Used to hold e-mail that is in the process of being sent

(Note that three additional default folders—Junk E-mail, RSS Feeds, and Search Folders—are not covered here. You can learn more about these folders by searching for them in Outlook Help.)

You may create additional folders and subfolders to further organize e-mail. For example, you can create folders for special projects or for specific people.

You can also rename or delete folders (with the exception of the default folders listed earlier), or copy or move folders. All of these options are available in the context menu (pictured here) when you right-click a folder in the navigation pane.

Creating a New Folder

1. Right-click anywhere in the navigation pane.
2. Choose New Folder from the menu. The Create New Folder dialog box opens.
3. Type a name for the new folder in the Name field.
4. Select a location for the new folder from the list at the bottom of the dialog box. (Typically, new folders are stored within the Inbox.) To expand a folder in the list, click the triangle icon next to the folder name.
5. Click OK.

Moving E-mail into a Folder

There are several ways to move e-mail from one folder to another:

- Drag one or more messages from the E-mail List into any of the folders listed in the navigation pane (use the CTRL key to select multiple messages).
- Right-click a message in the E-mail List, choose Move, and then select a folder from the list.

- Select one or more messages in the E-mail List. In the Move group on the Home ribbon, choose Move and then select a folder from the list.

- Select one or more messages in the E-mail List, and use the CTRL-X keyboard shortcut (Cut). Then select the folder where you want the e-mail(s) moved to and use the CTRL-V keyboard shortcut (Paste).

Working in the Deleted Items Folder

The Deleted Items folder is a temporary holding place for mail you have deleted. All deleted e-mail stays in this folder until you permanently empty it. This means that if you accidentally deleted an item, it is possible to restore it as long as you have not yet emptied the Deleted Items folder.

Restoring a Deleted Item

1. Click the Deleted Items folder in the navigation pane. The folder contents will be displayed in the E-mail List.

2. Click and drag the message(s) you wish to restore out of the Deleted Items folder and into any other folder (such as Inbox).

Permanently Emptying the Deleted Items Folder

1. Right-click the Deleted Items folder in the navigation pane.

2. Choose Empty Folder from the menu. You will be prompted to confirm the deletion.

3. Confirm the deletion by clicking Yes. Cancel the deletion by clicking No.

TIP *Are you the neat and tidy type? You can choose to have the Deleted Items folder emptied whenever you exit Outlook. On the File ribbon, click Options and then click Advanced. Under the Outlook Start And Exit heading, select the Empty Deleted Items Folder When Exiting Outlook check box, and then click OK. When you exit Outlook, you will be asked if you want to empty the Deleted Items folder.*

Using the Outlook Social Connector

The Outlook Social Connector lets you connect to your business and personal social networks, such as LinkedIn, Facebook, MySpace, SharePoint, or Windows

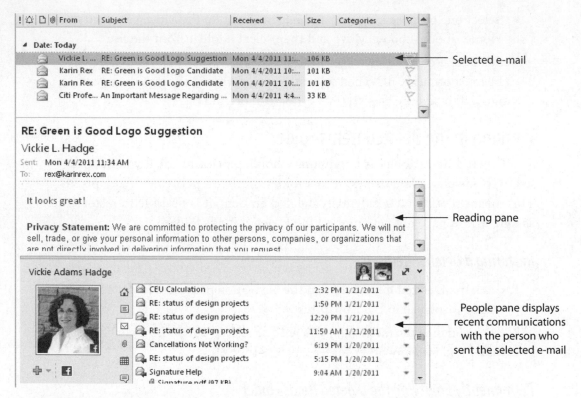

FIGURE 13-8 · The People Pane appears under the message list and/or Reading pane (if showing).

Live Messenger. If active, this information displays in a separate Outlook pane called the People pane (pictured in Figure 13-8 under the Reading pane). As you will learn, the People pane can be turned on and off via Outlook's View ribbon.

Exploring the People Pane

The Outlook Social Connector displays in the People pane, which is positioned just underneath the Reading pane (see Figure 13-9). The People pane is not only useful for keeping up with your social networks (it can display a contact's latest status update, for example), but it is also quite useful for centralizing all of your communications by person.

When an e-mail is selected, the People pane will display a list of recent communication between you and the person who sent the selected e-mail, including

Collapse/expand
People pane

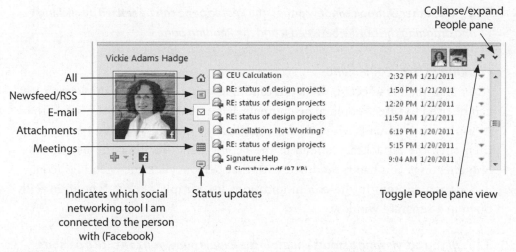

All

Newsfeed/RSS

E-mail

Attachments

Meetings

Indicates which social
networking tool I am
connected to the person
with (Facebook)

Status updates

Toggle People pane view

FIGURE 13-9 · The People Pane gives you a sneak peek at your social connections.

other e-mails, meetings, attachments, and social network updates. You can filter the list to view only what you want to see by using the icons on the left side. Clicking an item in the list opens the communication in a separate window.

Hiding and Showing the People Pane

1. Click the View ribbon.
2. Click the People pane button menu.

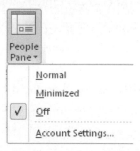

3. Do one of the following:
   - Click Normal to view the People pane.
   - Click Minimized to make the People pane as small as possible but still visible.
   - Click Off to hide the People pane.

TIP *Like other Outlook window panes, the People pane can be resized by clicking and dragging the border between it and the Reading pane.*

Working in the People Pane

After an e-mail is selected, the icons on the left side of the communication list can be used to filter People pane contents. For example, to filter the list so that it displays only e-mails with attachments, click an e-mail from that person, and then click the Attachments icon in the People pane. To filter the list to view only meetings you have scheduled with that person, click the Meetings icon.

To open an item in the communications list, simply click it. The item will open in a separate window.

TIP *If you are viewing a status update in the People pane, you can click a person's name to launch the social network in a new browser window.*

Still Struggling

Can't find Outlook Social Connector? If the Social Connector add-in was dese-lected during installation of Office 2010, then you will have to install it.

1. In the Windows Control Panel, click Program And Features.

2. In the Programs And Features dialog box, select Microsoft Office 2010.

3. At the top of the dialog box, click Change. The Microsoft Office 2010 Setup dialog box opens.

4. Click Add Or Remove Features, and then click Continue.

5. In the Installation Options list, click the plus sign next to Microsoft Outlook.

6. Click the plus sign next to Outlook Add-In.

7. Click the Outlook Social Connector down arrow, and choose Run From My Computer.

8. Click Continue.

9. Finish the Microsoft Office 2010 configuration process, and then exit and restart Outlook.

Connecting to a Social Network

Outlook supports several of the most popular social networks: Facebook, LinkedIn, MySpace, and Windows Live Messenger. A separate add-in program, available free from Microsoft, must be installed for each network.

TIP   *If your organization uses Microsoft SharePoint 2010, Outlook Social Connector can connect with your organization's SharePoint sites so you can see your colleagues' activity items.*

1. Click the View ribbon.
2. Click the People Pane button menu, and choose Account Settings.

3. Click the View Social Providers Available Online link near the top of the dialog box. A list of social network providers displays.
4. Click the social network that you want to add, and follow the on-screen instructions. This may include any or all of the following:
   - Downloading and installing software
   - Agreeing to a user license agreement
   - Selecting a folder location for installation
   - Exiting and restarting Outlook multiple times

- Using a Microsoft Outlook Social Connector Provider Wizard (pictured here)

After network providers are installed, a list of available social network accounts appears.

5. In the network list, select the check box next to each network to which you wish to connect.

6. Type your user name and password for each network, and then click Connect. After you have connected the Outlook Social Connector to a social network, the People pane will display social network information (such as status updates) about an e-mail sender if they belong to the same network as you.

Still Struggling

Remember to refer back to Chapter 2 for common program functionality, such as Backstage View (document properties and permissions, opening existing files, and saving files); using undo and redo; working with the Office Clipboard (cut, copy, and paste); working with themes; and getting help.

Summary

This chapter got you started with Outlook E-mail. You learned how to set up an e-mail account and how to send, format, read, reply, and forward mail. You also learned how to attach a file to an e-mail, create an e-mail signature, and organize your Outlook Inbox. Finally, you were introduced to the Outlook Social Connector. In Chapter 14 you will learn about Outlook Calendar, Contacts, and Tasks functionality.

QUIZ

1. True or False: To send and receive e-mail messages in Outlook, you must add and configure an e-mail account.
   A. True
   B. False

2. When connecting to a social network using Outlook Social Connector, which of the following might you have to do?
   A. Download and install software
   B. Agree to a user license agreement
   C. Select a folder location for installation
   D. Exit and restart Outlook multiple times
   E. All of the above

3. E-mail formatting options are available in the _____ group of the _____ ribbon. (Fill in the blanks using the following choices.)
   A. Home
   B. Message
   C. Quick Steps
   D. Basic Text
   E. View

4. Which Outlook ribbon provides tools for formatting an e-mail message? (Choose all that apply.)
   A. Home
   B. Message
   C. View
   D. Insert
   E. Format Text

5. True or False: If you choose a signature in the New Message drop-down list in the Signatures And Stationery dialog box, you will have to manually insert a signature into an e-mail.
   A. True
   B. False

6. Which of the following methods can be used to move an e-mail message into a folder?
   A. Drag a message into a folder
   B. Right-click a message and use the Move command
   C. Use the Move command on the Home ribbon
   D. Use copy and paste keyboard shortcuts
   E. All of the above

7. **True or False: New unread messages in the E-mail List appear in bold text. By contrast, read messages are in plain text.**
   A. True
   B. False

8. **To reply to an e-mail, you will use either the _____ or _____ button in the _____ group. (Fill in the blanks using the following choices.)**
   A. Reply All
   B. Move
   C. Respond
   D. Editing
   E. Reply

9. **Match each Outlook folder (lettered) with its correct content description (numbered).**

A. Inbox	1. Used for e-mail you have deleted from the E-mail List
B. Drafts	2. Used for e-mail you have sent to others
C. Sent Items	3. Used for e-mail you've started to create but have not yet sent
D. Deleted Items	4. Used for incoming e-mail
E. Outbox	5. Used to hold e-mail that is in the process of being sent

10. **True or False: You may create only one e-mail signature.**
    A. True
    B. False

chapter 14

Working with Outlook Calendar, Contacts, and Tasks

As you learned in Chapter 1, Outlook is a full-featured personal information management (PIM) program that provides you with e-mail, scheduling (Calendar), contact management (Address Book), and task-tracking capabilities. This chapter gets you started using Outlook Calendar, Contacts, and Tasks. You will learn how to create and work with new appointments, contacts, and tasks, including viewing and printing options.

CHAPTER OBJECTIVES

In this chapter, you will learn how to

- Create, modify, and delete calendar appointments
- View and print your calendar
- Create, modify, and delete contacts
- View and print your contacts
- Create, modify, and delete tasks
- View and print tasks

Working with the Outlook Calendar

Calendar is the datebook and scheduling component of Outlook 2010 and is fully integrated with e-mail, contacts, and tasks. Calendar features are rich and varied. This chapter only covers the most frequently used calendar features. Be sure to explore the many articles and videos on the topic in the Help file.

To access Calendar view, click Calendar in the bottom of the Outlook Navigation pane (pictured here).

Creating a New Appointment

1. In Calendar view, click New Appointment. The Appointment dialog box opens (pictured in Figure 14-1).

2. In the Subject field, type a meaningful name for the appointment.

3. In the Location field, type a location for the appointment, if necessary.

4. Modify the start time and end time for the meeting, or select the All Day Event check box if the event takes place all day.

5. In the meeting notes area, type any additional information for the meeting. For example, you might copy and paste directions to the meeting place, or a reminder to bring a document to the meeting.

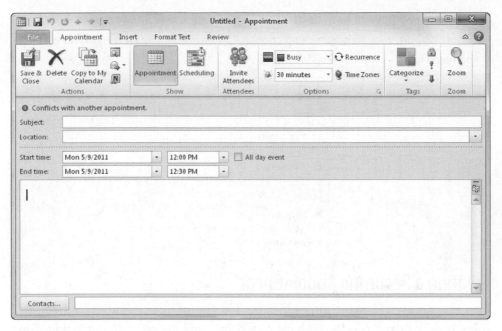

FIGURE 14-1 · The Appointment dialog box is where you will specify details for a new meeting or engagement.

6. To be reminded ahead of time for a meeting, choose the desired reminder time from the Reminder drop-down menu in the Options group on the Appointment ribbon. (The default reminder time is 30 minutes.)

7. Use the Show As dropdown menu in the Options group to choose how the appointment timeslot should appear in your calendar (Free, Tentative, Busy, or Out Of Office). (The default is Busy.)

8. To invite somebody else to the appointment, click the Invite Attendees button on the Appointment ribbon and add an e-mail address to the To field. (This field only appears if you click the Invite Attendees button.)

9. Click Save & Close to save and close the Appointment dialog box.

TIP   *You don't have to be in Calendar view to create a new appointment. On the Home ribbon, click New Items and choose Appointment. The New Items menu is pictured here.*

Creating a Recurring Appointment

You can create recurring appointments for any of your regularly scheduled meetings. For example, if you have a staff meeting every Friday morning, you can create a recurring appointment for that event, which will place it on your calendar for however many weeks you specify.

1. In Calendar view, click New Appointment and complete all of the necessary appointment fields as outlined previously.

2. Click the Recurrence button to open the Appointment Recurrence dialog box (pictured here).

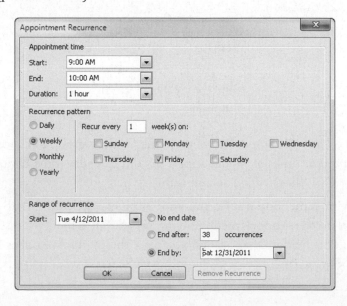

3. Under the Recurrence Pattern heading, select the desired pattern for the recurring appointment (Daily, Weekly, Monthly, or Yearly), and specify the recurrence rate and day.

4. Under the Range Of Recurrence heading, choose the start date for the recurring appointment and then designate an end date, keeping the following in mind:

   • To have the recurring appointment never end, click the No End Date option.

   • To indicate a specific number of occurrences, click the End After option and type a number in the Occurrence field.

   • To specify a specific date for the recurring appointments to end by, type a date in the Date field.

5. Click OK to close the Appointment Recurrence dialog box.

6. Click Save & Close to save and close the Appointment dialog box.

Modifying an Appointment

In Calendar view, the Appointment ribbon (pictured here) offers controls for working with appointments.

1. In Calendar view, click the appointment you want to modify.

2. On the Appointment ribbon, click Open. If the appointment is recurring, a menu (pictured here) will prompt you to open the single occurrence of the appointment (which would allow you to modify only that occurrence) or to open the series (which would allow you to modify all of the recurring appointments). If the appointment is not recurring, the Appointment dialog box will open as soon as you click Open.

3. Modify each of the necessary appointment fields as outlined previously.

4. Use options on the Appointment ribbon to designate the appointment as Private, High Importance, or Low Importance if desired.

5. Click Save & Close to save and close the Appointment dialog box.

TIP   *To quickly open an appointment, double-click it and choose an option from the Open Recurring Item dialog box (pictured here).*

Deleting an Appointment

1. In Calendar view, click the appointment you want to delete.

2. On the Appointment ribbon, click Delete. If the appointment is recurring, a menu (pictured to the right) will prompt you to delete the single occurrence of the appointment or the series. If the appointment is not recurring, the appointment will be deleted as soon as you click Delete.

TIP   *To quickly delete an appointment, right-click it and choose Delete from the menu (pictured here). If the appointment is recurring, a menu will prompt you to delete the single occurrence of the appointment or the series.*

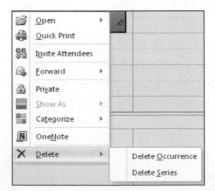

Exploring Calendar Views

In Calendar view, the View ribbon (pictured here) offers options for viewing a calendar.

Modify Calendar view options on the View ribbon as follows:

- In the Current View group, advanced options for customizing calendar views are available by using the Change View and View Settings buttons. Read more about these options in the Help file by searching on "custom views." The Reset View button resets the current view to the default setting.

- In the Arrangement group, use the Day, Work Week, Week, and Month buttons to view specific calendar timeframes. The Month button menu will let you decide the level of detail you want the month view to display: low, medium, or high. To see multiple calendars side by side horizontally, use Schedule view. (Note that these options are also available on the Home ribbon.) Use the Time Scale button menu to increase or decrease the calendar time grid intervals (the default is 30 minutes).

- In the Color group, click the Color button to choose a background color for your calendar.

- In the Layout group, use the Daily Task list, Navigation pane, Reading pane, and To-Do bar buttons to determine how—or if—these panes appear on screen.

- In the People Pane group, use the People Pane button to determine how—or if—the People pane appears on screen.

- From the Windows button menu, use the Reminders window button to open the Reminders window. Use the Open In New Window button to open an item in a new window. Use the Close All Items button to close all open items.

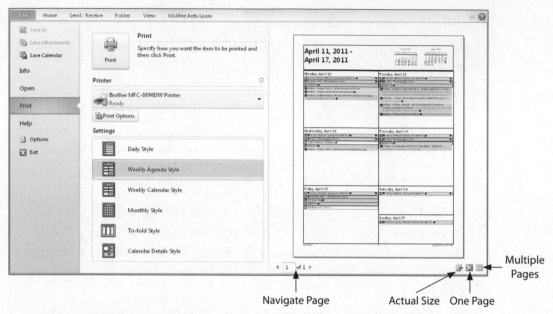

FIGURE 14-2 · For a hardcopy version of your calendar, use the options on the Print tab.

Printing a Calendar

The Print tab of the File ribbon (pictured in Figure 14-2) offers numerous options for printing a hardcopy of a calendar.

Outlook defaults to printing the current day, week, or calendar month. To print a specific range of dates, click the Print Options button to open the Print dialog box where you can specify a date range.

1. On the File ribbon, click Print.

2. Under Settings, choose a style (Daily, Weekly, etc.). The style will be previewed on the right side of the window. Navigate the preview using the Navigate Pages, Actual Size, One Page, and Multiple Page buttons.

3. To set additional options, including page range, specific date range, page setup options, and styles, click Print Options to open the Print dialog box (pictured in the following illustration).

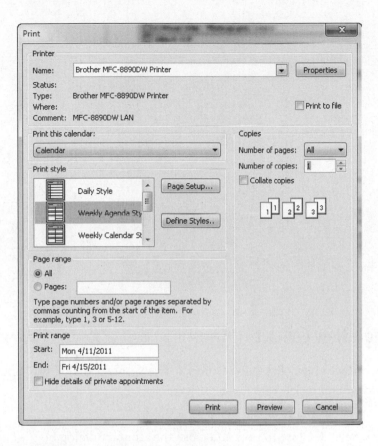

4. Click Preview to preview the calendar.

5. Click Print to print the calendar.

TIP   *Use the CONTROL-P keyboard shortcut to quickly open the Print window.*

Working with Outlook Contacts

Contacts is the address book component of Outlook 2010 and is fully integrated with all other Outlook features. To access Contacts view, click Contacts in the bottom of the Outlook navigation pane (pictured in the following illustration).

Creating a New Contact

1. In Contact view, click New Contact. The Contact dialog box opens (pictured in Figure 14-3).

2. Complete as many of the fields as desired.

3. Click Save & Close to save and close the Contact dialog box.

TIP   *You don't have to be in Contact view to create a new contact. On the Home ribbon, click New Items and choose Contact. The New Items menu is pictured here.*

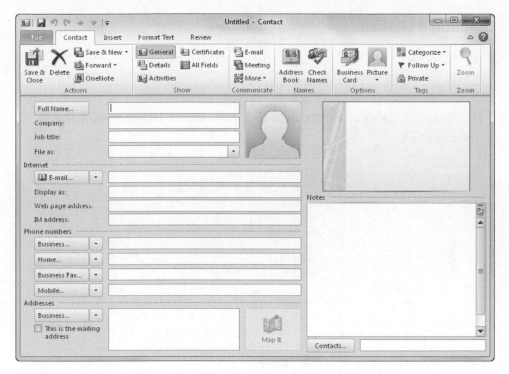

FIGURE 14-3 • The New Contact dialog box lets you add details to a contact.

Modifying a Contact

In Contacts view, the Contact ribbon (pictured here) offers a variety of controls for working with contacts.

1. In Contact view, double-click the contact you want to modify.

2. Modify each of the contact fields as necessary.

3. Use options on the Contact ribbon to designate the contact as private, if desired (located on the Tags group).

4. Click Save & Close to save and close the Contact dialog box.

Deleting a Contact

1. In Contact view, click the contact you want to delete.

2. On the Contact ribbon, click Delete.

TIP   *To quickly delete a contact, right-click it and choose Delete from the menu (pictured here).*

Working with Suggested Contacts

The Suggested Contacts feature in Outlook 2010 provides a quick and easy way to add contacts to a contacts list. In Contact view, the Navigation pane (pictured in Figure 14-4) displays a folder called Suggested Contacts. This folder contains a searchable list of recently used e-mail addresses that are not currently in your Contacts folder. This can include e-mail addresses for those you have either sent mail to or received mail from.

TIP   *If you have more than one Outlook e-mail address there will be a separate Suggested Contacts folder for each address.*

Suggested Contacts folder(s) (one for each e-mail address)   Search field

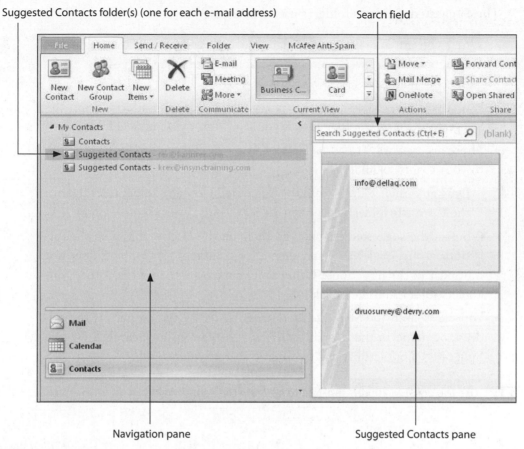

Navigation pane   Suggested Contacts pane

FIGURE 14-4 • Outlook suggests contacts to add to your contact list.

Still Struggling

Wondering what the difference is between Suggested Contacts and AutoComplete? Suggested Contacts can be searched; AutoComplete entries cannot be searched. AutoComplete has a maximum of 1,000 entries; Suggested Contacts has no such limit.

The Suggested Contacts folder is useful in several ways:

- When you are addressing an e-mail, Outlook will look in the Suggested Contacts folder as well as your Contacts folder when suggesting Auto-Complete names.

- When you are addressing an e-mail, you can select an address from the Suggested Contacts folder, just as you can from the Contacts folder.

- There are two ways to add a contact from the Suggested Contacts folder to your Contacts folder:

  - Drag an e-mail address from the Suggested Contacts folder directly into the Contacts folder.

  - Select the suggested contact and then, on the Home ribbon, in the Actions group, click Move and then click Contacts. (If Contacts does not appear in the list, choose Other Folder, navigate to and select the Contacts folder, and then click OK.)

- You can search the Suggested Contacts folder by typing part of the address or name in the Search field. As you type in the Search field, the Suggested Contacts list will be filtered to suit your search.

TIP   *Use the CTRL-E keyboard shortcut to activate the Search field.*

Still Struggling

The Suggested Contacts feature is active by default in Outlook 2010. However, if you synchronize contacts with other devices, some synchronization programs may attempt to synchronize the Suggested Contacts list, which could be quite large. First, check your synchronization program documentation to learn how you might prevent a folder from synchronizing. If you cannot do this in your synchronization program, exclude the Suggested Contacts folder as part of the Outlook Address Book instead:

1. In Contacts view, click the Suggested Contacts folder.
2. On the Folder ribbon, in the Properties group, click Folder Properties.

Still Struggling (continued)

3. Click the Outlook Address Book tab (pictured here).

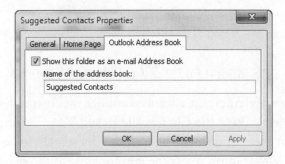

4. Clear the Show This Folder As An Email Address Book check box.

Alternatively, you could turn off the Suggested Contacts Feature completely.

1. On the File ribbon, click Options and then click Contacts.
2. Under the Suggested Contacts heading, clear the Automatically Create Outlook Contacts For Recipients That Do Not Belong To An Outlook Address Book check box (pictured here).

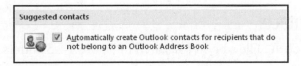

Deleting Suggested Contacts

- To delete a single suggested contact, click it and then click the Delete button on the Home ribbon.
- To delete all suggested contacts, use the CTRL-A keyboard shortcut to select all of the suggested contacts, and then click the Delete button on the Home ribbon.

Exploring Contact Views

In Contact view, the View ribbon (pictured here) offers options for viewing your contacts.

Modify contact view options on the View ribbon as follows:

- In the Current View group, advanced options for customizing contact views are available by using the Change Views and View Settings buttons. Read more about these options in the Help file by searching on "custom views." The Reset View button resets the current view to the default setting.

- In the Arrangement group, use the Categories, Company, and Location buttons to sort a contact list by those fields. (You can also sort the contact list by clicking a column heading.) Use the Reverse Sort button to change the order of the sort (from A through Z to Z through A, for example). To add category columns to your contact list, use the Add Columns button. If you are viewing contacts in groups, use the Expand/Collapse button to expand or collapse groups.

Printing Contacts

The Print tab of the File ribbon (pictured in Figure 14-5) offers numerous options for printing one or more contacts.

1. On the File ribbon, click Print. The contacts table style will be previewed on the right side of the window. Navigate the preview using the Navigate Pages, Actual Size, One Page, and Multiple Page buttons.

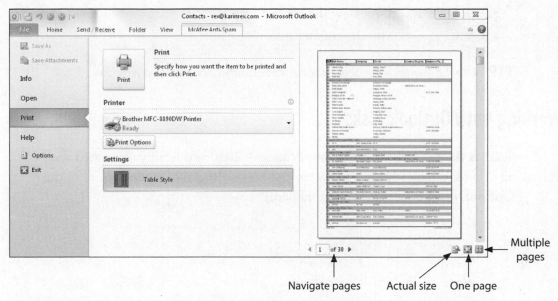

FIGURE 14-5 • The Print pane lets you preview and choose options for printing one or more contacts.

2. To set additional options, including page range, print range, page setup options, and styles, click Print Options to open the Print dialog box (shown here).

3. Click Preview to preview the contact list.

4. Click Print to print the contact list.

TIP   *Use the CONTROL-P keyboard shortcut to quickly open the Print window.*

Working with Outlook Tasks

Tasks is the to-do list component of Outlook 2010 and is fully integrated with all other Outlook features. To access Task view, click Tasks in the bottom of the Outlook Navigation pane (pictured here).

Creating a New Task

1. In Tasks view, click New Task. The Task dialog box opens (pictured in Figure 14-6).

2. In the Subject field, type a meaningful name for the task.

3. Modify the start date and due date for the task.

4. Choose the current status for the task (Not Started, In Progress, Completed, Waiting On Someone Else, or Deferred) from the Status drop-down menu.

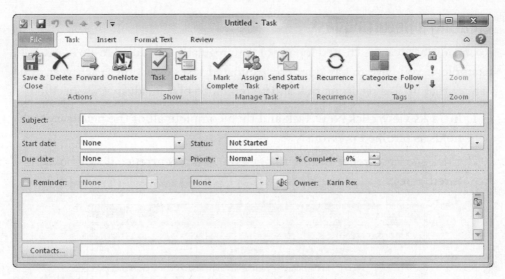

FIGURE 14-6 · The New Task dialog box lets you provide details on your to-do item.

5. Choose a priority level for the task (Low, Normal, or High) from the Priority drop-down menu.

6. If applicable, type the task's current percentage of completion in the % Complete field.

7. To be reminded ahead of time for a task, select the Reminder check box and then choose a date and time for the reminder. (The default is None.)

8. In the task notes area, type any additional information for the task.

9. If a task involves one of your contacts, you can create a link to the contact by clicking Contacts and choosing the name.

10. Click Save & Close.

TIP *YYou don't have to be in Task view to create a new task. On the Home ribbon, click New Items and choose Task. The New Items menu is pictured here.*

Creating a Recurring Task

Recurring tasks can be created for any of your regularly scheduled to-do items. For example, if you have to pay quarterly estimated taxes four times each year, you can set that up as a recurring task and be reminded of it in advance as specified.

1. In Tasks view, click New Task and then complete all of the necessary task fields as outlined previously.

2. Click the Recurrence button to open the Task Recurrence dialog box (pictured here).

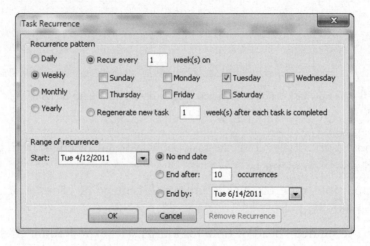

3. Under the Recurrence Pattern heading, select the desired pattern for the recurring task (Daily, Weekly, Monthly, or Yearly), and specify the recurrence rate and day.

4. To create a new task after a task has been marked as done, select the Regenerate New Task option, and specify the time period for when the new task should be regenerated.

5. Under the Range Of Recurrence heading, choose the start date for the recurring task and then designate an end date, keeping the following in mind:

   • To have the recurring task never end, click the No End Date option.

   • To indicate a specific number of occurrences, click the End After option and type a number in the Occurrence field.

   • To specify a specific date for the recurring task to end by, type a date in the Date field.

6. Click OK.

Modifying a Task

The Daily Task List ribbon (pictured here) offers a variety of controls for working with tasks. This section covers a few of the more popular options available on the Daily Tasks List ribbon. For additional topics, explore the Help file.

1. In Tasks view, double-click the task you wish to modify.

2. Modify each of the necessary task fields as outlined previously.

3. Apply flags (Today, Tomorrow, etc.) from the Follow Up group if desired. These flags are visual cues that alert you when a task is due.

4. Click Save & Close to save and close the Task dialog box.

Marking a Task as Complete

1. In Task view, click the task you wish to mark as complete.

2. On the Home ribbon, click Mark Complete. If the task was a recurring one and you selected the Regenerate New Task option in the Task Recurrence dialog box, the recurring task will be generated as soon as you mark the current task as complete.

TIP *To quickly mark a task as complete, click in the Complete column next to the text in Task view (pictured here).*

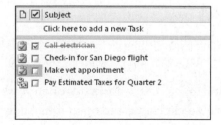

Deleting a Task

1. In Task view, click the task you wish to delete.

2. On the Home ribbon, click Delete. If the task is recurring, a menu will prompt you to delete the single occurrence of the task or the series. If the task is not a recurring one, the task will be deleted as soon as you click the Remove From List button.

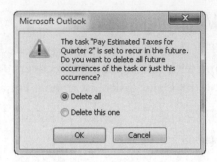

TIP *To quickly delete a task, right-click on it and choose Delete from the menu (pictured below).*

Exploring Task Views

Tasks can be displayed in three locations: Task view, the To-Do bar, and in the Daily Task List in Calendar view. To view tasks, do any of the following:

- In the Navigation pane, click Tasks to open Tasks view (pictured in Figure 14-7). Double-click a task to open it in a new window; single-click a task to view it in the Reading pane.

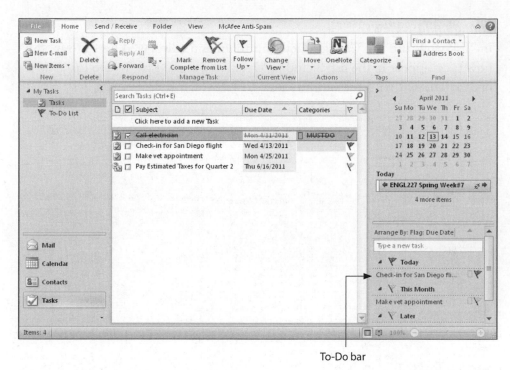

FIGURE 14-7 · The Task List and To-Do bar let you view and work with all of your tasks.

- In any Outlook view, click the View ribbon and then the To-Do button to display the To-Do bar. Choose Options from the To-Do button menu to specify which items should appear in the To-Do bar (Task List, Appointments, and/or Date Navigator).

- In Calendar view, click the View ribbon, and in the Layout group choose Daily Task List. From the Daily Task List button menu (pictured here), choose Minimized or Normal. This will display the task list at the bottom of the calendar when you are in Day or Week view.

Changing Task Views

In Task view, use the Change Views button menu (displayed here) to modify how tasks appear in the list, including Detailed, Simple List, To-Do List, and so on. Experiment with the various views to see which style you like best.

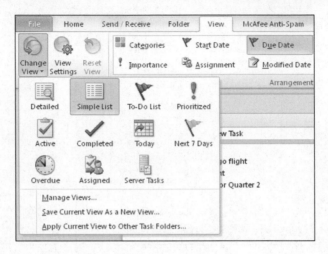

Sorting Tasks

In Task view, you can sort tasks in the Arrangement group (pictured here). You can sort by category, start date, due date, importance, and more. (You can also sort the task list by clicking a column heading.) Use the Reverse Sort button to change the order of the sort (from displaying the oldest due date first to displaying the earliest due date first, for example). To add category columns to your task list, use the Add Columns button. If you are viewing tasks in groups, use the Expand/Collapse button to expand or collapse groups.

Printing Tasks

The Print tab of the File ribbon (pictured in Figure 14-8) lets you print a hardcopy of your to-do list.

1. In Task view, click the File ribbon and then click Print. The tasks table style will be previewed on the right side of the window. Navigate the preview using the Navigate Pages, Actual Size, One Page, and Multiple Page buttons.

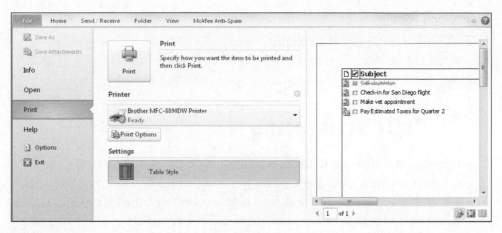

FIGURE 14-8 · The Print pane lets you preview and print a task list.

2. To set additional options, including page range, print range, page setup options, and styles, click Print Options to open the Print dialog box (pictured here).

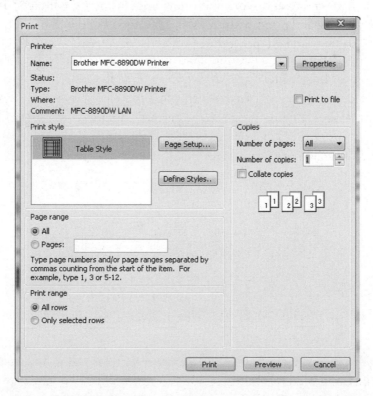

3. Click Preview to preview the task list.

4. Click Print to print the task list.

Still Struggling

Remember to refer back to Chapter 2 for common program functionality, such as Backstage View (document properties and permissions, opening existing files, and saving files); using undo and redo; working with the Office Clipboard (cut, copy, and paste); working with themes; and getting help.

Summary

In this chapter, you learned about Outlook Calendar, Contacts, and Tasks. You learned how to create and work with new appointments, contacts, and tasks, including viewing and printing options. In Chapter 14 you will begin to explore the Office suite's database powerhouse: Microsoft Access.

QUIZ

1. **True or False: If an appointment is a recurring appointment, clicking the Delete button will produce a menu prompting you to choose whether to delete the single occurrence or the entire series.**
   A. True
   B. False

2. **Which Outlook feature is used to set up a meeting that occurs the same day and time every week?**
   A. Arrangement
   B. Delete Appointment
   C. Recurring Appointment
   D. To-Do List
   E. View ribbon

3. **In _____ view, the _____ ribbon offers options for viewing your calendar. (Fill in the blanks using the following choices.)**
   A. Send/Receive
   B. Contacts
   C. Calendar
   D. Tasks
   E. View

4. **What types of e-mail addresses will you find in the Suggested Contacts folder?**
   A. E-mail addresses that you have sent e-mail to but that are not in your contact list
   B. E-mail addresses from your Contact list
   C. Old e-mail addresses for contacts
   D. E-mail addresses that you have received e-mail from, but that are not in your contact list
   E. None of the above

5. **True or False: You cannot create a new contact unless you are in Contact view.**
   A. True
   B. False

6. **Tasks can be displayed in which three locations? (Choose three.)**
   A. Daily Task List in Calendar
   B. File ribbon
   C. To-Do bar
   D. View ribbon
   E. Task view

7. True or False: In Outlook, as in all other Office 2010 applications, printing is managed on the Print tab of the File ribbon.

    A. True
    B. False

8. On the View menu, use the _____ button to change the order of the sort (from A through Z to Z through A, for example).

    A. Time Scale
    B. Reverse Sort
    C. Reset View
    D. People Pane
    E. Reminders Window

9. In which view does the Daily Task List button appear?

    A. Email
    B. Contacts
    C. Calendar
    D. Tasks
    E. None of the above

10. True or False: Double-click a task to open it in a new window; single-click a task to view it in the Reading pane.

    A. True
    B. False

Part VI

Microsoft Access

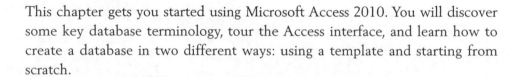

chapter 15

Getting Started with Access

This chapter gets you started using Microsoft Access 2010. You will discover some key database terminology, tour the Access interface, and learn how to create a database in two different ways: using a template and starting from scratch.

CHAPTER OBJECTIVES

In this chapter, you will learn how to

- Distinguish between a relational database and a flat file database
- Use key database terminology
- Navigate the Access interface
- Create a database from a template
- Create a database from scratch

Database Basics

As you may recall from Chapter 1, Access is the Office suite's database power-house, helping you manage your endless mounds of data. A database is a collection of related data (bits of information). These bits of information can be about people (e.g., names, addresses, credit card numbers, purchasing preferences); numbers (e.g., dates, income, expenses, time); things (e.g., inventory, product SKU numbers, prices, colors); or any combination of these.

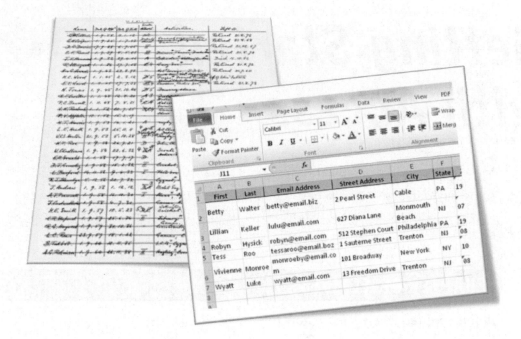

Many databases start as a simple handwritten list on paper or in a word processing or spreadsheet program. Eventually, the list grows larger and the data becomes difficult to contain and manage in such a simple format. For example, you might need to be able to reorganize the list or break it into sublists; you may spot inconsistencies, such as duplicate or out-of-date items; or you may start to have difficulties finding a specific piece of data in the list. This is where using a database program becomes advantageous. Placing your data in a database gives you the power to manipulate and organize your information in almost any way possible.

Database Terminology Primer

Access uses some terminology that you may be unfamiliar with unless you've worked in a database program before. If you are already database-savvy, feel free to skip this section of the chapter; if you aren't, then familiarize yourself with the following database terms and definitions.

Access lets you manage all related data in a single *database file*. Within the file you can use one or more *tables* to store data; use *queries* to locate and retrieve specific information; use *forms* to view, add, and update individual *records*; and use *reports* to study or print data in an attractive layout. Each of these terms, plus a few others you will encounter, is defined in Table 15-1.

This illustration shows an Access table with records, fields, and values labeled.

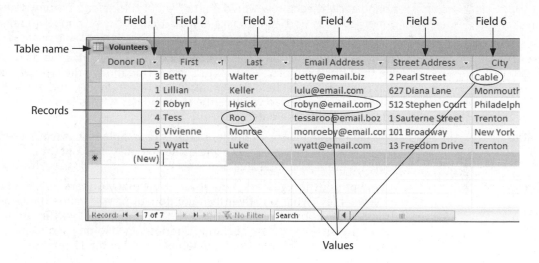

Database Types

There are two main types of database models: *flat file* and *relational*. Which type you choose to use depends on how you need to organize your data. Access can be used to create both flat file and relational databases.

As you read earlier, in a database, related data is organized into *tables*. Tables provide a systematic way to access, manage, and revise data. A *flat file database* consists of a single table. A *relational database* consists of one or more interrelated tables. A relational database is more flexible than a flat file database, but also a bit more complex to design. Luckily, Access makes the process fairly painless.

TABLE 15-1 Access 2010 Terminology

Term	Definition
Database management system (DMS)	An application used to manage a database, such as Microsoft Access, FileMaker Pro, SQL Server, or Oracle.
Database/database file	A collection of related data plus everything needed to work with that data, including tables, records, queries, forms, reports, and so on. Access database files are saved with an .accdb file extension.
Table	A collection of data with a particular focus stored in rows and columns. For example, you could create a Donor table to track information about those who have donated to a nonprofit organization. The table might contain names, contact information, amount of donation, and so on.
Record	A single row within a table. For example, in the Donor table mentioned earlier, each row would contain all of the details about a single donor, such as first name, last name, e-mail address, phone number, and so on. You may have as many records in a database as necessary.
Field	A single column within a table. A field definition includes the name of the field (for example, "First," "Last," and "Donation"); the type of data that is stored in the field (for example, text or number); and any validation rules needed to validate the stored data. Access lets you define up to 255 fields in a database.
Value	One data element. For example, in the Donor table discussed earlier, where one row (record) meets one column (field), the content contained therein would be a value.
Query	A type of question you ask a database. How many donors do we have in New Jersey? What was their average donation? Who made the largest donation? You have to ask the question in the right way in order to get the answer you are seeking. Queries can also be used to modify information retrieved from a database. In Chapter 17 you will learn more about queries.
Form	A graphical user interface for data, letting you view, add, or edit one record at a time. Access lets you work with data in tables (which consist of rows and columns like those found in a spreadsheet) or forms, which are a bit more graphically pleasing and easier to navigate.
Report	A way to show case data by displaying information retrieved from a table or query in an organized and attractive way. For example, for your organization's monthly board meeting you could create a donor report that summarizes all of the donations that came in that month. Access offers a Report Wizard that makes reporting quick and easy, and offers the flexibility to create and format your own custom reports.

Flat File Database

If you think back to the chapters on Excel, you saw that Excel stores information in rows and columns. That's how a database stores data as well. Each column represents a field and each row represents a record. A flat file database stores each piece of information in separate fields (columns) of every record (rows). This arrangement often causes repeated categories of information over several records, which can make working with data more difficult. Using a flat file database can make reporting challenging, as it can be tricky to group information easily. In addition, a flat file database can get huge, sometimes to the point of taxing a computer's system resources. For example, opening a really large flat file database or running a report can be very time-consuming.

Relational Database

A relational database, which can be composed of multiple related tables, stays nice and lean by cutting down on redundant data, letting you categorize available data and store each category in a separate table (for example, customers, products, and vendors). You can store these multiple tables in a single database and then combine the data from different tables to retrieve exactly the information you want. The tables in a relational database relate to one another through special key fields. (You will learn more about key fields in Chapter 17.)

Flat File vs. Relational Database

To better understand the two types of databases, imagine two nonprofit organizations that are funded by donations: Organization Red and Organization Green. Both organizations need to keep track of their contributors (names, contact information, amount and date of donation, etc.). Organization Red uses one flat file database with a single table named Donors-Donations to record information about contributors and their gifts. Organization Green uses a single relational database consisting of two tables: one table for Donors and one table for Gifts.

When a contributor sends a gift to Organization Red, a new record (or row) in the Donors-Donations table is created. Since Organization Red has just a single data table, all the information pertaining to that donation must be put into a single record (or row). This means that the contributor's basic information (name, contact details, etc.) is stored in the same record (or row) as the donation information (amount, method of payment, etc.). If multiple gifts come from a single contributor, their basic information will be reentered for each donation. (See how flat files can get fat fast?)

	ID	Name	Address	City	State	Zip	Gift	Date	Method
	4	Kristian Kellne	54 Studio Way	New York	NY	10021	$300.00	4/13/2011	Check
	3	Wilson David	877 Scooter Street	Lakewood	NJ	08701	$100.00	4/13/2011	Check
	1	John Smith	1 Main Street	Anytown	PA	19128	$50.00	5/9/2011	Check
	2	Lulu Dianamo	54 Annendale Driv	Staten Island	NY	10301	$125.00	6/27/2011	Credit Card
	7	John Smith	1 Main Street	Anytown	PA	19128	$100.00	7/23/2011	Check
	5	Beth Kirkland	2 Avocette Way	New York	NY	10021	$75.00	8/17/2011	Credit Card
	8	John Smith	1 Main Street	Anytown	CA	19128	$25.00	11/1/2011	Check

Org Red Donors-Donations

The same donor appears three times in the table (once with the incorrect state)

Whenever this type of redundant data entry exists, discrepancies can occur when queries are run. In the example pictured above, a three-time contributor's state was typed incorrectly as "CA" in one of the three records and correctly as "PA" in the other two records. Running a report of donations by state would result in a misleading report, as one of the donations would incorrectly appear in the California total while the other two would appear in the Pennsylvania total. In addition, to process a simple change of e-mail address for that particular donor, you would have to find all three of the donation records and make the change three times.

Organization Green's relational database will help them be much more efficient in tracking donors and gifts. Each contributor has a single record containing basic information stored in the Donors table, and each record is identified by a unique donor code, which serves as the primary key that relates the Donors table to the Gifts table (you will learn more about primary keys in Chapter 16). When a contributor makes a gift to Organization Green, the record in the Gifts table simply has to point to the contributor's unique code in the Donors table, because all of that person's basic information is already stored there—there is no need to enter it again. This approach to entering data solves potential glitches with duplicate records and makes updating donor information easy. You would only need to change one record in the Donors table to update an e-mail address, for example.

Org Green Donatio...	**Org Green Donors**								
Donor ID	Name	Address	City	State	Zip	Gift	Date	Method	
1	John Smith	1 Main Street	Anytown	PA	19128	$50.00	5/9/2011	Check	
2	Lulu Dianamo	54 Annendale I	Staten Island	NY	10301	$125.00	6/27/2011	Credit Card	
3	Wilson David	877 Scooter Str	Lakewood	NJ	08701	$100.00	4/13/2011	Check	
4	Kristian Kellner	54 Studio Way	New York	NY	10021	$300.00	4/13/2011	Check	
5	Beth Kirkland	2 Avocette Wa	New York	NY	10021	$75.00	8/17/2011	Credit Card	

The Donor ID field serves as a primary
key to relate the two tables

Org Green Donations		Org Green Don...			
Gift ID	Donor ID	Gift	Date	Method	
1	3	$300.00	4/13/2011	Check	
4	4	$300.00	4/13/2011	Check	
6	1	$50.00	5/9/2011	Check	
3	1	$50.00	5/9/2011	Check	
5	2	$125.00	6/27/2011	Credit Card	
2	5	$75.00	8/27/2011	Credit Card	
7	1	$25.00	11/1/2011	Check	

Exploring the Access Interface

The Microsoft Access interface is quite similar to all of the other Office 2010 applications in that it uses ribbons, dialog boxes, and button menus to issue commands, but there are a few differences to be aware of:

- When Access is launched using the Access application icon (as opposed to an existing database icon), Backstage View (which is located on the File ribbon) is the default view.

- The File ribbon Info pane offers a different set of options from the other programs, offering commands for compacting and password-protecting a database.

- When a database is open, a navigation pane on the left side of the window provides access to all of the database's objects.

Each of these points is discussed further in the following sections.

About Backstage View

When you launch the Microsoft Access 2010 application, the program opens in Backstage View (AKA the File ribbon). As you may recall from Chapter 2, an easy way to remember what features you will find in Backstage View is to understand that it provides commands that will allow you to do things *to* a database (such as opening, saving, or printing), while all of the other ribbons provide commands that allow you to do things *within* a database (such as querying it or editing it).

To underscore that distinction, the File ribbon and Backstage View look different from any of the other ribbons in one very noticeable way: the database you are working in is hidden from view when the Backstage View is active. If no database is open, most of the commands on the other ribbons (Home, Create, External Data, and Database Tools) are grayed out, meaning you cannot use those commands. Figure 15-1 shows an example of the File ribbon with the New tab displayed.

The left pane of Backstage View displays a list of commands (Save, Open, New, Help, etc.), as well as a list of the last four database files that were used. The right side of Backstage View displays related information or additional options for whatever command is currently selected in the left pane.

FIGURE 15-1 · Backstage View provides commands that will allow you to do things *to* a database (such as opening, saving, or printing).

TIP   *Since the File ribbon looks so different from the other ribbons, you may be tempted to click the Close button in the top-right corner of the window when you want to leave Backstage View. Don't do it! Instead, press the ESC key or simply click any of the other ribbons (e.g., Home, Create, etc.). Clicking the Close button in the top-right corner of the screen or the Exit link in the left margin will close the database (as well as the application if only a single database was open). You will be prompted to save the file if you've made any changes.*

About the Info Pane

In all of the other Office 2010 applications, clicking the Info Pane command in Backstage View gave you access to information about the currently opened file, including document properties, permissions, preparation for sharing, and versions. Instead of these, the Access Info pane offers options for compacting and repairing a database and password-protecting it. Figure 15-2 shows an example of the Access Info pane in Backstage View.

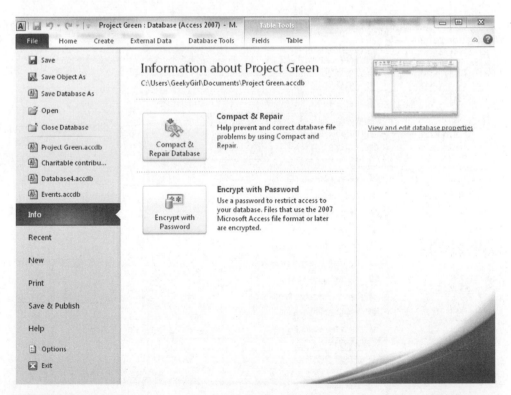

FIGURE15-2 • The Info pane lets you view and modify database properties as well as use the Compact & Repair and Encrypt with Password features.

About the Navigation Pane

When a database is opened in Access 2010, a Navigation pane (pictured in Figure 15-3) displays on the left side of the window. The Navigation pane, which lists all of the database's objects, including queries, forms, reports, and tables, is your primary way of navigating within the database. Each object has a unique icon that helps identify the type of object it is.

TIP   *Click the Hide/Show button located at the top-right corner of the Navigation pane to either hide or show the pane. Click a Collapse/Expand button to either collapse or expand a group within the Navigation pane.*

Double-clicking an object opens it in a new window on the right side of the screen. Multiple objects can be opened simultaneously. With the exception of

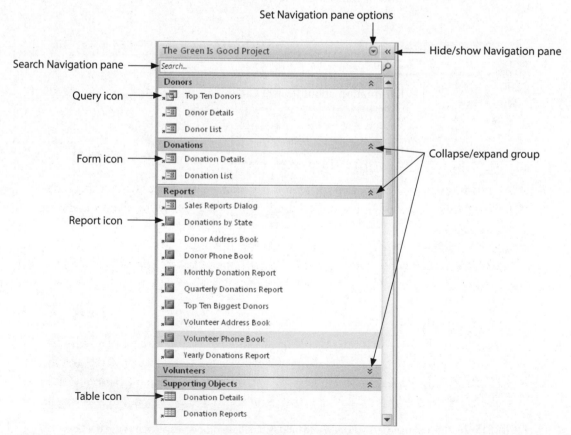

FIGURE 15-3 · The Navigation pane lets you navigate through database objects.

forms, objects will open in a tabbed window on the right side of the screen, and you can switch between open objects by clicking a tab. Forms open in a separate window, which can be floated anywhere on screen.

Viewing options for the Navigation pane can be set using the Options menu (pictured here) at the top of the pane. By default, the Navigation pane list displays the names of all of the tables in the open database, but you can choose to display other types of objects, filter the list of objects, or group objects using the Options menu.

Creating a New Database

Access offers two ways to create a database: using a template or creating a database from scratch. Whichever method you choose, you will always begin in Backstage View.

TIP *Use the CTRL-N keyboard shortcut to quickly open the New pane in Backstage View.*

Using a Template

The Access 2010 New pane (pictured in Figure 15-1) offers the option of starting with a completely blank database, starting with a sample template (installed with the application), or starting with a template from the Microsoft Office website. An Access template is a preformatted database layout that serves as the basis for a brand-new database. Some Access database templates include the following:

- Assets Database
- Projects Web Database
- Expense Reports and Tracker
- Contacts Database
- Sales Pipeline
- Student List
- Inventory Tracker
- Charitable Contributions Database
- Personal or Business Account Ledger

Using a template can save loads of time and ensure a professional look and feel to your database. If this cookie-cutter design approach doesn't quite appeal to you, you can still save time by customizing an existing template to suit your own needs and then saving it with a new name.

In addition to the sample templates available under the Available Templates heading, there are hundreds of templates available from the Office.com website.

1. Click the File ribbon.

2. Choose New.

3. Navigate to and select the desired template under the Available Templates or Office.com Templates headings (pictured in Figure 15-4).

4. Type a name for the database in the File Name field.

5. To change the current location for saving the file (displayed under the File Name field), click the folder icon to navigate to and select a new save location.

6. Click the Create button. How the new database displays when it is first created depends on which template you are using. In some cases, a table will be displayed; in others, a form or login screen may appear. Read the on-screen instructions to know how to proceed.

7. Begin working in the new database.

TIP *Use the Search field in the New pane to search for a template by name or keyword.*

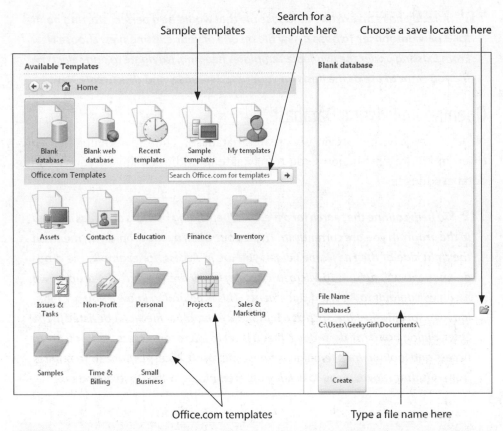

Sample templates   Search for a template here   Choose a save location here

FIGURE 15-4 · The New tab in Backstage View lets you start with a blank database or from a template.

Starting from Scratch

1. Click the File ribbon.

2. Choose New.

3. Under the Available Templates heading, click Blank Database (pictured in Figure 15-4).

4. Type a name for the database in the File Name field.

5. To change the current location for saving the file (displayed under the File Name field), click the folder icon to navigate to and select a new save location.

6. Click the Create button. The new database will open with a new, blank table displayed.

7. Begin working in the new database.

TIP *Already have an existing database file that would be a perfect starting point for a new database? To base a new file on one of your existing files, choose New From Existing under the Available Templates heading. Navigate to and select the file you want to use as the basis for your new database, and click Create New.*

Opening an Existing Database

Need to work with a previously created database? The Open dialog box (pictured in Figure 15-5) allows you to navigate to and open any of your existing database files.

TIP *To help confine the search for a file, the Open dialog box lists only files created in the program you are currently in. This is controlled by the drop-down menu on the right side of the File Name field. If you are in Access, for example, the drop-down menu will default to Microsoft Access; if you are in Word, the drop-down menu will default to All Word Documents. This is helpful to know if you are looking for a specific file type, such as a template. A template file won't be listed in the Open dialog box if the drop-down menu is set to Microsoft Access. So if you are in Access and looking for a template, choose Microsoft Access Database Templates from this drop-down menu to display only templates in the Open dialog box.*

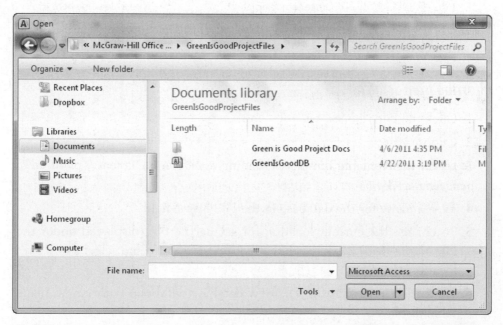

FIGURE 15-5 · The Open dialog box lets you navigate to and open any database you have access to.

Opening an Existing Database

1. Click the File ribbon.
2. Choose Open. Figure 15-5 shows an example of the Open dialog box.
3. Navigate to the folder where the file is stored, and select it.
4. Click Open.

TIP *Use the CTRL-O keyboard shortcut to quickly access the Open dialog box.*

Opening a Recently Viewed Database

If you've recently worked with a database, the File ribbon makes it easy for you to locate and open that file. If the file you wish to open is one of the last few database files you worked in, it will be listed on the left side of the File ribbon and you can open it simply by clicking it. The Recent pane provides access to a greater number of recent databases.

1. Click the File ribbon.
2. Choose Recent Databases.
3. Click a file from the Recent list.

TIP *You can control the number of database files that appear in the left margin of the File ribbon (the default is 4) as well as in the Recent Databases pane (the default is 17). To set the number of database files that will appear on the left side of the File ribbon, click Recent Databases. At the bottom of the Recent Databases list, modify the number in the Quickly Access This Number Of Recent Databases number field (pictured here).*

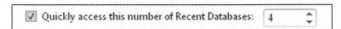

To set the number of database files that will appear in the Recent Databases pane, on the File ribbon, click Options and then click Client Settings. Scroll down to the Display heading (pictured here). Modify the number in the Show This Number Of Recent Documents number field.

Display

Show this number of Recent Documents: 17

☑ Status bar
☑ Show animations
☑ Show Action Tags on Datasheets
☑ Show Action Tags on Forms and Reports

Closing a Database

When you are finished working with a database, save the file (see Chapter 2 if you've forgotten how to save a Microsoft Office file) and then close it using either of the following methods:

- Click the File ribbon and choose Close Database (pictured here).

- Double-click the Close button in the top-right corner of an open object window (pictured here). A single click closes the current object; a double click closes all objects and the database.

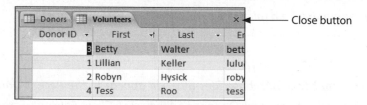

Close button

TIP *If you forget to save before closing a database, Access will remind you.*

Still Struggling

Remember to refer back to Chapter 2 for common program functionality, such as saving a file; using undo and redo; working with the Office Clipboard (cut, copy, and paste); working with themes; and getting help.

Summary

In this chapter, you became familiar with Microsoft Access 2010. You learned common database terminology, briefly explored the Access interface, and learned how to create a new database. In Chapter 16, you'll learn how to create and work with Access tables.

QUIZ

1. **True or False: Microsoft Access is a spreadsheet program best used for working with numeric data.**
    A. True
    B. False

2. **In a table, where one row (record) meets one column (field), the content contained therein would be a _____ . (Fill in the blank using the following choices.)**
    A. File
    B. Query
    C. Value
    D. Report
    E. Database file

3. **Within a database file you can use one or more _____ to store your data and _____ to locate and retrieve specific information. (Fill in the blanks using the following choices.)**
    A. Queries
    B. Files
    C. Values
    D. Reports
    E. Tables

4. **What is the default number of databases that will appear on the File ribbon to allow quick access to your most recently used databases?**
    A. 17
    B. 6
    C. 4
    D. 3
    E. None

5. **True or False: A field is a single column within a table.**
    A. True
    B. False

6. **What lists all of the database's objects, including queries, forms, reports, and tables, and is your primary way of navigating within the database?**
    A. Home ribbon
    B. Navigation pane
    C. File ribbon (Backstage View)
    D. Create ribbon
    E. None of the above

7. **True or False: Database templates can be searched by name or keyword.**
   A. True
   B. False

8. **A _____ consists of a single table. A _____ consists of one or more inter-related tables. (Fill in the blanks using the following choices.)**
   A. Relational database
   B. Flat file database

9. **Which of the following is an example of an Access database template?**
   A. Assets database
   B. Expense reports and tracker
   C. Contacts database
   D. Student list
   E. All of the above

10. **True or False: The File ribbon provides commands that will allow you to do things to a database, while all of the other ribbons provide you with commands that allow you to do things within a database.**
    A. True
    B. False

chapter **16**

Working with Access Tables

This chapter gets you started creating and working with Microsoft Access tables. You will become familiar with basic database and table design considerations, and learn how to create and work with an Access table in both Design view and Datasheet view. You will also learn to add and work with fields and records.

In this chapter, you will learn how to

- Plan database tables
- Create an Access table
- Work in an Access table in Design view and Datasheet view
- Create and work with fields
- Add, edit, and delete records

Design Considerations for Access Tables

As you may recall from the previous chapter, a *table* is a collection of data with a particular focus stored in rows and columns. For example, a nonprofit organization might create a Donor table to track information about those who have contributed to their organization. The table might contain names, addresses, phone numbers, and other related data. Tables consist of records, fields, and values.

A *record* is one single row within a table. For example, in the Donor table, each row would contain all of the details about a single contributor, such as first name, last name, mailing address, phone number, and so on. You can have as many records in a database as necessary.

A *field* is a single column within a table. When you define a field, you will give it a unique name (for example, "FirstName," "LastName," and "Donation"), specify the type of data that will be stored in the field (for example, text or number), and add any validation rules needed to validate the stored data. Access lets you define up to 255 fields in a database.

Where one row (record) meets one column (field), the content contained therein is called a *value*. Figure 16-1 illustrates these table concepts.

Planning Ahead

A successful database begins with the end result in mind. Carefully assess the information you want to track and imagine the tables you might need to contain that data, as well as the reports you will need to pull from those tables. Do not make the "newbie" mistake of assuming that you can start creating tables

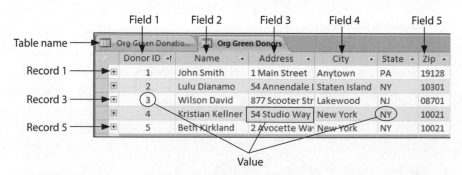

FIGURE 16-1 · It's helpful to understand basic database table terminology when planning a database.

and their relationships without having done some careful prep work ahead of time. Even experienced database designers will usually begin the design process on paper instead of in Access, arranging information into related tables and then sketching out the relationships between them. Planning ahead is crucial to a successful outcome and can save loads of time in the long run, as it is a much better investment of time than having to painfully retrofit a database after it has already been built and populated.

Still Struggling

Need a crash course in database design? In the Access Help file, search on the phrase "database design basics" for a comprehensive overview. Additional resources are available by performing the same search in your favorite Internet search engine, as well as on websites that house instructional videos, such as YouTube, lynda.com and eHow.com.

If the database you are developing is being created to replace either an existing paper-based list or electronic file (such as a Word table, Excel worksheet, or flat file database), then you may already have the basic blueprint for the new database. (Although you will definitely want to identify the limitations of the existing system to make sure you don't make any of the same mistakes!)

If starting from scratch, try to identify exactly what you want from the database. How do you want to retrieve data? What "buckets" do your data fit into comfortably? What types of reports might you need? What data management pain are you trying to relieve or avoid? You may need to collect copies of existing management reports, customer invoices, tax forms, billing statements, and any other documents that contain some or all of the information you want to track in your database. Consider collaborating with anyone else who will have a stake in either using the database (such as entering data or pulling reports) or using data pulled from the database (such as managers, CEOs, and field or sales representatives).

TIP *Database and table design, as well as the topic of table relationships, can quickly become complicated. While this chapter serves as an introduction to these topics, it merely scratches the surface. To learn more, use the Access Help files and the Microsoft Office website, as well as other Internet-based resources. In addition, you might consider a more thorough book on the topic of databases, such as* Databases Demystified *by Andy Oppel (McGraw Hill Professional, 2011).*

Table Design

A well-designed database will cleverly allocate related information into separate tables to help cut down on duplicate data. (As you learned in the previous chapter, redundant data not only fattens up a database file, but also makes it prone to errors.) These tables will be related (hence the name "relational database") to one another through the use of a primary key to comprise one cohesive database file from which a variety of reports can be built and data analysis needs can be artfully accommodated. Some things to think about when designing tables include the following:

- Determine the "why" behind the database and gather together any related materials that might be needed to help define your tables.

- Decide how many tables will be required and what the overriding theme of each table will be (for example, a nonprofit organization might want one table to track contributors, another to track donations, and yet another to track volunteers).

- Figure out what data will be tracked in each table and identify field names for each piece of data (for example, first name, last name, address, city, state, ZIP code).

- Think about how the data in one table will relate to the data in the other tables, and identify primary keys and foreign keys for each table.

Understanding Keys: Primary and Foreign

A *primary key* is a single field in each table that uniquely identifies each record in that table. The following illustration shows fields in two tables: Donors and Donations. The Donor ID field has been designated as the primary key in that table (note the key icon next to it). This field uniquely identifies each of the records in the Donors table by automatically assigning a number to each new donor. This primary key is what will relate the Donors table with the Donations table and allow a report to be built based on data pulled from both tables (for example, a report showing donations by state).

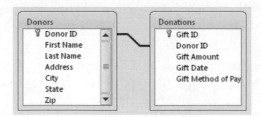

Note that the Donor ID field also appears in the Donations table. This was done to establish the relationship between the two tables. When a primary key field appears in another table, it is known as a *foreign key*. In the illustration, the Donor ID field is a foreign key in the Donations table.

In the Donations table, the Gift ID field uniquely identifies each of the records in that table. This field, marked with the primary key icon, could be used to relate donations-specific data with other tables in the database if needed.

Each table in a database must have a primary key. Without one, it is not possible to create relationships and extract meaningful information from a database. Typically, an automatically numbered field with a unique name is used as a primary key in each table. To help ensure that you remember to establish a primary key in each new table, an ID field is automatically created as the first field in any new table and is designated as the primary key. It's a good idea to rename this field so that it has a unique name within your database structure.

If you are migrating existing data into a database, you may already have a field that could be used as the primary key. Any unique identification number, such as an employee number or a serial number or code, can act as the primary key in a table.

Creating an Access Table

When you create a new database from scratch (covered in Chapter 15), the first thing you will see is a new, blank table (like the one pictured here) waiting for you to name and define fields in it. The table appears in the navigation bar, and the Table Tools Fields and Table ribbons are both available for use when working in the table. By default, the table displays in Datasheet view; you can also work in Design view. Each view is described later in this chapter.

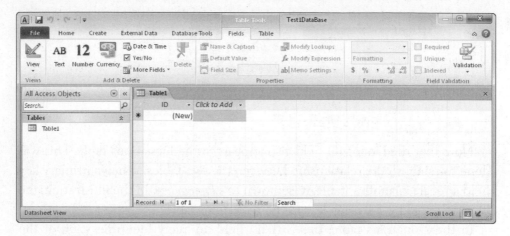

TIP *When starting with a template, the first screen you encounter depends on the chosen template, and may or may not be a table. For example, a template could open with a form or a log-in dialog box. In some cases, you can click the Help button (the question mark icon at the top-right corner of the window) to find helpful information about using that particular template. For example, the Marketing Project Management Database offers such a link (pictured here).*

Marketing project management database
View more information about this template
Rating: ⭐⭐⭐⭐☆ (1590)

Building a New Table

The Create ribbon (pictured here) lets you create a new table in an existing database.

1. Click the Create ribbon.

2. In the Tables group, do one of the following:

- Click Table Design to create a new table and have it open in Design view.

- Click Table to create a new table and have it open in Datasheet view.

TIP *For optimal results (especially for beginners), it's best to build a table in Design view, as you will be more likely to remember to consider and set field properties since they are right there on the screen.*

Understanding Table Views

Access provides several table views: Datasheet view, Pivot Table view, Pivot Chart view, and Design view. To change views while in a table, use the Views button menu (pictured to the right), which is available on both the Home and Design ribbons.

Datasheet view can be used to scroll through records and add, modify, or view data in a table. Design view gives you complete control over a table's structure, including adding and modifying field details.

PivotTable view enables interactive data analysis, and PivotChart view enables you to create dynamic, interactive charts. These topics are not covered in this chapter. For information on these views, search on "create a PivotTable or PivotChart view" in the Access Help file.

Changing Views

1. Click the Home or Design ribbon. (The Home ribbon is available, regardless of what view you are in; the Design ribbon is only available when you are in Design view.)

2. Click the View button.

3. Choose a view from the menu provided.

TIP *You can also change views using the View buttons (pictured here) which are located near the bottom-right corner of the Access window.*

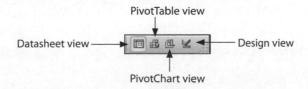

About Datasheet View

Datasheet view (pictured in Figure 16-2) closely resembles an Excel worksheet, in that it appears as a grid composed of rows (which will become the database's records once you add data) and columns (in which you will define your fields). Column headings (where you will add field names) come equipped with a drop-down arrow that opens a menu of sorting and filtering options (also pictured in Figure 16-2).

If you are an experienced Excel user, you may feel quite at home working in Datasheet view. Inserting, deleting, and moving rows are all accomplished using the same methods as in Excel. In Datasheet view, you can add and rename fields, change a field's data type and format properties, and change a few other field properties.

Navigate through records in the table using the navigation tools provided at the bottom of the table. You will learn how to add and work with fields in Datasheet view later in this chapter.

About Design View

Design view (pictured in Figure 16-3) provides three columns for adding and working with fields: Field Name, Data Type, and Description. The Field

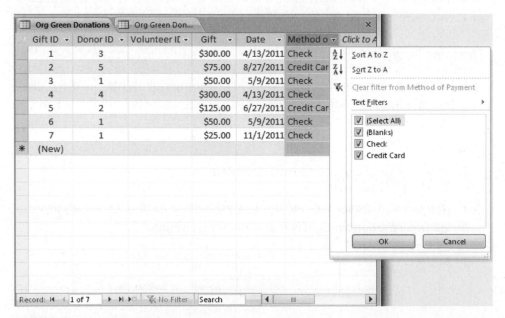

FIGURE 16-2 · Datasheet View consists of rows and columns.

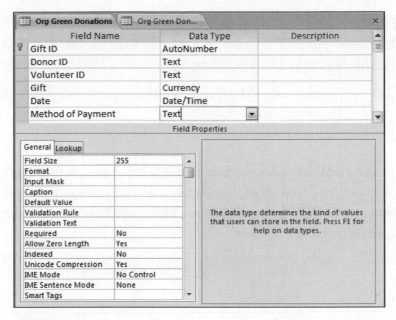

FIGURE 16-3 · Design View displays three columns: Field Name, Data Type, and Description.

Properties pane, displayed in the lower-left corner of Design view, allows you to set properties to control every possible aspect of a field's appearance and behavior. For example, you can dictate how data will appear in a field, set up rules to prevent incorrect data entry, define default values, and speed up searching and sorting. While you can set some of these field properties in Datasheet view, to work with the complete list of field properties, you must use Design view. Clicking a field or property in this view produces a helpful tip in the lower-right corner of the screen.

You will learn how to add and work with fields in Design view later in this chapter.

Working with Tables

Saving, opening, closing, renaming, navigating, deleting, and copying tables are each described below.

Saving a Table

As you begin to build tables and relationships and work with a database, Access will prompt you to save your work when necessary. In some cases, you will not be able to move on until you save as requested. You should, of course, save often to avoid losing work! To save a table, do one of the following:

- Click the File ribbon and choose Save.
- Click the Save button on the Quick Access toolbar (located at the top-left corner of the application window).
- Use the CTRL-S keyboard shortcut.

TIP *To save a table with a new name, click the File ribbon and use the Save Object As command. The Save As dialog box (pictured here) opens. Type a new name for the table in the Save To field, and make sure Table is selected in the As drop-down list. Click OK to complete the save.*

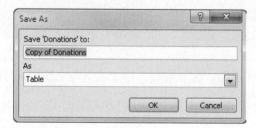

Opening and Closing a Table

Tables are opened from the Navigation pane. Simply double-click the table name to open that table. When multiple tables are open, use the tabs at the top of the window to switch between them. To close a table, first view it by clicking its tab and then click the Close button (the X) near the top-right corner of the window.

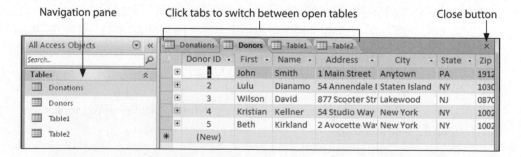

Navigating in a Table

In addition to using the mouse, you can navigate within a table using the keyboard, as described in Table 16-1.

TABLE 16-1 Navigating in a Table	
To Move To This	**Use This Keystroke/Keystroke Combination**
Next field	TAB
Previous field	SHIFT–TAB
Next record	DOWN ARROW
Previous record	UP ARROW
First field of current record	HOME
First field of very first record	CTRL–HOME
Last field of current record	END
Last field of very last record	CTRL–END
Up one page	PAGE UP
Down one page	PAGE DOWN

Renaming a Table

Tables can be renamed from the Navigation pane in one of two ways:

- Right-click the table you want to rename, and choose Rename from the menu. Type a new name and press ENTER.

- Right-click the table you want to rename and then press the F2 key on the keyboard. Type a new name and press ENTER.

TIP *If a table is open, it cannot be renamed. Access will prompt you to close the table and then try renaming it again (pictured here).*

Deleting a Table

Tables are deleted from the Navigation pane in one of three ways:

- Click the table you want to delete, and then, on the Home ribbon, click the Delete button (located in the Records group).

- Click the table you want to delete, and then press the DELETE key on your keyboard (the BACKSPACE key will not work).

- Right-click the table you want to delete, and choose Delete from the menu.

When prompted to confirm the deletion (pictured here), click Yes.

TIP *If a table is open, it cannot be deleted. Access will prompt you to close the table and then try deleting it again (pictured here).*

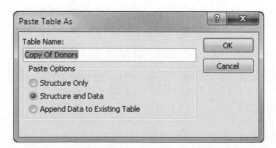

Copying a Table

1. In the Navigation pane, right-click the table you want to copy.
2. Choose Copy.
3. On the Home ribbon, click Paste. The Paste Table As dialog box opens (pictured here).

4. In the Paste Table As dialog box, select one of the Paste Options, and then click OK. Keep in mind the following:

- Choose Structure Only to create a new, empty table based on the design of the copied table.

- Choose Structure And Data to create an exact replica of the copied table, including data.

- Choose Append Data To Existing Table to add the data from the copied table to the bottom of another table (you will be prompted to choose which table to paste into).

TIP *If you prefer keyboard shortcuts, you can use CTRL-C to copy a selected table and CTRL-V to paste it (this pastes the structure only).*

Defining Fields

As you may recall, Design view (pictured in Figure 16-4) gives you complete control over a table's structure, including adding and modifying field details. It is recommended that you add and define fields in Design view instead of Datasheet view. While Datasheet view can be used to add a field and define its data type, it does not provide access to any other field properties. Datasheet view is best used for scrolling through records and adding, modifying, or viewing data in a table structure.

TIP *Using Design view to add tables is not a hard and fast rule—it's just a suggestion. You can add fields in Datasheet view if you are more comfortable in that environment and then switch to Design view to modify field properties.*

Working with the ID Field

As you learned earlier, to help ensure that you establish a primary key in each new table, an ID field is automatically created as the first field in any new table and is designated as such. It is a good practice to rename this field so that it has a unique name within your database structure. For example, if you are in a table called Volunteers, you could rename this field "VolunteerID."

1. In Design view, under the Field Name heading, click in the ID field and rename it to suit the table. The default data type for this field is AutoNumber. This should not be changed, since you want to be able to identify each record in the table by a unique number and this is the easiest way to do it. (See "Field Naming Conventions" later in this chapter for guidelines on naming fields.)

Click in a Field Name cell to add a new field

Use the Data Type drop-down list to select a data type

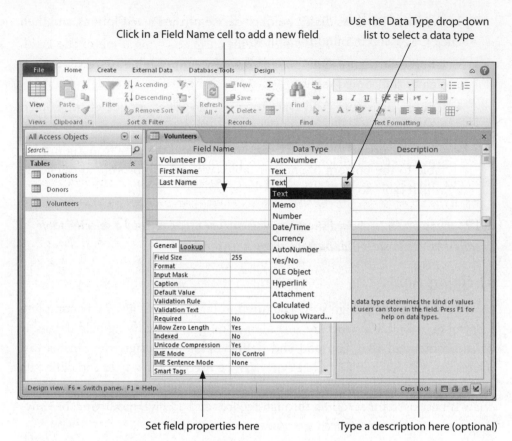

Set field properties here

Type a description here (optional)

FIGURE 16-4 · Fields can be added or modified in Design View.

2. Add a description in the Description column (optional).

3. Set additional field properties as desired in the General tab of the Field Properties area. Clicking in a field produces a brief description of it on the right side of the window. For additional information on these properties, search on "field properties" in the Access Help file.

Adding a New Field (Row) in Design View

1. To add a new field, click in the next empty Field Name cell, and type a name for the field.

2. Click in the Data Type field, and choose a data type. (See Table 16-2 later in this chapter for descriptions of all data types.)

3. Add a description in the Description column (optional).

4. Set additional field properties as desired in the General tab of the Field Properties area. Clicking in a field produces a brief description of it on the right side of the window. For additional information on these properties, search on "field properties" in the Access Help file.

5. Repeat steps 2 through 7 for each additional field.

TIP *You may add fields in Datasheet view or Design view at any time, either before or after the database has been populated. In either view, to add a new field after all of the other fields, simply click in the next available row (Design view) or column (Datasheet view). To add a new field in between two other fields, right-click the field where you want the field to be added. Then in Datasheet view, choose Insert Field; or in Design view, choose Insert Rows.*

For example, in Figure 16-5, a field is being added between the existing Name and Address fields. In either view, the Address field is selected before inserting the field.

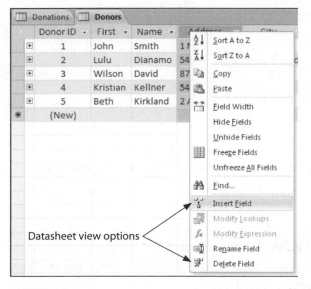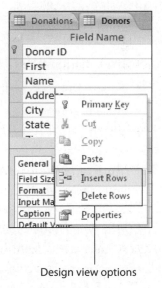

FIGURE 16-5 · The right-click menu in Datasheet View and Design View lets you insert and delete fields or rows.

Deleting a Field (Row)

You can delete a field from either Datasheet view or Design view:

- In Datasheet view, right-click the field you wish to delete, and choose Delete Field.
- In Design view, right-click the field you wish to delete, and choose Delete Rows.

Field Naming Conventions

In Design view, field names are placed vertically in the first column of the table. In Datasheet view, field names are placed horizontally in the very top row of the table.

When choosing field names, be concise but descriptive. You want short field names (which will save you some typing later if you add validation rules to the field or use it in a calculation), but you also want to ensure that others working in the database will be able to easily recognize what that field is going to hold. A field name can contain between 1 and 64 characters, including letters (upper- and lowercase), numbers, and some special characters. Field names cannot begin with a space, but can contain spaces between words. Field names cannot contain any of the following:

- Period (.)
- Exclamation point (!)
- Square brackets [ ]
- Accent grave (`)
- ASCII values 0 through 31

TIP   *For a complete list of ASCII characters, search on "ASCII table" in your favorite Internet search engine.*

The Data Type Field Property

Access has categorized the various types of data that a field can hold into a dozen distinct categories, as pictured in Figure 16-6 and described in Table 16-2. Each field must have a data type defined.

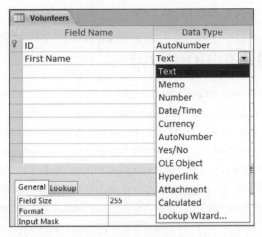

FIGURE 16-6 • The Table Data Type Menu lets you choose from a list of data types.

TABLE 16-2 Field Data Types

Field Name	Use to Store
Attachment	A link to an external file.
AutoNumber	An automatically generated incremented number.
Calculated	The result of two or more calculated fields (for example, multiplying the price of an item by the number of items sold).
Currency	Data dealing with money (prices, wages, tax, etc.)—numbers will not round up or down.
Date/Time	Date and time data (or combinations of the two).
Hyperlink	A link to an Internet website.
Lookup & Relationship	A link to pull data in from another table.
Memo	Any combination of letters, symbols, and numbers, up to 65,535 characters in length (which equals approximately 20 pages of this book!).
Number	Numbers only (use this data type for numbers that may be involved in calculations such as quantities sold or inventory; do not use for ZIP codes or phone numbers). Note that there is a separate data type for monetary values: Currency.
OLE Object	Object Linking or Embedding (OLE) objects, such as Excel spreadsheets, charts/graphics, and pictures.
Text	Any combination of letters, punctuation, and numbers, up to 255 characters in length.
Yes/No	Logical values (yes/no or true/false).

Still Struggling

It is easy to become confused by the text, number, and currency data types. A text field can store data consisting of either words or numbers (or combinations thereof). The numbers in a text field are numbers that won't ever be needed for a calculation. For example, you would never add two ZIP codes or telephone numbers together. A number field can only contain numerical data. Use this data type if the data is something you might possibly use as part of a calculation, such as a quantity. If you are dealing with money numbers, then you should always use the currency data type so the numbers will always be formatted properly.

The Field Size Property

The Field Size property is set on the General tab. This field will only appear on the tab if the data type is one in which the field size is able to be modified. When this field does appear on the tab, it will contain a default value that can be changed to suit your data storage needs. For example, when Text is the data type for a field (as pictured in Figure 16-6), 255 (referring to characters) appears in the Field Size field by default. This number can be modified to suit the field. For example, you probably would not need 255 characters to store somebody's first name. Changing the field size adjusts the amount of space that each record in a table uses. This has a space-saving impact on number fields, but minimal impact on text fields.

For fields defined with the Number data type, the Field Size property (as pictured in Figure 16-7) determines the possible range of field values that the field can house. For example, a one-bit number field can store only integers ranging from 0 to 255. The Field Size property also determines how much disk space each number field will take up. Long Integer is the default choice when the number data type is selected. However, Long Integer takes up twice as much disk space to store a value than the Integer field size and four times the disk space as the Byte field size. Typically, there is no need for you to change the Long Integer default; however, if you are working in a large database with lots of number fields, this small difference can impact the database's performance. Table 16-3 describes each of the number field size choices.

Number data type field size option   Note tips below

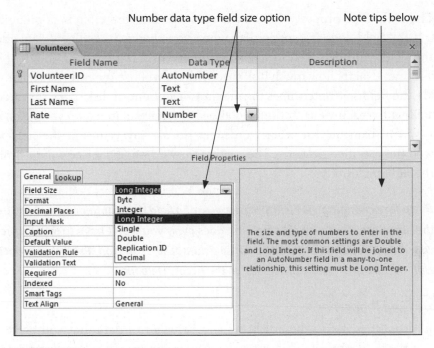

FIGURE 16-7 · The Number Data Type/Field Size Options lets you choose the size and type of numbers to enter in the field.

TABLE 16-3 Field Size Choices and Storage Requirements for the Number Data Type

Field Size	Description	Storage Requirement
Byte	Use for integers that range from 0 to 255.	A single byte
Integer	Use for integers that range from –32,768 to +32,767.	2 bytes
Long Integer	Use for integers that range from –2,147,483,648 to +2,147,483,647.	4 bytes
Single	Use for numeric floating–point values that range from –3.4 × 1038 to +3.4 × 1038 and up to seven significant digits.	4 bytes
Double	Use for numeric floating–point values that range from –1.797 × 10308 to +1.797 × 10308 and up to 15 significant digits.	8 bytes
Replication ID	Use for storing a globally unique identifier (GUID) that is required for replication of your database (for example, to make a backup copy).	16 bytes
Decimal	Use for numeric values that range from –9.999 . . . × 1027 to +9.999 . . . × 1027.	12 bytes

The Field Size property can be changed whether the table is populated or not. If the field doesn't contain data when you change it, any new data added to the field will be limited to the set number. For number fields, the field size determines exactly how much disk space Access will use for each value. For text fields, the field size determines the maximum amount of disk space that Access will allow for each value. If the field already contains data when you change it, Access will truncate (in other words, get rid of) any values in the field that exceed the specified field size. Then, going forward, the field size will be limited to the new parameters.

TIP   *Before changing the Field Size property of a field that contains data, back up the database. That way, if something goes awry you won't have to reconstruct your data. For details on how to back up a database, search on "Protect your data with backup and restore processes" in the Access Help file.*

Other Field Properties

Field properties define the attributes and behavior of data that will be stored within the field. You already learned about two important field properties: data type and field size. Naturally a field's chosen data type property determines what kind of data the field can hold, and this property must be defined for every field. Other field properties include such attributes as what formats can be used in the field, how the field can be used in expressions, and whether a field can be indexed.

TIP   *For additional information on data types, as well as a more thorough introduction to other field properties, search on "introduction to data types and field properties" in Access Help.*

Designating a Primary Key

As you read earlier in this chapter, a *primary key* is one field in each table that uniquely identifies each record in that table. A table's primary key is used to relate tables to one another and allow a report to be built based on data pulled from both tables. You might also recall that when a primary key field appears in another table (thereby relating the two tables), it is known as a *foreign key*.

1. Click the Home ribbon.
2. Click the View button, and choose Design View.

3. Select the field you wish to use as the primary key.

4. Click the Design ribbon.

5. In the Tools group, click the Primary Key button (pictured here). Note that this button is a toggle, meaning you can use the same button to define and undefine a primary key. Access will warn you if you try to delete a primary key that has an existing relationship. You will not be permitted to delete the primary key until you have deleted the relationship.

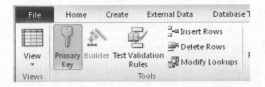

TIP   *To quickly assign the primary key to a field, right-click on in the field and choose Primary Key from the menu (pictured here). Note that this command is a toggle, meaning you can use the same command to define and undefine a primary key. Access will warn you if you try to delete a primary key that has an existing relationship. You will not be permitted to delete the primary key until you have deleted the relationship.*

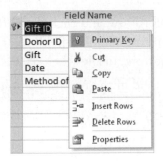

TIP   *You will learn more about the topic of relating tables through a primary key in Chapter 17.*

Populating a Database

A database can be populated with records in either Datasheet view or by using a form. Forms are covered in Chapter 18. In this chapter, you will learn to add and work with records in Datasheet view.

Adding Records in Datasheet View

In the illustration below, the Donors table contains five existing records. The cursor is placed in the First field to begin adding a new record. The Donor ID field will be completed automatically as soon as the first bit of data is added to the record.

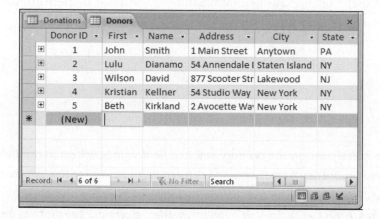

1. Open the table you want to add records to, and change to Datasheet view if necessary.

2. Locate the (New) record row, and click in the first cell. (Note that if your primary key field is an AutoNumber field, you cannot type in that field, as it will be populated automatically when data is added to the record.)

3. Provide data in each field of the record as applicable.

Navigating Between Records in a Table

In addition to using the scroll bar to navigate between records, you can use the navigation bar near the bottom of the screen (pictured in Figure 16-8). Use the

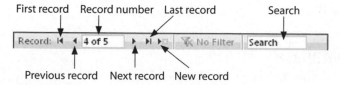

FIGURE 16-8 · The navigation bar at the bottom of screen can be used to move between and search within records.

Previous and Next buttons to move between records one at a time. Use the First and Last buttons to move to the very first or very last record in the table.

Working with Records in Datasheet View

Working with records in Datasheet view, including editing, selecting, copying, moving, deleting, and searching, are covered here.

Editing Records in Datasheet View

1. Open the table you want to edit, and change to Datasheet view if necessary.

2. Locate the record you want to edit, and click in the cell that needs editing.

3. Modify the data as necessary.

Selecting Records in Datasheet View

To select an entire record (row) in Datasheet view, click a gray selection button at the very beginning of the record (pictured here). Click and drag to select adjacent records.

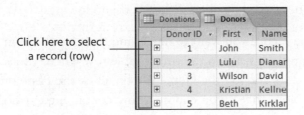

Click here to select a record (row)

Copying Records in Datasheet View

A record can be copied by doing either of the following:

- Select the record you want to copy and choose Copy button. Click in the empty table row where you want the copied data to be placed, and, on the Home ribbon, click the Paste button (pictured here).

- Right-click the record you want to copy, and choose Copy. Right-click in the empty table row where you want the copied data to be placed, and choose Paste (pictured here).

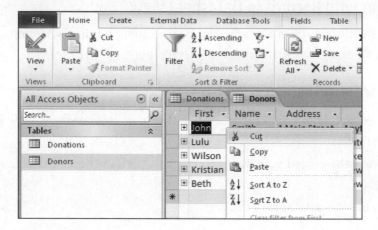

TIP *If you prefer keyboard shortcuts, you can use CTRL-C for Copy and CTRL-V for Paste.*

Moving Records in Datasheet View

A record can be moved by doing either of the following:

- Select the record you want to move, and then, on the Home ribbon, click the Cut button. Click in the empty table row where you want the data to be moved to, and, on the Home ribbon, click the Paste button (pictured earlier). Note that if you choose a row containing existing data, the cut data will replace the existing data. If you do not want this to happen, insert a new row before pasting.

- Right-click the record you want to move and choose Cut. Right-click in the empty table row where you want the data to be moved to and choose Paste. Note that if you choose a row containing existing data, the cut data will replace the existing data. If you do not want this to happen, insert a new row before pasting.

TIP *If you prefer keyboard shortcuts, you can use CTRL-X for Copy and CTRL-V for Paste.*

Deleting Records in Datasheet View

A record can be deleted by doing either of the following:

- Select the record(s) you want to delete, and then, on the Home ribbon, click the Delete button. When asked to confirm the deletion, click Yes.

- Right-click the selection button of the record you wish to delete, and choose Delete from the menu. When asked to confirm the deletion, click Yes.

Searching Records

To find a record, type a search term in the Search field on the navigation bar (pictured in Figure 16-8). As you type, the first record containing the search term will be highlighted. Press ENTER to move to the next field containing the search term.

Still Struggling

Remember to refer back to Chapter 2 for common program functionality, such as Backstage View (document properties and permissions, opening existing files, and saving files); using undo and redo; working with the Office Clipboard (cut, copy, and paste); working with themes; and getting help.

Summary

In this chapter, you started to create and work with Microsoft Access tables. You became familiar with basic database and table design considerations, and learned how to create and work with an Access table in both Design view and Datasheet view. You also learned to work with fields and records. In Chapter 17, you'll learn how to create and work with queries—a type of question you can ask your database.

QUIZ

1. True or False: Each table in a database must have a primary key.
   A. True
   B. False

2. A single row within a table is known as a _____. (Fill in the blank using the following choices.)
   A. Foreign key
   B. Database
   C. Primary key
   D. Record
   E. Field

3. A _____ is one field in each table that uniquely identifies each record in that table. When a primary key field appears in another table (thereby relating the two tables), it is known as a _____. (Fill in the blanks using the following choices.)
   A. Foreign key
   B. Data type
   C. Naming convention
   D. Primary key
   E. Secondary key

4. Choose two Access table views from the views listed below.
   A. Design view
   B. Database view
   C. Record view
   D. Display view
   E. Datasheet view

5. True or False: A database can be populated with records in either Datasheet view or by using a form.
   A. True
   B. False

6. Which of the following would be an acceptable field name in an Access table? (Choose all that apply.)
   A. First.Name
   B. Address
   C. Zip!
   D. [Size]
   E. Zip Code

7. **True or False: An open table can be renamed or deleted.**
   A. True
   B. False

8. **_____ can be used to scroll through records and add, modify, or view data in a table. _____ gives you complete control over a table's structure, including adding and modifying field details. (Fill in the blanks using the following choices.)**
   A. Database view
   B. Design view
   C. Display view
   D. Datasheet vlew
   E. Record view

9. **Which of the following are table data types? (Choose all that apply.)**
   A. Text
   B. Number
   C. Record
   D. Primary key
   E. Currency

10. **True or False: A well-designed database will cleverly allocate related information into separate tables to help cut down on duplicate data.**
    A. True
    B. False

chapter **17**

Working with Access Queries

This chapter gets you started creating and working with Microsoft Access query objects. You will become familiar with select queries and learn how to plan and create a simple select query and a complex select query. You will also explore Query Design view as well as the Query Wizard.

In this chapter, you will learn how to

- Differentiate between query types
- Define types of table relationships
- Describe join types
- Create a simple select query
- Create a complex select query

Understanding Queries

The word "query" comes from the Latin word "quaerere," which means "to ask or inquire." As you may recall from Chapter 15, a query is a type of question you ask a database. To pose a question to an Access database, you create a query object. While Access supports numerous types of query objects, the two more common types to be aware of include *select queries* and *action queries*. A select query is the most commonly used Access query as well as the simplest. It is used to select and display data from one or more tables in a database. An action query is a more complex type of query that causes a specific action to take place within the database. For example, an action query might cause a new table to be created or cause rows to be deleted from existing tables. This chapter focuses on select queries. To learn more about action queries, search on "action query" in the Access Help file.

Select Queries

A select query asks the database a question. The database's answer consists of a set of records pulled from the database (called a *record set*). There are two types of select queries: *simple* and *complex:*

- A simple select query pulls information from a single table in the database.
- A complex select query pulls information from multiple tables in the database.

Access displays the record set as a table in Datasheet view. You can work with the data in this table in the same way that you work with any other table in the database. If you add or modify data within the record set, Access will make those same changes to the table(s) from which the record set was pulled (known as the *record source*).

The previous two chapters in this section used the example of a nonprofit organization's database to illustrate concepts. In that example, there were two tables in the database: Donors and Donations. The illustration displays the fields in each of the two tables. Note that basic information about contributors, including name and address, is maintained in the Donors table, while details specific to donations are maintained in the Donations table.

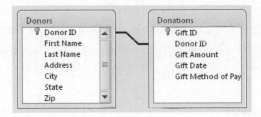

Simple Select Query Example

The nonprofit organization might want to "ask" (i.e., create a query object) the database which contributors come from a certain state. The "answer" to the query is a record set displaying a list of contributors from that state. Since the answer is pulled from a single table, this is an example of a simple select query.

Complex Select Query Example

The organization might also want to "ask" (i.e., create a query object) the database who its top ten contributors are. The "answer" to that query is a record set displaying a list of its most generous contributors. Since the record set is pulled from multiple tables, this is an example of a complex select query.

Organizing a Query

In thinking through and organizing a query, you will want to do the following:

1. **Identify the record source**   Identify which table(s) the information is coming from (i.e., the *record source*). For example, in the simple select query example, the record source would be the Donors table. In the complex select query example, the record source would be both the Donors table and the Donations table.

2. **Specify how the answer to the query should look**   Identify the fields you want included in the record set that answers the query. In the simple select query example, you might want first and last names as well as state included in the resulting record set. For the complex select query example, you might want first and last names, states, and total donation amount.

3. **Stipulate how the answer is to be organized**   Decide how the fields in the resulting record set should be organized. In the simple select query example, you might want the list sorted alphabetically by last name. For the complex select query example, you might want the list sorted by largest to smallest donation amount.

Once you have created a query object, run the query to test it and then adjust it as necessary. You can refine a query by adding or removing fields, or by changing the selection criteria until you have exactly the data needed. Nothing is set in stone—you can keep trying until you get it right!

Creating a Select Query

Access provides two methods for creating a query object: Query Design view and the Query Wizard. The Queries group on the Create ribbon (pictured here) is where both of these commands are located. Both methods are detailed in this chapter.

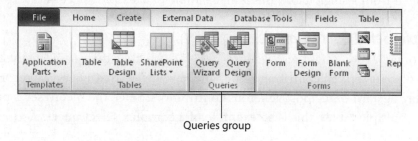

Queries group

Exploring Query Design View

Query Design view (pictured in Figure 17-1) allows the most flexibility when creating a query and is the easiest to use when creating a simple select query. In Query Design view, the screen is divided into four separate areas:

- The Query Design ribbon displays at the top of the window, offering tools and commands for use when working with queries.

- The Navigation pane is positioned along the left side of the window as usual, letting you navigate between database objects as needed.

- The Record Source area in the middle of the window is blank at first, but once a record source is identified, it will appear in this area.

- The Query By Example grid along the bottom of the window is where additional settings can be specified for a query, such as sort order, whether or not a field displays in the record set, and field criteria.

Query Design ribbon   Record Source area

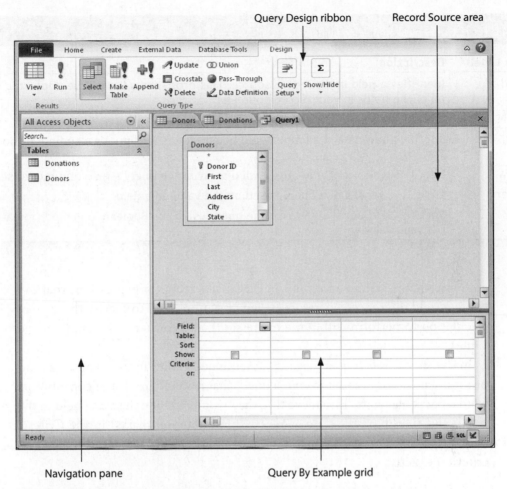

Navigation pane   Query By Example grid

FIGURE 17-1 · Query Design View lets you create and work with Access queries.

Working in the Query by Example Grid

The query by example grid gives you ultimate control over a query. Each column in the grid allows you to specify sort, show, and criteria settings for each field in the query's resulting record set. Table 17-1 describes how these settings work.

Specifying Criteria

To limit the results of a query based on the values in a field, you use query criteria. A query criterion is simply an expression that Access compares against values in the field to decide whether or not to include a record in the resulting record set.

TABLE 17-1	Query by Example grid fields
Row Label	**Description**
Field	Identifies a field in the record source. This drop-down list will be populated with all of the fields in your record source(s).
Table	Identifies a field's record source.
Sort	Specifies how data in a field should be sorted (ascending, descending, or not sorted).
Show	Specifies whether or not a field will display in the query's resulting record set.
Criteria	Limits the results of a query based on the value in a field.
or	Specifies additional criteria for the query using the Boolean logic "Or" operator between values.

A criterion is akin to a formula, in that it is a string (or expression) that can contain field references, operators (a sign or symbol used to specify the type of calculation to perform within the expression), and constants (a noncalculated value).

In the simple select query example mentioned earlier in this chapter, a non-profit organization wanted to craft a query that resulted in a list of contributors from a particular state. To achieve this, they would include the State field in the query and then type the state name (within quotation marks) in the Criteria field, as pictured here. The quotation marks tell Access to match the specified criterion exactly.

Field:	First	Last	City	State	
Table:	Donors	Donors	Donors	Donors	
Sort:					
Show:	☑	☑	☑	☑	
Criteria:				"NJ"	
or:					

And Multiple criteria in the same row can be used to create an "and" expression. For example, if the organization in the example wanted to craft a query that resulted in a list of contributors from a particular city and state, they would add values to both the City and State Criteria fields, as shown in the following illustration.

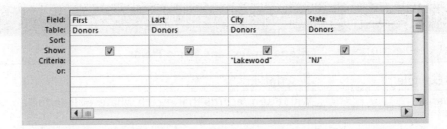

Or The "or" row can be used to create a "this or that" expression. For example, if the organization wanted to craft a query that resulted in a list of contributors from two different states, the second state would be added to the "or" row, as pictured here.

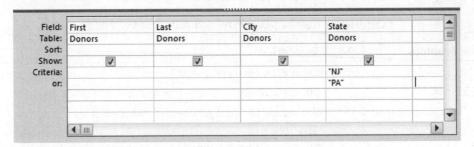

As mentioned earlier, quotation marks are used to tell Access to match a specified criterion exactly. Examples of a few other such conventions for specifying criteria are outlined in Table 17-2.

Note that the table does not contain all possible conventions. For a complete list, search on the following in Access Help:

- Criteria for text, memo, and hyperlink fields
- Criteria for number, currency, and autonumber fields
- Criteria for date/time fields
- Criteria for other fields

Query Tools Design Ribbon

In Design view, the Query Tools Design ribbon (pictured in Figure 17-2) offers commands for working with queries.

TABLE 17-2 Criterion Examples

Criteria for Text and Memo Fields	
Criterion Example	**Description**
"Pennsylvania"	Will return records that match whatever is in the quotation marks.
Not "Pennsylvania"	Will omit whatever is specified in the quotation marks.
Like P*	Will look for values that begin with the letter P.
Not Like P*	Will omit values that begin with the letter P.
Like *nia	Will look for values that end with nia.
Not Like *nia	Will omit values that end with nia.
Is Null	Will look for records with that field empty.

Criteria for Number, Currency, and AutoNumber Fields	
Criterion Example	**Description**
525	Will match the typed number.
Not 525	Will omit records where the number specified matches.
<525	Will return records where the number is less than the number specified.
<=525	Will return records where the number is less than or equal to the number specified.
>525	Will return records where the number is greater than the number specified.
>=525	Will return records where the number is greater than or equal to the number specified.

Criteria for Date and Time Fields	
Criterion Example	**Description**
#5/09/2011#	Will return records that match the date within the pound sign.
Not #5/09/2011#	Will omit records with dates that match the date within the pound sign.
< #5/9/2011#	Will return records with a date prior to the date specified.
> #5/9/2011#	Will return records with a date after the date specified.
> #5/9/2011# and < #6/9/2011#	Will return records where the data occurs between the two dates specified.

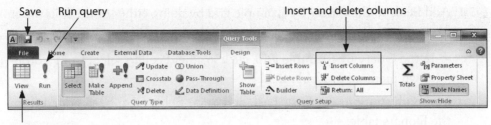

Save   Run query   Insert and delete columns

Change views

FIGURE 17-2 · The Query Tools Design ribbon (partially pictured here) lets you work with queries.

Creating a Simple Select Query Using Design View

1. Click the Create ribbon.

2. Click the Query Design button. The Show Table dialog box (pictured here) opens, asking you to define your record source. For a simple select query, this would be a single table. Using the simple select query example discussed earlier in this chapter (in which the goal was to know which contributors come from a certain state), this would mean choosing the Donors table.

3. Choose a record source (a single table), click Add, and then click Close. The chosen table appears in the Record Source area. Note that you can resize the table if necessary by clicking and dragging any edge.

4. Add fields to the Query By Example grid by doing either of the following:

- In the Record Source table, double-click a field.
- In the Query By Example grid, click in a field cell to select from a drop-down menu of available fields.

In the illustration, the First, Last, and State fields have been added from the Donors table.

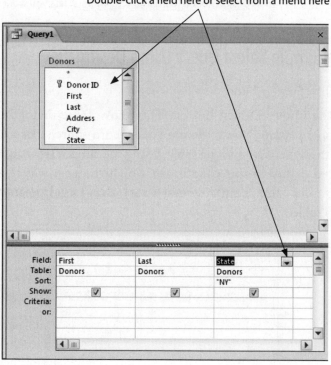

Double-click a field here or select from a menu here

5. To specify a sort order based on this field, click in the Sort field, and choose Ascending or Descending from the drop-down menu.

6. To have this field appear in the query's resulting data set, leave the check mark in the Show check box. If you prefer that the field not show, deselect the Show check box.

7. To limit the results of the query based on the value in this field, add a criterion to the Criteria field.

8. Repeat steps 4 through 7 as necessary for each field.

9. When you have added all of the fields and settings for the query, click the Save button in the Quick Access toolbar, and type a name for the query in the Query Name field (pictured here).

10. On the Query Tools Design ribbon, click the Run button to run the query. The query's resulting record set opens in its own table. In the illustration, the query asked for contributors in New York.

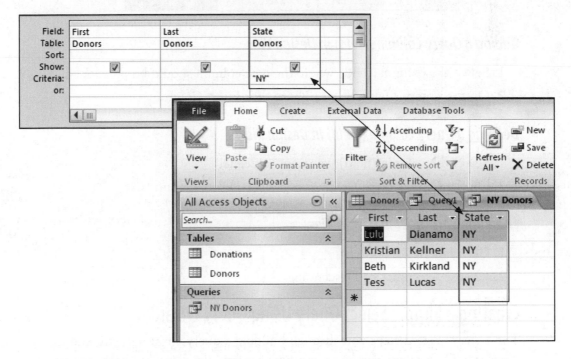

11. Adjust the query as necessary to obtain the desired results.

TIP *To switch between query results in Datasheet view and the Query By Example grid in Design view, use the View button on the Home ribbon.*

Selecting a Query Column (Field) in Design View

To select an entire field in the Query By Example grid (Design view), click in the thin gray bar near the top of the column, just above the field name. The cursor appears as a down arrow when you are in the correct location (pictured here). The column turns black when selected.

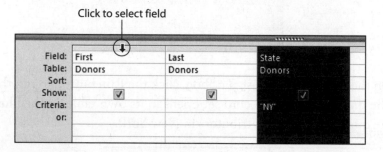

Click to select field

Adding a Query Column (Field) in Design View

1. Select the column (field) where the new column should be positioned.
2. On the Query Tools Design ribbon, click Insert Columns.

Deleting a Query Column (Field) in Design View

1. Select the column (field) you want to delete.
2. On the Query Tools Design ribbon, click Delete Columns.

Changing Sort Order in Design View

1. Click in a field's Sort row.
2. Choose Ascending or Descending.

Creating a Simple Select Query Using Query Wizard

The Query Wizard steps you through building a query. (You will still end up going into Query Design view to fine-tune a query, which is why that topic was covered first in this chapter.)

1. Click the Create ribbon.
2. Click the Query Wizard button. The New Query dialog box opens, asking you what type of query you want to build.

3. Click Simple Query Wizard, and then click OK. The Simple Query Wizard opens (pictured here) asking you to specify the table and fields you want included in the query.

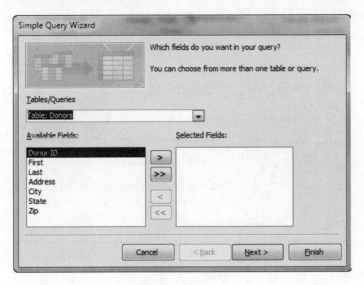

4. Select your record source from the Tables/Queries drop-down menu. A record source can be a table or an existing query. For a simple select query, you can only work with a single table.

5. Select fields to be included in the query, keeping in mind the following:

   • Available fields in the currently selected table or query will be listed in the Available Fields list on the left side of the dialog box. Click a field to select it, and then click the single right arrow to move it to the Selected Fields list. (Click the double right arrow to move all fields into the Selected Fields list.) To remove a field from the Selected Fields list, select it and then click the single left arrow to move it back into the Available Fields list.

6. Click Next. The Simple Query Wizard prompts you for a query name and asks whether you want to open or modify the query. Keep in mind the following:

   • Type a brief yet descriptive name for the query in the What Title Do You Want For Your Query? field. The name will appear in the Navigation pane along with your other database objects, so you want to be able to differentiate it from other objects.

- To run the query, click the Open The Query To View Information option.
- To go right to Design view to further modify the query, click the Modify The Query Design option.

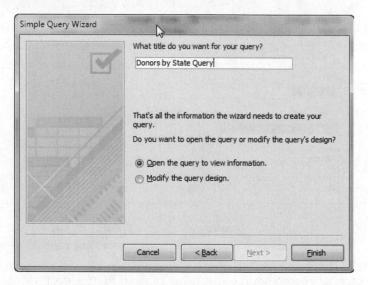

7. Click Finish. If you chose Open The Query To View Information in the previous step, the query runs and opens in its own table. If you chose Modify The Query Design in the previous step, the query opens in Design view.

8. Adjust the query as necessary to obtain the desired results. For example, the Query Wizard did not prompt you to add sorting preferences or criteria to the query, so you will need to modify the query in Design view as you did in the previous section of this chapter.

TIP   *To switch between query results in Datasheet view and the Query By Example grid in Design view, use the View button on the Home ribbon.*

Creating a Complex Select Query

Earlier in this chapter you learned that a simple select query pulls data from a single table in the database while a complex select query pulls data from multiple tables. To create a complex select query, you must have a basic grasp of *table relationships* and *joins*. You began learning about table relationships in Chapter 16, when you read about primary and foreign keys.

You may recall that a *primary key* is a single field in a table that uniquely identifies each record in that table. Each table in a database should have a primary key. Without one, it is not possible to create relationships and extract meaningful information from your database.

The illustration below shows fields in two tables: Donors and Donations. The Donor ID field has been designated as the primary key in that table (note the key icon next to it). This field uniquely identifies each of the records in the Donors table by automatically assigning a number to each new contributor. This primary key is what will help relate the Donors table with the Donations table and allow a query object to be built that will pull data from both tables (for example, a record set showing contributor names alongside their gift amounts).

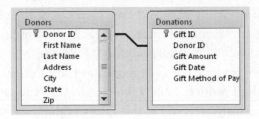

Note that the Donor ID field also appears in the Donations table. This was done to help establish the relationship between the two tables. When a primary key field appears in another table, it is known as a *foreign key*. In the illustration, the Donor ID field is a foreign key in the Donations table. A join line appears between these two fields signifying the relationship.

A relationship can be created using the Database Tools Relationship tool, or it can be created while defining a query object. Either way, you drag a field from one table on top of a field in another table and then define the relationship. In this chapter, the table relationship will be defined as you create the complex select query.

Types of Relationships

Three different types of relationships can be established between database tables: one-to-many, many-to-many, and one-to-one. Each relationship type is described in the sections that follow.

One-to-Many Relationship Using the nonprofit organization database as an example, you will recall that there is a Donors table and a Donations table. One contributor can donate many times. Therefore, for each contributor in the Donors table, there can be multiple gifts listed in the Donations table, making the relationship between the two tables a one-to-many relationship.

To establish a one-to-many relationship in a database, the primary key on the "one" side of the relationship is added as a field (i.e., foreign key) in the table on the "many" side of the relationship. In this case, for example, you add the Donor ID field from the Donors table as a field in the Donations table. Access can then use the Donor ID number in the Donations table to locate the correct contributor for each gift.

Many-to-Many Relationship In a many-to-many relationship, there needs to be a third table (called a junction table). The junction table breaks down the many-to-many relationship into two one-to-many relationships. The primary key from each of the first two tables is inserted into the third table. Doing this means that the third table will record each instance of the relationship.

As an example, consider a database that tracks customers, orders, and products. An order can include multiple products. Likewise, a product can make an appearance in many orders. For each record in the Orders table, there can be many records in the Products table. Likewise, for each record in the Products table, there can be many records in the Orders table. See the many-to-many relationship? For any given product, there can be many orders, and for any given order, there can be many products.

One-to-One Relationship In a one-to-one relationship, each record in the first table can have only one matching record in the second table, and each record in the second table can have only one matching record in the first table. This type of relationship is rare, because data related in this manner is usually stored within the same table.

Types of Joins

When a relationship is created between tables, a *join line* appears between the tables as a visual cue alerting us to the relationship. Double-clicking the join line opens the Join Properties dialog box (pictured here).

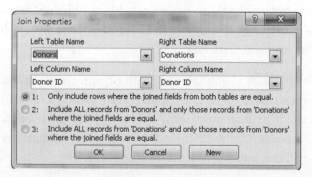

There are three types of joins: inner, left outer, and right outer. Each join type is described in the sections that follow.

Inner Join   An inner join (which is the default, number 1) will display data only when there are matching values in both of the join fields. Using the nonprofit database as an example, it might be possible that there are people in the Donors database who have not yet made a donation (call them *potential contributors*). Therefore, there will not be a matching record for these potential contributors in the Donations table. If you created a query that included the Donors table and the Donations table, using the Donor ID field as the join, contributors who have not yet made a donation would not be listed in the query's resulting record set. This may be exactly what you want to happen. However, if you want the query to display all records from one table regardless of whether it has matching records in the other table, you can change the join type to one of two outer joins.

Left Outer Join   A left outer join displays all records from the table on the left side of the join and only matching records from the table on the right side of the join.

Right Outer Join   A right outer join displays all records from the table on the right side of the join and only matching records from the table on the left side of the join.

Creating a Complex Select Query Using Design View

These instructions assume that you have already identified primary and foreign keys in your tables as discussed in Chapter 16.

1. Click the Create ribbon.
2. Click Query Design. The Show Table dialog box opens (pictured here).

3. Double-click each table you want to define relationships between. (Alternatively, add tables one at a time by selecting a table and then clicking Add.)

4. Click Close to close the Show Table dialog box. The tables are added to the top half of the Query Design view. Keep in mind the following:

   - If two tables have fields with the same exact name and one of the fields is a primary key in a table, Access will auto-join the tables. (This is one of the benefits of establishing primary and foreign keys with the same names when creating your tables.) In this case, a join line will already appear between the two tables (as pictured here), and you can skip the next step.

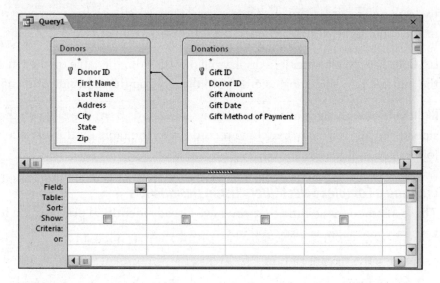

   - If these conditions do not exist, you will create the relationship manually in the next step.

5. Establish a relationship between tables by dragging the primary key field from one table on top of the foreign key field in the other table. A join line will now link the two tables.

6. If desired, double-click the join line to open the Join Properties dialog box and modify the join type.

7. You can add fields to the query grid in one of two ways:

   - In the Record Source table, double-click a field.

   - In the Query By Example grid, click in a field cell to select from a drop-down menu of available fields.

In the illustration, the First Name and Last Name fields have been added from the Donors table and the gift amount has been added from the Donations table.

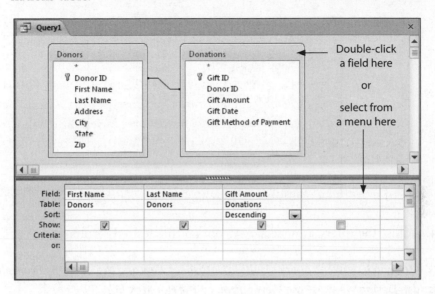

8. To specify a sort order based on a field, click in the Sort field, and choose Ascending or Descending. For example, in the illustration, the Gift Amount field has a sort order of Descending. This means that the largest gifts will be at the top of the record set.

9. To have a field appear in the query's resulting data set, leave the check mark in the Show check box. If you prefer that the field not show, deselect the Show check box. In the illustration, all three fields will display in the record set.

10. To limit the results of the query based on the value in this field, add a criterion to the Criteria field. For example, if I added the State field to the example illustrated, I could then specify a particular state to have the record set display contributors and donations in that state.

11. Repeat steps 4 through 7 as necessary for each field.

12. When you have added all of the fields and settings for the query, click the Save button in the Quick Access toolbar, and type a name for the query in the Query Name field (pictured here).

13. On the Query Tools Design ribbon, click the Run button (see Figure 17-2) to run the query. The query's resulting record set opens in its own table. In the example pictured here, the query asked for contributors and donations.

Donors & Donations Query		
First Name ▾	Last Name ▾	Gift Amount ▾
Lulu	Dianamo	$350.00
Peg	Brennan	$300.00
Lorraine	Wilson	$125.00
John	Fitzgerald	$125.00
Wilson	David	$75.00
Tess	Lucas	$55.00
Kristian	Kellner	$50.00
Robin	Denbeigh	$50.00
Beth	Kirkland	$25.00
*		

14. Adjust the query as necessary to obtain the desired results.

TIP *To switch between query results in Datasheet view and the Query By Example grid in Design view, use the View button on the Home ribbon.*

Still Struggling

Remember to refer back to Chapter 2 for common program functionality, such as Backstage View (document properties and permissions, opening existing files, and saving files); using undo and redo; working with the Office Clipboard (cut, copy, and paste); working with themes; and getting help.

Summary

In this chapter you started creating and working with Microsoft Access query objects. You were introduced to select queries and learned how to plan and create a simple select query and a complex select query. You also explored Query Design view as well as the Query Wizard. In Chapter 18 you'll begin working with Access forms and reports.

QUIZ

1. **True or False: Query Design view allows you the most flexibility when creating a query.**
   A. True
   B. False

2. **Which of the following is a type of Access query? (Choose all that apply.)**
   A. Join query
   B. Action query
   C. Tool query
   D. Select query
   E. And/Or query

3. **To pose a question to the database, you create a _____. (Fill in the blank using the following choices.)**
   A. Layout object
   B. Query object
   C. Join object
   D. Relationship object
   E. Design object

4. **Which criteria would return records whose state is Pennsylvania?**
   A. "PA"
   B. Like *nia
   C. Like P*
   D. All of the above
   E. None of the above

5. **True or False: The Query By Example grid along the bottom of the window allows you to specify additional settings for a query, such as sort order, whether or not a field displays in the record set, and field criteria.**
   A. True
   B. False

6. **Which of the following is a type of select query? (Choose all that apply.)**
   A. Difficult
   B. Easy
   C. Simple
   D. Complex
   E. Complete

7. True or False: A complex select query pulls information from a single table in the database.

   A. True

   B. False

8. To switch between query results in Datasheet view and the Query By Example grid in Design view, use the _____ on the _____ . (Fill in the blanks using the following choices.)

   A. Home ribbon

   B. Filter button

   C. Find button

   D. View button

   E. Database Tools ribbon

9. Multiple criteria in the same row can be used to create an _____ expression. (Fill in the blank using the following choices.)

   A. Or

   B. And

10. True or False: A select query is used to select and display data from one or more tables in the database.

   A. True

   B. False

chapter 18

Working with Forms and Reports

This chapter provides an introduction to two essential Access topics: data forms and reports. You will learn to ease data entry by creating data forms using the Form tool and the Form Wizard. You will also learn how to harness the power of a database by creating meaningful and attractive reports using the Report tool and the Report Wizard.

CHAPTER OBJECTIVES

In this chapter, you will learn how to

- Create a form using the Form tool
- Create a form using the Form Wizard
- Populate a database using a form
- Create a report using the Report tool
- Create a report using the Report Wizard
- Preview and print a report

Working with Access Forms

In Chapter 16, you learned to add and work with data records in Datasheet view. Datasheet view (pictured in Figure 18-1) closely resembles an Excel worksheet in that it appears as a grid composed of rows (i.e., records) and columns (i.e., fields).

If you are an experienced Excel user, you may feel quite at home working in Datasheet view. However, for larger tables, all that scrolling back and forth and up and down can become bothersome. In addition, if others who may be providing data input duties are not familiar with navigating and working in a spreadsheet-like environment, they can quickly do more harm than good!

Access data forms make populating a database much more straightforward, allowing you to work with a single record at a time. Figure 18-2 displays a form in Form view. This is the same table that is displayed in Datasheet view in Figure 18-1. Note that the same navigation tools appear at the bottom of both views.

There are several ways to create forms in Access 2010: the Form tool, the Form Wizard, the Blank Form tool, and Design view. These commands are all located in the Forms group on the Create ribbon (pictured here). This chapter covers the Form tool and the Form Wizard.

Donors							
Donor ID	First Name	Last Name	Address	City	State	Zip	Click to Add
1	John	Smith	1 Main Street	Glen Rock	PA	19128	
2	Lulu	Dianamo	54 Annendale Drive	Staten Island	NY	10301	
3	Wilson	David	877 Scooter Street	Lakewood	NJ	08701	
4	Kristian	Kellner	54 Studio Way	New York	NY	10021	
5	Beth	Kirkland	2 Avocette Way	New York	NY	10021	
6	John	Fitzgerald	101 West Avenue	North Wales	PA	19454	
7	Peg	Brennan	36 Northfield Avenue	Lansdowne	PA	10301	
8	Lorraine	Wilson	200 Scooter Street	Lakewood	NJ	08701	
9	Tess	Lucas	100 A Street	New York	NY	10021	
10	Robin	Denbeigh	10 Hatfield Street	Glen Rock	PA	10021	
*	(New)						

Record: I◄ ◄ 11 of 11 ► ►I ►* ⊱ No Filter | Search

FIGURE 18-1 · A table in Datasheet View resembles an Excel worksheet.

FIGURE 18-2 • You may find Form view easier to work with, especially if you are new to database creation.

Creating a Form Using the Form Tool

The Form tool lets you create a simple yet attractive form from any table or query object in a single click. All of the fields (also called "controls" in forms lingo) that were in the table or query will be included on the form. The form in Figure 18-2 was created with the single click of a button using the Form tool.

1. Open the table or query object that you want to base the form on.
2. Click the Create ribbon.
3. In the Forms group, click Form. The form is created and displayed in Layout view. (Layout view is discussed later in this chapter.)

TIP *If Access finds a single table that has a one-to-many relationship with the table or query you based the form on, a datasheet will be added to the form that is based on the related table or query. For example, if you create a simple form that is based on the Donors table and there is a one-to-many relationship between the Donors table and the Donations table, the datasheet displays all the records in the Donations table that relate to the current Donor record. It is okay to delete the datasheet from the form if you don't need it. If there are multiple tables with a one-to-many relationship to the table the form is based on, Access does not add any datasheets to the form.*

Creating a Form Using the Form Wizard

The Form Wizard walks you through some basic form design decisions. For example, using the wizard, you can define how data is grouped and sorted, and use fields from more than one table or query (as long as you have defined the relationships beforehand, as covered in Chapter 17).

1. Click the Create ribbon.
2. In the Forms group, click Form Wizard. The Form Wizard opens (pictured here).

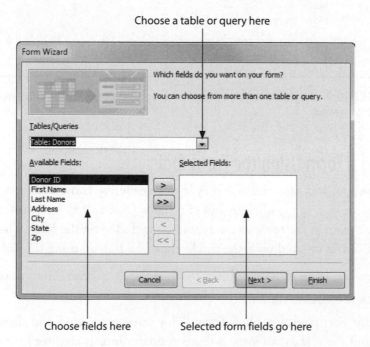

3. Choose a table or query from the Table/Queries drop-down list. Fields from that table or query will populate the Available Fields list.

4. Double-click a field in the Available Fields list to move it into the Selected Fields list. Alternatively, click the double right arrow between the two lists to move all of the fields from Available Fields into Selected Fields.

5. Repeat the previous two steps if you are creating a form from multiple tables or queries.

6. Click Next. Access prompts you to choose a layout for the form (pictured here).

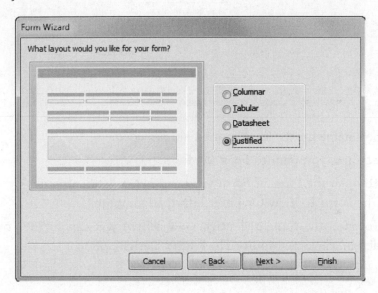

7. Choose a layout for the form. There are four layout choices:

- Columnar shows one record per page with fields laid out in columns.
- Tabular shows multiple records per page with fields in columns and records in rows.
- Datasheet shows the default datasheet view.
- Justified shows field names above their controls with fields arranged across and down the form.

8. Click Next. Access prompts you for a name for the form (pictured here).

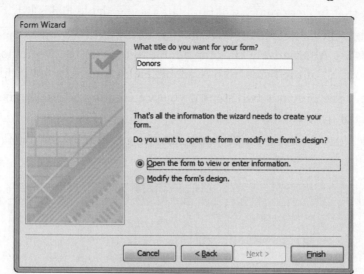

9. Type a name for the form in the field provided.

10. Select how you want to open the form:

- To open the form in Form view and begin data entry, click the Open The Form To View Or Enter Information option.

- To open the form in Design view, where you can further tweak its design, click the Modify The Form's Design option.

11. Click Finish.

Exploring Form Views

Once a form has been created, it can be viewed in several ways: Layout view, Form view, and Design view. Layout view and Design view both let you make design changes to a form; Form view is used for data entry. To change between views, use the View drop-down menu on the Home or Design ribbon or the view buttons located at the bottom-right corner of the Access window (pictured in Figure 18-3).

Layout View

In Layout view (pictured in Figure 18-3), data is displayed and simple layout changes can be made to the form controls. For example, you can resize controls, add or delete fields, add a logo, and change fonts and/or font sizes and more using the three Form Layout Tools ribbons: Design, Arrange, and Format.

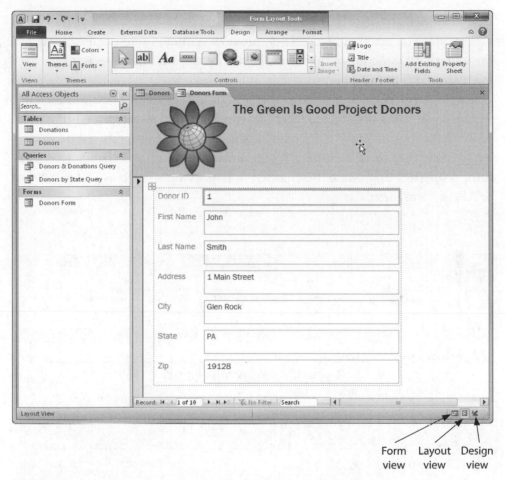

Form   Layout   Design
view   view   view

FIGURE 18-3 · Form Layout view lets you make simple layout changes to form controls.

Controls are form features that allow you to view and work with data in a database. The most frequently used control is the text box, but other controls include command buttons, labels, check boxes, and subform/subreport controls. *Layouts* are guides that provide horizontal and vertical alignment options within a form to give it a uniform appearance.

Because data is displayed in Layout view, it is a bit more visually oriented than in Design view, and this nuance can be useful when setting the size of controls or carrying out other tasks that affect the visual appearance and usability of the form.

TIP   *Certain form modifications cannot be accomplished in Layout view. When this is the case, Access will display a message letting you know that you need to be in Design view.*

Design View

Design view, pictured in Figure 18-4, provides a much more detailed view of the underlying structure of the form. Header, Detail, and Footer sections for the form are all visible. Data is not visible in Design view.

A few design tasks are easier to accomplish in Design view than in Layout view, such as being able to add labels, images, lines, and rectangles; editing text box control sources in the text boxes (without using the property sheet); resizing form sections (e.g., the header, footer, and detail areas); and changing certain form properties that cannot be changed in Layout view (such as Default view or Allow Form view).

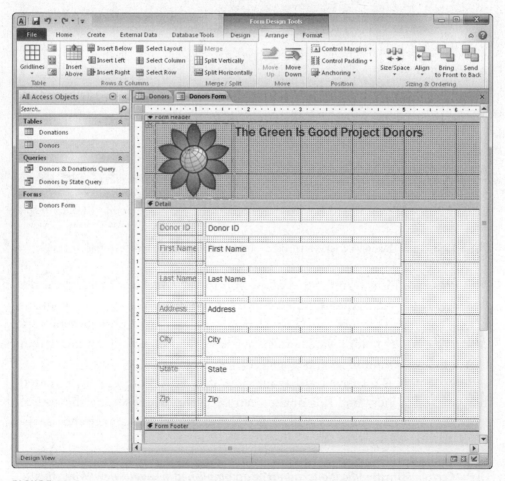

FIGURE 18-4 · Design view offers a more detailed view of a form's structure.

You can also fine-tune your form's design in Design view. You can add new controls to the form by adding them to the design grid. The property sheet (pictured here) gives you access to numerous properties that you can set to customize the form:

Property Sheet	
Selection type: Form	
Form	▼

Format	Data	Event	Other	All

Caption	
Default View	Single Form
Allow Form View	Yes
Allow Datasheet View	No
Allow PivotTable View	No
Allow PivotChart View	No
Allow Layout View	Yes
Picture Type	Embedded
Picture	(none)
Picture Tiling	No
Picture Alignment	Center
Picture Size Mode	Clip
Width	7.8958"
Auto Center	No
Auto Resize	Yes
Fit to Screen	Yes
Border Style	Sizable

- Press F4 to display the form's property sheet, and then use it to modify properties for the form.

- To add fields from the underlying table or query, click the Design ribbon and then click the Add Existing Fields button. Drag fields from the Field list onto the form to add them.

TIP   *Designing forms can be as rich and complex as you want it to be. For additional information on modifying forms and working with controls, explore the Forms topic in the Access Help file table of contents or search on "controls."*

Form View

Form view (pictured in Figure 18-5) displays the form in its final configuration, ready for data input. You will learn more about using Form view for data entry later in this chapter.

Data Entry Using a Form

A form can be used for data entry as well as editing records. Data is automatically saved as you move between fields and records.

Entering Data in a Form

1. Open the form you want to add records to, and change to Form view.

2. In the navigation bar at the bottom of the form (pictured here), click the New Record button. A new, empty record opens.

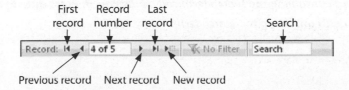

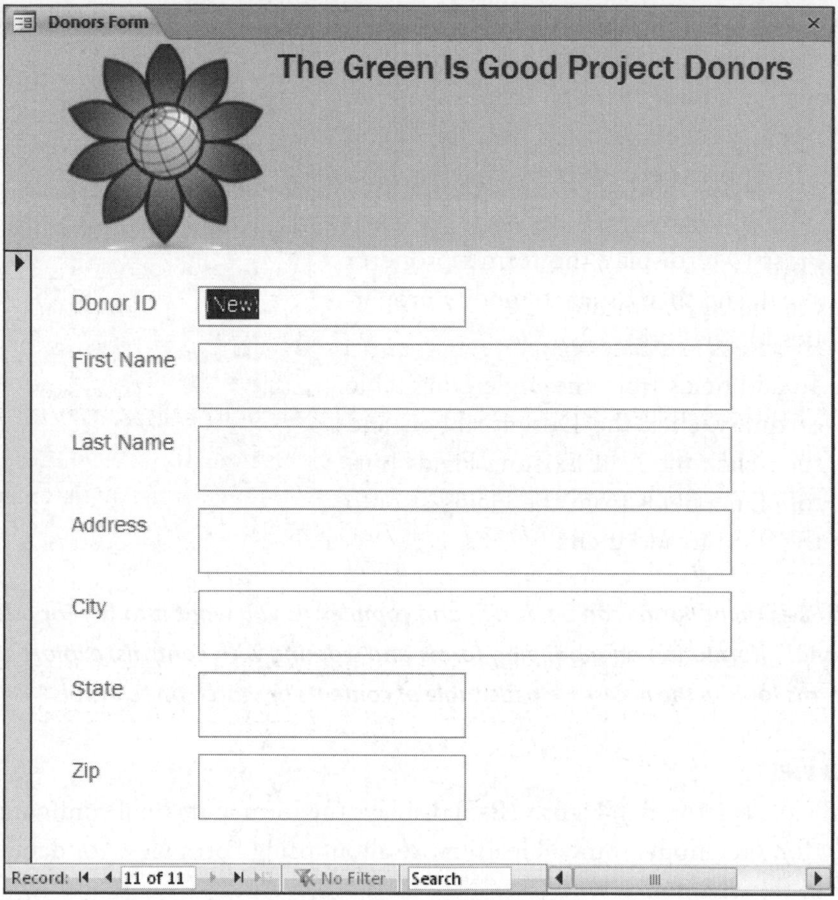

FIGURE 18-5 • Form view lets you preview the finished form.

3. Provide data in each field of the record as applicable. (Note that a list of data entry shortcuts is provided later in this chapter.)

TIP   *Use the navigation bar near the bottom of the screen to navigate between records. Use the Previous and Next buttons to move between records one at a time. Use the First and Last buttons to move to the very first or very last record in the table. To find a record, type a search term in the Search field. As you type, the first record containing the search term will be displayed. Press* ENTER *to move to the next field containing the search term.*

TABLE 18-1 Access 2010 Data Entry Shortcuts

To Do This	Keyboard Shortcut
Insert the current date	CTRL-; (semicolon)
Insert the current time	CTRL- SHIFT-: (colon)
Insert whatever value was in the same field in the previous record	CTRL-' (apostrophe)
Add a new record	CTRL-+-+ (plus sign)
Save changes to the current record	SHIFT-ENTER
Switch between values in a check box or option button	SPACEBAR
Insert a new line	CTRL-ENTER

Data Entry Shortcuts To save time (and keystrokes) when populating a database, try some of the data entry shortcuts listed in Table 18-1.

Editing Records in a Form

1. Open the form you want to edit, and change to Form view.
2. Locate the record you want to edit, and click in the cell that needs editing.
3. Modify the data as necessary.

Selecting a Record in a Form

To select an entire record in a form, click in the record's selection bar, located along the left margin of the form.

Copying Records in a Form

A record can be copied by doing either of the following:

- Select the record to copy, and then, on the Home ribbon, click the Copy button. Create a new record and, on the Home ribbon, click the Paste button.
- Right-click in the selection bar of the record to copy, and choose Copy from the context menu. Create a new record, right-click in the selection bar of that record, and choose Paste from the context menu.

TIP *If you prefer keyboard shortcuts, you can use CTRL-C for Copy and CTRL-V for Paste (the record must be selected first).*

Deleting Records in a Form

To delete a single record, select the record(s) to delete, and then, on the Home ribbon, click the Delete button. When asked to confirm the deletion, click Yes.

Still Struggling

You can choose one of your forms to open automatically each time the database file is opened. On the File ribbon, click Options and then click Current Database. Under the Application Options heading, click the Display Form drop-down list (pictured here) and choose the form you wish to have automatically displayed.

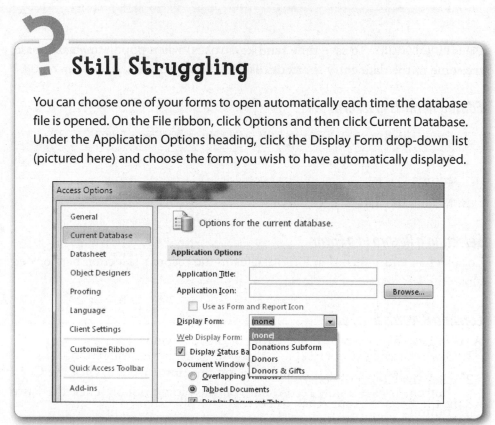

Working with Access Reports

Reports help data come alive by organizing key business data and answering key business questions in a visually appealing way. A well-designed report can have a terrific impact on those who read it by creating interest, illustrating points that are difficult to explain, and increasing the reader's ability to absorb and retain the important data takeaway points.

There are several ways to create reports in Access 2010: the Report tool, Report Wizard, Blank Report tool, and Report Design view. These commands are all located in the Reports group on the Create ribbon (pictured here). This chapter covers the Report tool and the Report Wizard.

Creating a Report Using the Report Tool

The Report tool lets you create a simple yet attractive report from any table or query object in a single click. All of the fields (also called "controls" in reports lingo) that were in the table or query will be included in the report. The form shown here was created with the single click of a button using the Report tool.

Donors				Thursday, May 05, 2011 4:52:12 PM	
Donor ID	First Name	Last Name	Address	City	State
1	John	Smith	1 Main Street	Glen Rock	PA
2	Lulu	Dianamo	54 Annendale Drive	Staten Island	NY
3	Wilson	David	877 Scooter Street	Lakewood	NJ
4	John	Smith	1 Main Street	Glen Rock	PA
5	Beth	Kirkland	2 Avocette Way	New York	NY
6	John	Fitzgerald	101 West Avenue	North Wales	PA
7	Peg	Brennan	36 Northfield Avenue	Lansdowne	PA
8	Lorraine	Wilson	200 Scooter Street	Lakewood	NJ
9	Tess	Lucas	100 A Street	New York	NY
10	Robin	Denbeigh	10 Hatfield Street	Glen Rock	PA
14	Peg	Brennan	36 Northfield Avenue	Lansdowne	PA

1. Open the table or query object that you want to base the report on.
2. Click the Create ribbon.
3. In the Reports group, click Report. The form is created and displayed in Layout view.

Creating a Report Using the Report Wizard

The Report Wizard walks you through making some basic design decisions for a report. For example, using the wizard, you can define how data is grouped and sorted, and you can use fields from more than one table or query, as long as you have defined the relationships beforehand, as covered in Chapter 17.

1. Click the Create ribbon.

2. In the Reports group, click Report Wizard. The Report Wizard opens (pictured here).

Choose a table or query here

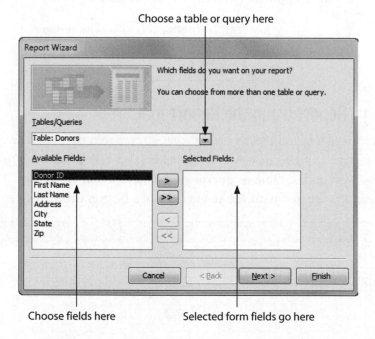

Choose fields here   Selected form fields go here

3. Choose a table or query from the Table/Queries drop-down list. Fields from that table or query will populate the Available Fields list.

4. Double-click a field in the Available Fields list to move it to the Selected Fields list. Alternatively, click the double right arrow between the two lists to move all of the fields from Available Fields into Selected Fields.

5. Repeat the previous two steps if you are creating a form from multiple tables or queries.

6. Click Next. Access prompts you to add grouping levels:

   • If you have selected fields from a single table, Access lists those fields on the left side of the window, inviting you to add your own grouping levels. Double-click a field to set it as a group. In the illustration, I double-clicked the Last Name field to set that as its own grouping level.

- If you have selected fields from more than one table, Access will automatically set up the groups for you, grouped on tables. For example, in the illustration, since I chose fields from both the Donor and Donations tables, Access automatically grouped the fields according to table.

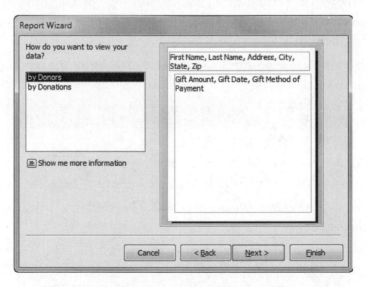

7. Click Next. Access prompts you to add sorting details (pictured here). This step is optional.

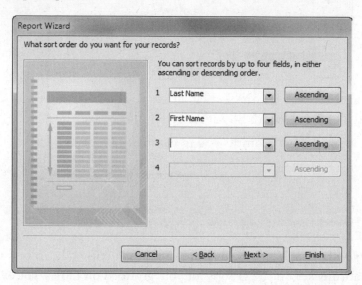

8. To choose a sort order, select the first field you want to sort on from the top drop-down list and then choose a sort type by using the Ascending/ Descending toggle button next to the field. Repeat for each subsequent field as desired.

9. Click Next. Access prompts you to select a layout for the report (pictured here).

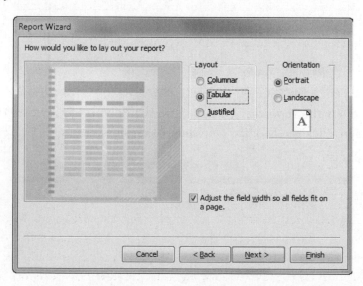

10. Choose a layout for the report. If you are creating a report from a single form, there will be three layout choices: Columnar, Tabular, and Justified. If you are creating a report from multiple tables, there will be three different layout choices: Stepped, Blocked, and Outline. Click a layout option for a quick preview of that layout on the left side of the window.

11. Choose a page orientation for the report (Portrait or Landscape).

12. To "force-fit" field widths so that all fields fit on a single page, select the Adjust The Field Width So All Fields Fit On A Page check box.

13. Click Next. Access prompts you to name your report (pictured here).

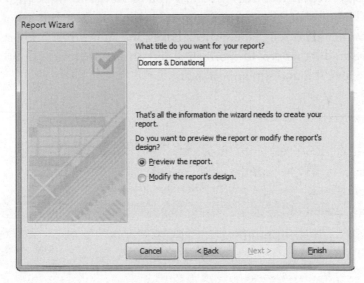

14. Type a name for the report in the field provided.

15. Choose whether you want to preview the report or modify its design:

   - To preview the report, click the Preview The Report option.

   - To open the report in Design view, where you can further tweak its design, click the Modify The Report's Design option.

16. Click Finish.

Exploring Report Views

Once a report has been created, it can be viewed in several ways: Layout view, Report view, Print Preview, and Design view. Layout view and Design view both let you make design changes to a report; Report view is used for viewing the report on-screen. Print Preview allows you to preview how a report will print and is discussed later in this chapter. To change between views, use the View drop-down menu on the Home or Design ribbon or the view buttons located at the bottom-right corner of the Access window (pictured in Figure 18-6).

Layout View

In Layout view (see Figure 18-7), data is displayed, and you can make simple layout changes to the report controls. For example, you can resize controls, add or delete fields, add a logo, change fonts and/or font sizes, and more using the four Report Layout Tools ribbons: Design, Arrange, Format, and Page Setup.

Controls are report features that allow you to view and work with data in a database. The most frequently used control is the text box, but other controls include command buttons, labels, check boxes, and subform/subreport controls. *Layouts* are guides that provide horizontal and vertical alignment options within a report to give it a uniform appearance.

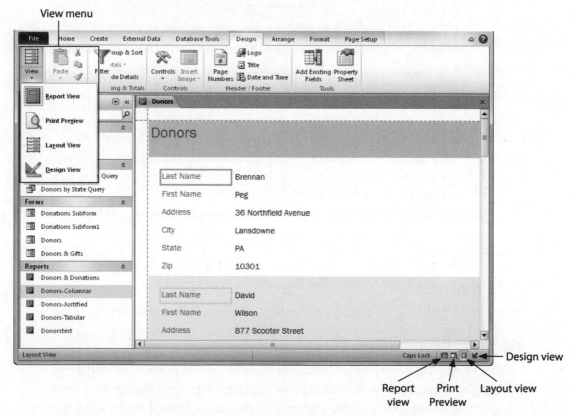

FIGURE 18-6 · Report Layout view lets you make design changes to a report.

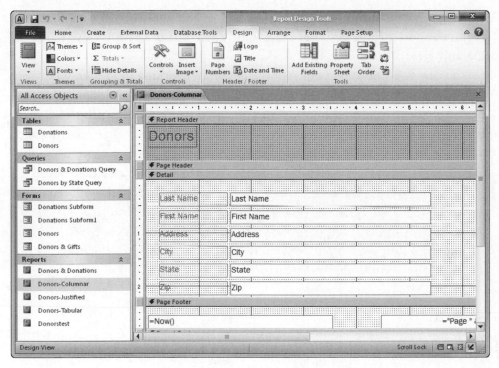

FIGURE 18-7 • Report Design view offers a detailed view of a report's structure.

Because data is displayed in Layout view, it is a bit more visually oriented than in Design view, and this nuance can be useful when setting the size of controls or carrying out other tasks that affect the visual appearance and usability of the report.

TIP *Certain report modifications cannot be accomplished in Layout view. When this is the case, Access will display a message letting you know that you need to be in Design view.*

Design View

Design view, pictured in Figure 18-7, provides a much more detailed view of the underlying structure of the report. Header, Detail, and Footer sections for the report are all visible. Data is not visible in Design view.

A few design tasks are easier to accomplish in Design view than in Layout view, such as being able to add labels, images, lines, and rectangles; editing text box control sources in the text boxes (without using the property sheet);

resizing report sections (e.g., the header, footer, and detail areas); and changing certain report properties that cannot be changed in Layout view (such as Default view).

You can also fine-tune your report's design by working in Design view. You can add new controls to the report by adding them to the design grid. The property sheet (pictured here) gives you access to numerous properties that you can set to customize the report.

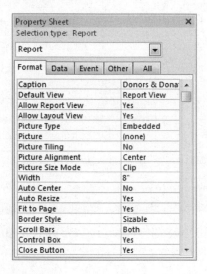

- Press F4 to display the report's property sheet, and then use it to modify properties for the report.
- To add fields from the underlying table or query, click the Design ribbon, and then click the Add Existing Fields button. Drag fields from the Field list onto the report to add them.

TIP *Designing and formatting reports can be as rich and complex as you wish it to be. For additional information on modifying and formatting reports and working with controls, explore the Reports topic in the Access Help file table of contents or search on "controls."*

Report View

Report view (pictured in Figure 18-8) displays the report in its final configuration.

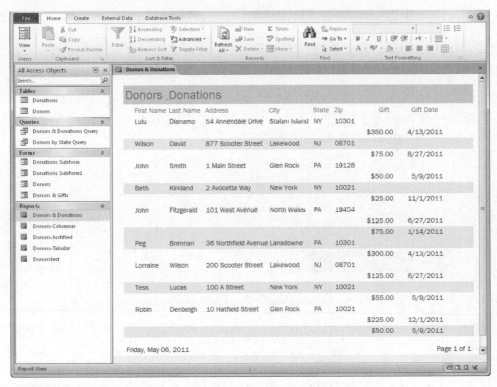

FIGURE 18-8 · Report view lets you see exactly how the final report will look.

Previewing and Printing a Report

Print Preview shows you exactly what a report will look like when printed. It is always a good idea to preview a report before printing.

Previewing a Report

There are two ways to preview a report:

- Click the Print Preview button in the lower-right corner of the window (see Figure 18-7).

- On the File ribbon (pictured in Figure 18-9), click Print and then click Print Preview.

In Print Preview (pictured in Figure 18-10), Access provides you with a Print Preview ribbon so you can adjust some of the aspects of the report before printing. For example, commands in the Page Size group allow you to change the

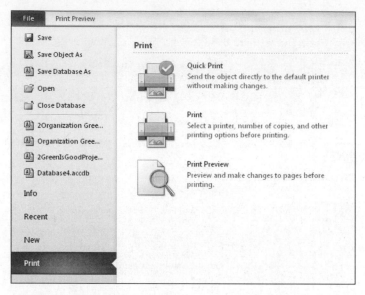

FIGURE 18-9 · The Print pane lets you specify settings for printing a report.

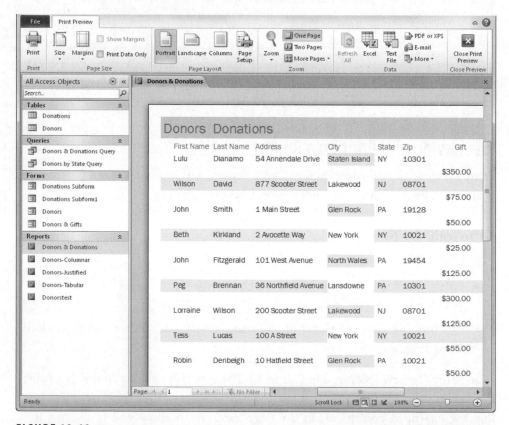

FIGURE 18-10 · The Print Preview pane lets you see what a printed report will look like before you print it out.

paper size and margins. Commands in the Page Layout group let you change the page orientation as well as access the Page Setup dialog box.

TIP *To exit Print Preview and return to the report, you must click the Close Print Preview button in the Print Preview ribbon or press the ESC key on your keyboard.*

Print a Report

There are two ways to print a report:

- On the File ribbon (scc Figure 18-10), click Print and then click Print or Quick Print.
- Use the CTRL-P keyboard shortcut.

Summary

This chapter provided an introduction to two key Access topics: data forms and reports. You learned how to ease data entry by creating data forms using both the Form tool and the Form Wizard. You also learned how to harness the power of your database by creating meaningful and attractive reports using both the Report tool and the Report Wizard.

QUIZ

1. True or False: You can choose one of your forms to open automatically each time the database file is opened.
   A. True
   B. False

2. Which of the following is a form view? (Choose all that apply.)
   A. Design
   B. Data Entry
   C. Form
   D. Layout
   E. Wizard

3. The _____ lets you create a simple yet attractive form from any table or query object in a single click. (Fill in the blank using the following choices.)
   A. Form Wizard
   B. Form tool
   C. Design view
   D. Report Wizard
   E. Datasheet view

4. When using the Form Wizard, which of the following is a layout option? (Choose all that apply.)
   A. Columnar
   B. Tabular
   C. Datasheet
   D. Justified
   E. None of the above

5. True or False: Records can be added to a database in either Datasheet view or Form view.
   A. True
   B. False

6. Which of the following are Access tools for building reports?
   A. Blank Report
   B. Report Tool
   C. Report Wizard
   D. Report Design view
   E. All of the above

7. **True or False: Report view and Design view both let you make design changes to a report.**
   A. True
   B. False

8. **In _____, data is displayed and you can make simple layout changes to the report controls. (Fill in the blank using the following choices.)**
   A. Report view
   B. Print Preview
   C. Layout view
   D. Form view
   E. None of the above

9. **Which of the following is not a report layout when using the Report Wizard?**
   A. Columnar
   B. Tabular
   C. Stepped
   D. Justified
   E. Professional

10. **True or False: When previewing a report in Print Preview, you can change margins as well as page size.**
   A. True
   B. False

Final Exam

Choose the correct responses to each of the multiple-choice questions.

Microsoft Office 2010

1. True or False: Microsoft Access is a spreadsheet program best used for working with numeric data.

   A. True

   B. False

2. Which of the following is a component of Outlook? (Choose all that apply.)

   A. E-mail

   B. Spreadsheet

   C. Contact management (address book)

   D. Calendar

   E. Task tracker

3. Microsoft PowerPoint is best used for which of the following?

   A. Keeping an appointment calendar

   B. Writing a memo

   C. Tracking product inventory

   D. Creating a photo slide show

   E. Writing a letter

4. Which of the following elements can a PowerPoint presentation contain?

  A. Charts

  B. Tables

  C. Graphics

  D. Speaker notes

  E. All of the above

5. True or False: The number of commands displayed on the ribbons is dependent upon the screen real estate available.

  A. True

  B. False

6. Microsoft Word is best used for which of the following? (Choose all that apply.)

  A. Keeping an appointment calendar

  B. Writing a memo

  C. Tracking product inventory

  D. Creating a photo slide show

  E. Writing a letter

7. True or False: PowerPoint charts and tables cannot be animated.

  A. True

  B. False

8. Which of the following displays a formatted list of options within the ribbon?

  A. A drop-down menu

  B. A dialog box

  C. Ribbon gallery

  D. Split button

  E. None of the above

9. True or False: The Quick Access toolbar can be customized.

  A. True

  B. False

10. **What happens when you click a split button display?**

    A. A drop-down menu opens

    B. A dialog box opens

    C. A formatted list of options displays within the ribbon

    D. The application closes

    E. None of the above

11. **Which Office programs offer Backstage View?**

    A. Word

    B. PowerPoint

    C. Excel

    D. Access

    E. All of the above

12. **By default, Office 2010's AutoSave feature is set to automatically save a version of your document every _____ minutes. (Fill in the blank using the following choices.)**

    A. 30

    B. 5

    C. 15

    D. 10

    E. 3

13. **Which of the following is a keyboard shortcut for creating a new document in Word, Excel, PowerPoint, and Access?**

    A. CTRL-V

    B. F1

    C. CTRL-S

    D. F12

    E. CTRL-N

14. **True or False: A theme is a designer-coordinated collection of fonts, color combinations, table formats, and graphic concepts.**

    A. True

    B. False

15. **Which of the following best describes a template?**

    A. A blank document

    B. A designer-coordinated collection of fonts, color combinations, table formats, and graphic concepts

    C. A completed document

    D. A preformatted document that serves as the basis for a brand-new file

    E. None of the above

16. **True or False: Backstage View does not exist in Outlook.**

    A. True

    B. False

17. **What is a keyboard shortcut for copying text or graphics in a document?**

    A. CTRL-S

    B. F1

    C. CTRL-V

    D. F12

    E. CTRL-C

18. **Which of the following buttons appear in the Help Window toolbar? (Choose all that apply.)**

    A. Print

    B. Table Of Contents

    C. Change Font Size

    D. Save

    E. Back

19. **Which of the following is a keyboard shortcut for saving a document in Word, Excel, and PowerPoint?**

    A. F1

    B. CTRL-S

    C. CTRL-V

    D. CTRL-F7

    E. CTRL-N

    F. None of the above

20. True or False: A spreadsheet program displays a grid of rows and columns made up of numerous cells.

    A. True

    B. False

Microsoft Word 2010

1. What is the name of the template that a new, blank Word document is based on?

    A. Normal.doc

    B. Normal.docx

    C. Blank.doc

    D. Normal.dotx

    E. New.doc

2. True or False: In Word, most paragraph formatting commands can be found on the Paragraph group on the Home ribbon.

    A. True

    B. False

3. Which of the following methods can be used to change the size of selected text in a Word document?

    A. Use the CTRL-SHIFT-> or CTRL-SHIFT-< keyboard shortcut.

    B. Choose a size from the Size drop-down list.

    C. Type a size in the Size field.

    D. Click the Grow Font or Shrink Font button.

    E. All of the above

4. True or False: Word's Normal template can be customized to suit your own needs.

    A. True

    B. False

5. How does a spelling error appear in a Word document?

   A. The misspelled word has a squiggly green underline.

   B. The misspelled word has a squiggly red underline.

   C. The misspelled word has a double underline.

   D. The misspelled word has a dotted underline.

   E. The misspelled word appears in italic.

6. How does a grammar error appear in a Word document?

   A. The grammar error has a squiggly red underline.

   B. The grammar error has a double underline.

   C. The grammar error has a dotted underline.

   D. The grammar error appears in bold italic.

   E. The grammar error has a squiggly green underline.

7. True or False: In Word, you must press the ENTER key at the end of every line to move to the next line down.

   A. True

   B. False

8. Which of the following modifications can be done to a Word table?

   A. Making a column wider

   B. Increasing a row's height

   C. Adding or deleting columns

   D. Adding or deleting rows

   E. All of the above

9. True or False: When resizing a graphic by dragging, if you don't want the aspect ratio of a graphic to be retained, click the Size Dialog Box Launcher, deselect Lock Aspect Ratio on the Size tab, and click OK.

   A. True

   B. False

10. If all you need in a header or footer is a page number, using the
    _____ button on the Header & Footer Tools Design ribbon
    can be much more straightforward than using the Header or Footer but-
    ton. (Fill in the blank using the following choices.)

    A. Page Number

    B. Bullets

    C. Insert

    D. View

    E. Home

11. The Header and Footer buttons appear on which ribbon in Word?
    (Choose all that apply.)

    A. Home

    B. Insert

    C. Page Layout

    D. View

    E. Header & Footer Tools - Design

12. True or False: An inline graphic keeps its location relative to the text that
    surrounds it. A floating graphic keeps its location relative to the page and
    lets text wrap around it.

    A. True

    B. False

13. To undo any stylistic changes you made to a graphic, or to return it to its
    original size, use the _____ button on the _____
    ribbon. (Fill in the blanks using the following choices.)

    A. View

    B. Reset Picture

    C. Paste

    D. Picture Tools Format

    E. Page Layout

14. True or False: In Word, the Page Layout ribbon is where the most frequently used page-related commands, such as margins, orientation, and size, are accessed.

    A. True

    B. False

15. Which of the following is not a document view in Word?

    A. Print Layout

    B. Full Screen Reading

    C. Transparent

    D. Outline

    E. Draft

16. Which of the following can be found on the Page Layout ribbon? (Choose all that apply.)

    A. Margins

    B. Full Screen Reading

    C. Orientation

    D. Size

    E. Watermark

17. _____ page orientation refers to when a page is wider than it is tall; _____ page orientation refers to when the page is taller than it is wide. (Fill in the blanks using the following choices.)

    A. Narrow

    B. Even

    C. Landscape

    D. Letter

    E. Portrait

18. Which of the following displays in Full Screen Reading view? (Choose all that apply.)

    A. Pictures

    B. Page breaks

    C. Ribbons

    D. Status bar

    E. Task bar

19. True or False: Page background colors and images do not print in Word, unless you specify that you want them printed.

    A. True

    B. False

20. Which of the following is not an option in the Print pane of the File ribbon? (Choose all that apply.)

    A. Orientation

    B. Margin

    C. Breaks

    D. Watermark

    E. Printer

Microsoft Excel 2010

1. Which Excel feature lets you fill adjoining cells with a series?

    A. AutoFill

    B. AutoComplete

    C. Orientation

    D. Merge & Center

    E. Print

2. True or False: The formula bar is located just above the column headings in a worksheet and always displays the contents of the current cell.

    A. True

    B. False

3. The _____ feature lets you have cell content appear on multiple lines. (Fill in the blank using the following choices.)

A. Merge & Center

B. Orientation

C. Wrap

D. AutoFill

E. Top Align

4. Which of the following describes a method for changing the width of a column in Excel?

A. Clicking Format in the Cells group on the Home ribbon

B. Double-clicking the line separating two column headings

C. Dragging the line separating two column headings

D. Right-clicking a column heading and choosing Column Width

E. All of the above

5. In Excel, the _____ button shows more precise values by displaying more decimal places. (Fill in the blank using the following choices.)

A. Conditional Formatting

B. Decrease Decimals

C. Cell Styles

D. Increase Decimals

E. Format

6. True or False: In Excel, worksheet gridlines print by default.

A. True

B. False

7. In Excel, a formula consists of a(n) _____ that performs an operation on a worksheet. (Fill in the blank using the following choices.)

A. AutoSum

B. Screen tip

C. List of commands

D. Equation

E. Cell

8. In Excel, what symbol must a formula begin with?

   A. {

   B. =

   C. [

   D. (

   E. *

9. Which of the following elements can an Excel formula contain?

   A. Cell references

   B. Mathematical operators

   C. Values

   D. Functions

   E. All of the above

10. True or False: A function is a predefined built-in formula.

    A. True

    B. False

11. True or False: Excel requires that you have an excellent command of advanced math skills.

    A. True

    B. False

12. Which of the following are standard chart types in Excel?

    A. Pie

    B. Bar

    C. Column

    D. Line

    E. All of the above

13. When you copy a formula, cell references will change if you used
_____ cell references; cell references will not change if you used
_____ cell references. (Fill in the blanks using the following
choices.)

A. Sticky

B. Exact

C. Relative

D. Absolute

E. Temporary

14. A _____ is a tiny, cell-sized _____ that can be em-
bedded right next to the data it depicts. (Fill in the blanks using the following choices.)

A. Gadget

B. Sparkline

C. Chart

D. Picture

E. Weight line

15. Which of the following is a sparkline type? (Choose all that apply.)

A. Line

B. Trend

C. Pie

D. Column

E. Win/Lose

16. True or False: The Insert Function dialog box lets you search for a function by typing a description.

A. True

B. False

17. True or False: As data is added to a worksheet, page breaks are automatically inserted in accordance with the page's margins and page size.

A. True

B. False

18. Which of the following statements is not true? (Choose all that apply.)

A. Excel gridlines print by default.

B. Excel gridlines do not print by default.

C. Excel gridlines display on-screen by default.

D. Excel gridlines do not display on-screen by default.

Microsoft PowerPoint 2010

1. In PowerPoint's Normal view, which pane(s) display by default?

A. Slide

B. Outline Tab

C. Slide Tab

D. Notes

E. All of the above

2. True or False: In Normal view, the Notes pane that runs along the bottom of the slide provides a space for you to add slide notes to a presentation.

A. True

B. False

3. Which view does a PowerPoint presentation open in by default?

A. Notes

B. Normal

C. Slide Sorter

D. Reading view

E. None of the above

4. Which of the following is a default PowerPoint slide layout? (Choose all that apply.)

A. Title Slide

B. Title & Content

C. Notes Page

D. Two Content

E. Comparison

454   MICROSOFT OFFICE 2010 DeMYSTiFieD

5. True or False: Paragraph spacing is the spacing between each line in a paragraph. Line spacing is the extra spacing before and/or after paragraphs.

    A. True

    B. False

6. To modify PowerPoint proofing settings, which ribbon could you use?

    A. Home

    B. File

    C. View

    D. Design

    E. Transitions

7. True or False: Notes from the Notes pane can be printed.

    A. True

    B. False

8. Which of the following is not an option on the Print pane found on the File ribbon? (Choose all that apply.)

    A. Orientation

    B. Printer

    C. Margin

    D. Breaks

    E. Watermark

9. True or False: PowerPoint's Master View feature offers you the time-saving option of being able to make formatting changes to a set of master slides that can then be applied throughout the presentation.

    A. True

    B. False

10. Which of the following can be printed in PowerPoint 2010? (Choose all that apply.)

A. Slides

B. Handouts

C. Notes

D. Animations

E. Graphics

11. Which PowerPoint view displays the presentation for maximum ease of reading and hides the ribbons, status bar, and taskbar?

A. Normal view

B. Notes view

C. Reading view

D. Print Preview

E. Master view

12. Which of the following is a type of placeholder for a PowerPoint slide? (Choose all that apply.)

A. Handout

B. Content

C. Text

D. Picture

E. Chart

13. Which of the following is not a shape that is available in PowerPoint?

A. Butterfly

B. Block arrows

C. Stars

D. Equation shapes

E. Flowchart

14. True or False: The Editing group on the Audio Tools Playback ribbon lets you set fade-in/fade-out details for the audio clip as well as trim (shorten) it.

A. True

B. False

15. Which of the following is a type of SmartArt? (Choose all that apply.)

A. Cycle

B. Relationship

C. Stars

D. Process

E. Picture

16. True or False: The Video Tools Playback ribbon will become visible when a video is selected.

A. True

B. False

17. Which of the following is not a PowerPoint animation effect?

A. Entrance

B. Exit

C. Emphasis

D. Triangulate

E. Motion path

18. The _____ of the _____ ribbon let(s) you stipulate the start, duration, or delay timing for an animation. (Fill in the blanks using the following choices.)

A. Format

B. Animations

C. Advanced Animations group

D. Timing group

E. Playback

19. The _____ group on the Slide Show ribbon lets you view a presentation in Slide Show view, broadcast a presentation over the Internet, and create a custom show. (Fill in the blank using the following choices.)

    A. Monitors group

    B. Set Up group

    C. View group

    D. Start Slide Show group

    E. Table group

20. Which of the following options on the PowerPoint Slide Show ribbon allows you to prevent a slide from showing during a presentation?

    A. Hide Slide

    B. Broadcast Slide Show

    C. Set Up Slide Show

    D. From Beginning

    E. Rehearse Timings

21. Which PowerPoint feature makes it easy to create a self-contained representation of your presentation, including narration, animations, and timing of slide changes?

    A. Rehearse Timings

    B. Custom Slide Show

    C. Record Slide Show

    D. Presenter View

    E. Slide Sorter View

Microsoft Outlook 2010

1. True or False: To send and receive e-mail messages in Outlook, you must add and configure an e-mail account.

    A. True

    B. False

2. Most Outlook e-mail formatting options are available in the _____ group of the _____ ribbon. (Fill in the blanks using the following choices.)

A. Message

B. Home

C. Quick Steps

D. View

E. Basic Text

3. True or False: If you choose a signature in the New Message drop-down list in the Signatures And Stationery dialog box, you will have to manually insert a signature into an e-mail.

A. True

B. False

4. In Outlook, if you want to move an e-mail message into an existing folder, which of the following methods can be used?

A. Use the Move command on the Home ribbon.

B. Drag a message into a folder.

C. Right-click a message and use the Move command.

D. Use copy and paste keyboard shortcuts.

E. All of the above

5. True or False: New, unread messages in the Email List appear in italic text. By contrast, read messages are in bold text.

A. True

B. False

6. True or False: You may create multiple e-mail signatures.

A. True

B. False

7. **Which Outlook feature would allow you to set up a meeting that occurs the same day and time every other week?**

   A. Arrangement

   B. View ribbon

   C. Recurring Appointment

   D. Delete Appointment

   E. To-Do List

8. **True or False: In Calendar view, the View ribbon offers options for viewing your calendar.**

   A. True

   B. False

9. **Outlook's Suggested Contacts folder will contain which type of e-mail addresses? (Choose all that apply.)**

   A. E-mail addresses that you have received e-mail from but that are not in your contact list

   B. E-mail addresses that you have sent e-mail to but that are not in your contact list

   C. E-mail addresses from your contact list

   D. Old e-mail addresses for contacts

   E. None of the above

10. **In Outlook, where can tasks be displayed? (Choose all that apply.)**

    A. Daily Task List in Calendar

    B. File ribbon

    C. To-Do bar

    D. Task view

    E. View ribbon

11. On the View menu, which button can be used to change sort order (from A through Z to Z through A, for example)?

A. Time Scale

B. Reset View

C. Reverse Sort

D. People Pane

E. Reminders Window

Microsoft Access 2010

1. True or False: In a table, where one row (record) meets one column (field), the content contained therein would be a value.

A. True

B. False

2. Within a database file, one or more _____ are used to store data, and _____ are used to locate and retrieve specific information. (Fill in the blanks using the following choices.)

A. Files

B. Queries

C. Values

D. Reports

E. Tables

3. A field is a single _____ within a table. (Fill in the blank using the following choices.)

A. Row

B. Column

C. Query

D. Gridline

E. Value

4. A _____ consists of a single table. A _____ consists of one or more interrelated tables. (Fill in the blanks using the following choices.)

   A. Small database

   B. Flexible database

   C. Relational database

   D. Flat file database

   E. Large database

5. True or False: A foreign key is one field in each table that uniquely identifies each record in that table.

   A. True

   B. False

6. Which of the following is an Access table view? (Choose all that apply.)

   A. Database view

   B. Record view

   C. Design view

   D. Display view

   E. Datasheet view

7. Which of the following could be used as a field name in an Access table? (Choose all that apply.)

   A. Address

   B. First.Name

   C. ZipCode

   D. Zip!

   E. [Size]

8. In Access, you can use _____ to scroll through records and add, modify, or view data in a table. _____ gives you complete control over a table's structure, including adding and modifying field details. (Fill in the blanks using the following choices.)

   A. Design view

   B. Database view

   C. Display view

   D. Record view

   E. Datasheet view

9. To pose a question to the database, what type of object do you need to create?

   A. Layout

   B. Design

   C. Join

   D. Query

   E. Relationship

10. True or False: A complex select query pulls information from multiple tables in the database.

    A. True

    B. False

Answers to Quizzes and Final Exam

Chapter 1	Chapter 2	Chapter 3	Chapter 4
1. B	1. B	1. A	1. A
2. B	2. A	2. C	2. E
3. C, A	3. E, B	3. B, E	3. D, B
4. E	4. D	4. E	4. E
5. A	5. A	5. B	5. A
6. C	6. B	6. C	6. B, A
7. A, B, C	7. B	7. D	7. B, C
8. C	8. D	8. A	8. A
9. A	9. A	9. B	9. E, A
10. B	10. A	10. A	10. A

Chapter 5	Chapter 6	Chapter 7	Chapter 8
1. B	1. A	1. A	1. B
2. D	2. D	2. E	2. D
3. E, C	3. B, E	3. C, E	3. B, E (in any order)
4. F	4. B	4. A	4. C
5. A	5. B	5. B	5. A
6. C, D, E	6. E	6. C	6. B
7. B	7. A	7. B	7. B, C
8. C	8. B	8. B, C	8. A, C
9. C, D	9. A, D	9. A, B, E	9. D
10. B	10. A	10. A	10. A

Chapter 9	Chapter 10	Chapter 11	Chapter 12
1. B	1. B	1. A	1. B
2. E	2. E	2. E	2. C
3. C, E	3. B	3. C, A	3. D
4. B	4. C	4. D	4. E, B
5. A	5. C	5. A	5. A
6. C	6. A	6. C	6. A
7. A	7. E	7. E	7. E
8. D, B	8. D	8. D, A	8. A
9. A	9. C	9. E	9. C
10. B	10. A	10. A	10. A

Chapter 13	Chapter 14	Chapter 15	Chapter 16
1. A	1. A	1. B	1. A
2. E	2. C	2. C	2. D
3. D, B	3. C, E	3. E, A	3. D, A
4. B, E	4. A, D	4. C	4. A, E
5. B	5. B	5. A	5. A
6. E	6. A, C, E	6. B	6. B, E
7. A	7. A	7. A	7. B
8. A, E (any order), C	8. B	8. B, A	8. D, B
9. A-4, B-3, C-2, D-1, E-5	9. C	9. E	9. A, B, E
10. B	10. A	10. A	10. A

Chapter 17
1. A
2. B, D
3. B
4. D
5. A
6. C, D
7. B
8. D, A
9. B
10. A

Chapter 18
1. A
2. A, C, D
3. B
4. A, B, C, D
5. A
6. E
7. B
8. C
9. E
10. A

Final Exam

Microsoft Office 2010
1. B
2. A, C, D, E
3. D
4. E
5. A
6. B, E
7. B
8. C
9. A
10. A
11. E
12. D
13. E
14. A
15. D
16. B
17. E
18. A, B, C, E
19. B
20. A

Microsoft Word 2010
1. D
2. A
3. E
4. A
5. B
6. E
7. B
8. E
9. A
10. A
11. A, E
12. A
13. B, D
14. A
15. C
16. A, C, D, E
17. C, E
18. A, B
19. A
20. B, C, D

Microsoft Excel 2010
1. A
2. A
3. C
4. E
5. D
6. B
7. D
8. B
9. E
10. A
11. B
12. E
13. C, D
14. B, C
15. A, B, E
16. A
17. A
18. A, D

Microsoft PowerPoint 2010	Microsoft Outlook 2010	Microsoft Access 2010
1. E	1. A	1. A
2. A	2. E, A	2. E, B
3. B	3. B	3. B
4. A, B, D, E	4. E	4. D, C
5. B	5. B	5. B
6. B	6. A	6. C, E
7. A	7. C	7. A, C
8. A, C, D, E	8. A	8. E, A
9. A	9. A, B	9. D
10. A, B, C, E	10. A, C, D	10. A
11. C	11. C	
12. B, C, D, E		
13. A		
14. A		
15. A, B, D, E		
16. A		
17. D		
18. D, B		
19. D		
20. A		
21. D		

Index